FINDING A VOICE

The Practice of
Changing Lives
Through Literature

JEAN TROUNSTINE AND ROBERT P. WAXLER

Foreword by Elizabeth Mehren

2008   2007   2006   2005   4   3   2   1

Foreword

IT WAS 7 O'CLOCK AT NIGHT, and the small classroom at a community college in Lowell, Massachusetts, was filled with a sense of eagerness. The eight students—all women, as it happened, but they might just as easily have been men—were seated around a seminar table. Their books were placed neatly in front of them. When the professor, Jean Trounstine, called the class to order, the students reacted like racehorses ready to bolt through the gates at the Preakness. Hands shot up. Everyone—okay, almost everyone—wanted to talk about the week's reading assignment.

"You want me to toss it out the window right now?" asked Tina Berry.

Berry, 21, had attitude pouring out of her. She also had no use for Harper Lee's brilliant novel, *To Kill a Mockingbird*. So what if it was a classic, an enduring parable about justice in the American South?

"I hated it. I hated it," Berry said. "It was very complicated for me."

Fellow student Tracy Merritt, 37, fixed a firm gaze on Trounstine. "The print is too small. There are way too many words on every page," Merritt complained. But then she relented. She wanted to talk about Boo Radley, one of the most enigmatic characters in the book.

"I think I've met people like that nasty neighbor," Merritt said, "where you kick the soccer ball into his yard and you're afraid to go get it."

The discussion was off and running: Eight women, each convicted of one crime or another; their professor, Trounstine; their probation officer, Bobby Hassett; and the judge who sentenced every one of them, Presiding Justice of the Lynn District Court, Joseph Dever. The backgrounds of all the participants could scarcely have been more different. Berry was convicted of selling marijuana. Merritt had so many alcohol-related offenses she could not remember all the details—but malicious destruction of property was one of her more recent convictions. Trounstine, on the other hand, had a graduate degree and training in drama. And Dever, of course, went to law school.

Yet the playing ground in this particular session of the course known as Changing Lives Through Literature was entirely level. In fact, in order to sit in on this class session, I was required both to read Lee's novel and to participate in what turned out to be an animated—and amazingly egalitarian—discussion. Indeed, when probation officer Hassett wanted to dismiss *To Kill a Mockingbird* as a dated literary relic with little relevance to anyone in the room, Judge Dever leapt in with a stirring defense of the book.

"Take him down, Judge!" Merritt called out, earning a laugh from the very officer of the court who had given her an unusual choice of sentences: Sign on for the Changing Lives Through Literature seminar—or go to prison.

I will admit that I ventured into that classroom with a powerful sense of skepticism. As a journalist for nigh on three decades, I have covered scores of criminal trials. I have been in tiny jails in rural areas as well as huge prisons that house thousands of inmates. I have interviewed youthful offenders, including a teenager in Wisconsin who nearly killed her best friend for sleeping with her boyfriend. I have sat with wizened old men who have spent their lives behind bars. I have walked down long prison corridors with guards and wardens, grateful for the buffer they provided against catcalls and streams of obscenities.

What I know after all this is no different from what almost any criminologist in America would say without hesitation. The system is not working. Consider the U.S. Justice Department's own statistic from 2001: About 1.3 million people serving in state or federal prisons—more than the populations of Maine, Rhode Island, or New Hampshire; double the population of Vermont. Think of an entire state, filled with convicted criminals. No wonder the word "warehouse" comes to mind.

Between 1996 and 2001—again, according to the U.S. Justice Department—the number of drug offenders alone rose by 37 percent, putting a particular strain on local jails. In 2002, the Justice Department found that 39 percent of jail inmates had served three or more prior sentences.

As a culture, we remain deeply ambivalent about the purpose of incarceration. Only in the case of the most heinous offenses do Americans concur on severe punishment—and even there, we diverge on the value of the death penalty. Virtually since this country's founding, we have wrestled with what to do with those who break our laws. Do we throw them in the stocks—metaphorically or otherwise? Do we lock them away for long, hard sentences? Do we ship them off to facilities where they will learn to become even more dangerous? Or do we, as reformers have argued for more than a century, endeavor to rehabilitate our criminals—paving the way for possible re-entry to society at large? Do we, for example, sentence them to learn? Demand that they read some of the greatest works in the English language? Require that they meet regularly and participate in college-level conversations?

Such is the premise of Changing Lives Through Literature. When the program's founder, English professor Robert Waxler, first explained this concept to me, I was stunned by what seemed like transparent naivete. Give a criminal a book and it may turn his or her life around? How disingenuous.

But again, if not much else is working, why not give Shakespeare—or Norman Mailer—or Toni Morrison—or Russell Banks—a chance? Especially why not try it if you have a judge and a probation officer in the same room and on the same page, in every sense of that phrase.

A central theme in Changing Lives Through Literature is civility. The nature of the social covenant is another important motif. Another premise is that with the privilege of a free society comes responsibility. Oddly, perhaps—given the population for whom this course has been designed—optimism is also a recurring quality. For criminal offenders—for anyone, come to think of it—an intellectual meal made up of civility, social obligation, responsibility, and hope is a gourmet repast for the brain and soul.

Waxler and Trounstine—who expanded Changing Lives to serve female offenders as well as males—present literature as a tool to lend civility, and to humanize a population that may never have discovered fine writing as a vehicle for reflection. Waxler and Trounstine advocate literature as a method for finding one's voice: less the ability to speak, than the ability to speak sagely and with confidence won through knowledge. Literature, they are not the first to argue, can lead to enlightenment.

At the class session I attended in my capacity as New England Bureau Chief for the *Los Angeles Times,* Trounstine emphasized her belief that reading can be redemptive.

"There is something transformative about the power of the imagination to take on a character," she told me. "It's hard to measure, it's hard to really discuss, it's not magical—but there's something experiential that happens to a person in reading a book and then in talking about that book."

In turn, Waxler explained the reasoning that led him to develop this unusual program. Criminal offenders, he said, are completely marginalized. Not only is nobody in the greater society listening to them, but they have lost their own voice, Waxler contends. Without a voice, he continued, they stop believing in themselves. They lose their voice, and their place. Dwelling at the bottom becomes the only comfort zone they know.

"Literature in my mind is probably the most important tool we have to maintain a human society, to keep people human," Waxler told me.

Literature affords a vehicle for offenders to explore their own identities in the context of the world around them, he went on.

"It's a very important social experience," Waxler said. "That's what literature, I think, is all about."

In *Finding a Voice*, you will see that Waxler and Trounstine have established thoughtful, careful, and highly precise guidelines for putting their theory into practice. Whenever possible, the Changing Lives classes are held on college campuses—not in some dingy, makeshift space in a prison or courthouse. To be sure, all three are institutional settings. But the mere act of walking into a building that says "college" starts the course off with an air of legitimacy. Off campus, the participants may be lawbreakers. But for these two hours, they are college students.

Ideally, a Changing Lives student will at least have completed eighth grade. Although the participants may have done really awful things, rarely is a sex offender allowed to take part. The instructors do not know the exact nature of the students' crimes. That element raises the level of respect in the room. The students can be sure that there is no judgment from their instructors. The teachers can focus on teaching, not on wondering who did what, to whom. As in any good college class, the reading material quite properly becomes the center of attention.

The focus on the literature is steady and firm. Students are urged to reach inside themselves to interpret the material. Their opinions are valued. But they are not permitted to digress excessively, or to overpersonalize their reactions to the works they are reading. This is a literature course, not group therapy. And yet the curative value of literature is incontrovertible. Reading at once invites introspection and banishes self-absorption—for the book, after all, is written by someone else.

Over and over as they sit at their seminar tables, the participants are asked to examine how the characters in the books they read have changed. The message is unmistakable: Though it is often painful, change is always possible.

To hammer that point home still further, some students begin the first session of class by writing an essay titled "How I See Myself." At the last class session, they repeat the process. Invariably, something in how each person sees him or herself has changed.

Finally, a graduation ceremony caps each class series. This ritual of reward and validation also adds legitimacy.

In the smorgasbord of options known as "alternative sentencing," the Changing Lives Through Literature model is both young and relatively small. Though the program has been adopted by many states and at least one foreign country, the number of students who participate remains low. This is a labor-intensive effort, with small gatherings of carefully selected students and three supervisory professionals at each session.

Finding a Voice presents impressive data to suggest that introducing some offenders to literature in a highly structured environment can make a difference. But to return to my initial cynicism, so can the prospect of doing less time—the carrot that brings many students into the Changing Lives program in the first place.

Still, the presence of a judge and a probation officer assures that the charlatan students are almost always quickly weeded out. Moreover, these classes require work and commitment on the part of the participants. The syllabus options for Changing Lives Through Literature are vast and challenging. This is not the penal system's equivalent of a college gut course.

As you will learn in *Finding a Voice*, the variety of teaching strategies illustrates the evolutionary nature of this program. Although well-tested and thoughtfully structured, it is a work-in-progress, changing with every eight to ten offenders who are "sentenced to read." I hope those who read this book will be inspired to bring Changing Lives Through Literature to their own communities.

But for a final comment on all this, let's return to Trounstine's classroom. Tina Berry, the one who hated *To Kill a Mockingbird* so much, finally admitted there was one character she liked: the African-American housekeeper.

"I loved her because she brought the children to a black church," Berry said.

Trounstine was not about to let Berry get away with such a shallow answer.

"That's insightful, Tina, tell us more," Trounstine said.

Berry protested: "Come on, why do I have to speak up?"

"Because you do," Trounstine told her.

With that small phrase, she had summarized much of the philosophy of the entire program.

Berry told me she dropped out of high school at 16. She said she struggled when she started Trounstine's class. But taking part in the seminar prompted her to sign up to take her high school equivalency exam.

"Granted, we only have to read one book every two weeks," Berry said. "But reading one book is a whole lot better than nothing. And it's a whole, whole lot more than I ever read before."

Her classmate, Tracy Merritt, said that as a child, she was so uninterested in the printed word that she used to pay her sister in breakfast cereal to have her read the *TV Guide* to her. When Judge Dever proposed the literature seminar instead of jail, Merritt thought to herself, "What the hell is reading going to do for me?"

She signed up "because I wanted better than I had." She limped through Joyce Carol Oates' "Where Are You Going, Where Have You Been?" But she loved Sandra Cisneros' *The House on Mango Street* so much that she read it six times.

What had reading done for her? It had sent her to new places and introduced her to people she would never have met in a narrow world that centered on getting what she wanted, regardless of what she had to do to get it. Reading had illustrated the universality of certain social systems. It had explained to her that rules exist for good (and sometimes, ridiculous) reasons, and that responsible citizens strive to maintain those rules.

Delving into literature also had shown Merritt that whatever she thought was wrong with her own life, she was probably not the only person with such problems. Meeting women on the pages of novels who had experienced similar misfortunes made it harder for Merritt to hide behind the label of "victim." She saw that she was not the first person in history to be furious because life had not worked out quite the way she wanted. And she learned that people—even if they are fictional people—can pursue different avenues to make important changes.

Although she might not yet have realized it, Merritt also had tasted the lyric power of good writing. She had sampled the connection between language and expression. If she had not fully found her voice, she was certainly headed in that direction.

In class, at her generic little seminar table, in a room that was not much more glamorous than some prison cells, Merritt cast a fond glance at Trounstine.

"Because of her," Merritt said, "I read."

—Elizabeth Mehren
Hingham, Massachusetts
July 2005

Contents

Preface

ROBERT WAXLER ON *FINDING A VOICE*

CAN READING GOOD LITERATURE help us to find a voice? We believe it can—and this book offers a glimpse into that belief.

Start with the simple assumption, as we did back in 1991, that criminal offenders have been pushed to the margins and declared failures. They have an important story to tell, but no one will listen. Teachers have dismissed them as incompetent. Judges have sentenced them to confinement. They are disenchanted, struggling in an enormous present, without a past or a future, as if the human heart itself was surrounded by a frozen sea.

"A book must be an axe for the frozen sea within us. This is what I believe," Kafka wrote his friend Oskar Pollak. Perhaps he was thinking, as we are, that books can shock and surprise, return us to the voice lost, to the imagination forsaken.

Yes, books keep us off-balance, stir us to ask deep questions, and allow us to return to the enchantment of the heart. That is our belief.

A number of recent reports argue for the need to discover alternatives to the current approach to criminal justice. For us, such an argument invites a substantive conversation about the kind of society we want to live in, the values we respect and embrace, the way we judge ourselves as well as others in the community.

Back in 1991, we conducted a small experiment for criminal offenders at the University of Massachusetts, Dartmouth, based on just such thinking. The program was rooted in the simple idea that reading and discussing good literature could change lives. An engagement with language could help us find our voices in a world increasingly distracted by cold facts, ratios, and abstractions. Reading good stories, we believed, could re-awaken the interior life and bring us all closer to the beat of the human heart.

We believed then, as we do today, that the success of a democracy is best judged not by how many people are in jail, but by how many are able to speak out as productive citizens. And we knew that talking about books around a table on a college campus could give voice to those with little power—could in fact enhance the lives of everyone, including judges, probation officers, and professors.

In a good book, readers always discover the voice they seek, for in its language a book holds the future and the past, our hope and our memory. Such language makes us uneasy, calls us to question, and invites us to listen for something deeper in ourselves and in the world.

Since 1991, the Changing Lives Through Literature (CLTL) program has spread throughout Massachusetts and into several other states, including Texas where politically conservative judges, not unaccustomed to sentencing inmates to death, have embraced the program because they are convinced that great books can open the human heart and redeem us.

That is the power of CLTL. It has nothing to do with partisan politics and everything to do with democracy and education. It costs less than $500 per person to send an offender through CLTL, pocket cash compared to the $30,000 necessary to lock that same offender behind bars for a year.

Historically, often the first signs that a community has established itself appear when that community builds a jail and fashions gravestones for a cemetery. The jail serves as a temporary stay for citizens who have lost their way but who almost always return to the community. The cemetery offers no such hope. In its silence, it serves only as a final marker of our limitations, reminding us of the importance of the human voice and the need for justice and compassion.

But how we as a community make room for that human voice—how we provide that sense of justice and compassion—seems the crucial question. In my view, literature remains the best answer we have to keep ourselves, as individuals and as a society, human. Literature offers all of us the opportunity to find a voice deep within, the voice that names us and calls us home.

JEAN TROUNSTINE ON *FINDING A VOICE*

When I facilitated my first CLTL seminar, I was struck by how many of the women yearned, like me, to hear their dreams evoked what they read. As Zora Neale Hurston said, for women, "The dream is the truth." The women involved with CLTL came to the table with broken lives; they wanted to heal. In the characters who touched them most deeply, they often found a sense of connection, wisdom, safety, and hope. The conversations we had week after week were reflections of the texts we read. We took a book and held it up to our lives, bringing ideas, arguments, and many thought-provoking moments to the table. Many other CLTL practitioners have found the same truth: Our voices are enriched and deepened, not only from the readings but through all of the expression around the table. Our collective exploration into texts enlivens our voices.

It was 1973, on an early spring afternoon in Massachusetts that I first realized the transformational power of hearing my own voice inside a character. I was walking to the graduate student dorm at Brandeis University. The trees were just beginning to bloom, bushes breaking into yellow forsythia, grass becoming green. The pond was bursting with color. I was trying to sort out mixed feelings about playing Joan of Arc in my next scene class.

Acting was not something I had lucked into. I had been driven to the stage by the need to inhabit the soul of another, by the need to delve deep into behaviors that make each of us unique, and by an intuitive sense that the lives of others can teach us who we are and who we want to be. I read book after book, imagining myself inside the pages. In many ways, reading led me to corners that were hidden, through doors that were locked. As I listened to the voices of others, I found that I heard my own.

As a girl, I had not known exactly why I loved the world of the imagination. And as an adult, I knew my dream to be an actress was a long shot. Being cast at Brandeis had not been easy. I was short and chunky, more character than leading lady. I had a round face and long wild hair that kept me from getting dramatic leads like the stunningly beautiful Hedda Gabler and the sleek and sharp Sadie in *All the King's Men*. "You'll get more roles when you're older," one teacher had said. But that didn't console me. I wanted roles now, those that spoke to me: the intense and forthright Antigone in Anouilh's *Antigone;* the tall Rosalind who disguises herself as a man in Shakespeare's *As You Like It*; and the passionate believer, Joan, in George Bernard Shaw's *Saint Joan.* In their words, I found something of myself. I heard my voice.

So I rounded the pond thinking about the character I had chosen to play in a class monologue, Joan of Arc. I had just been on stage that day, trying out her words. During the scene where Joan tells her adversaries that it doesn't matter if they reject her, that she can take France to victory because she has God's help, my teacher had yelled "Crap!" From the back row, his voice resounded throughout the hall. Then, while the class sat in silence and shock, he told me that I was sentimentalizing Joan: "That kind of aloneness is unknown to you, to most of us. And it's not easy to play." I slunk away, feeling deep shame inside. I was, in his eyes, too weak to play such a dynamic character.

Later, I found myself thinking that if I was going to play Joan, I mustn't be beaten down. I had to believe in myself, no matter what he'd said. I gathered something like confidence or revenge or a combination of both, huffing and puffing, trying out thoughts, putting on a mantle of yes-I-can as I plodded through mud around that pond. Struggling against the wind, I could hear my boots clomping on the path beneath me. This next time, I would nail my part and surprise the lot of them.

My process that day was not unlike what our students undergo when they walk into a CLTL program, fraught with fear. My revelation was perhaps similar to their own when they encounter a character who sticks inside and, in spite of differences, touches a chord. I thought how Joan was a peasant girl who lived in the Middle Ages and became a soldier because the "voices" in her head told her to serve God. She was a military leader, a heretic, a national savior, a fighter, and according to George Bernard Shaw, an inspiration. I was a newly married woman, wanting a career that didn't want me; I was yearning to find my path in the world. In spite of the differences in our lives, Joan's words resonated with me; the very core of her character made me feel powerful and strong.

On that day in 1973, I realized Joan's epiphany. My voice became connected to what I read on the page, and I felt I could use her words to express my inner heart. With Joan, I could be anyone, play any part, no matter what the nay-sayers said. I practiced her words aloud as I walked around and around, and by the time it was dark, I felt somehow transformed. I understood that, like Joan, I must "dare and dare and dare" until I die.

When I performed Joan at the next class, I was solidly behind her words; I got a standing ovation. But more important, I began to see how a character could affect us.

When I first became a teacher, I told that story over and over again to my students because I wanted them to understand that there was much in stepping into the world of another, and that success is never easy. "Whose voice resonates with you?" I asked them, hoping to uncover what and who might be their touchstone. Through the years, I have asked that question many times, encouraging others to see that words have power, and that books can amuse, comfort, reveal, and teach. I tell students that we meet characters at different times in our lives and we need them at different times, but when we love a book, often what it means is that we have found our voice inside it. And I continue telling them until they start telling me.

CLTL allows all of us to be the teachers. It allows us to all share our epiphanies. It is a program of many voices, and in this book you will hear from students, probation officers, teachers, judges, and the text itself.

This book is about the how and why of Changing Lives Through Literature: It is through finding and sharing our voices and listening to the voices of others that we learn to hear more clearly, to see more deeply.

1

What Is *Changing Lives Through Literature?*

> *"This program was a changing point in my life. There were books that I couldn't put down. They kept me interested in the positive aspects of life."*
>
> —John, student,
> New Bedford Men's Program

HOW IT ALL BEGAN

CHANGING LIVES THROUGH LITERATURE (CLTL) is a program that began in Massachusetts in response to a growing need within the criminal justice system to find alternatives to incarceration. Burdened by expense and repeat offenders, prisons can rarely give adequate attention to inmates' needs and, thus, do little else than warehouse our criminals. Disturbed by the lack of real success by prisons to reform offenders and affect their patterns of behavior, Robert Waxler, a professor of English, and Judge Robert Kane, at the time, a Massachusetts District Court justice, discussed using literature to reach hardened criminals.

In the fall of 1991, as members of a team that also included Wayne St. Pierre, a New Bedford District Court probation officer (PO), the group initiated the first program at the University of Massachusetts, Dartmouth, where Waxler taught. Eight men were sentenced to probation instead of prison, with an important stipulation: *They had to complete a Modern American literature seminar run by Waxler and held on campus.* Believing that accessibility, language, and a good story were keys to unlocking the imagination, Waxler limited selections for this experiment to American short stories or novels from the 20th century.

One of the most important parts of the premise for the program that fueled Waxler and Kane was that the judge and PO St. Pierre would participate alongside the offenders. For twelve weeks, the men, many of whom had not graduated high school and who had 148 convictions among them for crimes such as armed robbery and theft, met in a seminar room at the university. Through a discussion of books, such as James Dickey's *Deliverance* and Jack London's *The Sea Wolf,* the men began to explore aspects of themselves, to listen to their peers, to increase their ability to communicate ideas and feelings to men of authority who they thought would never listen to them, and to engage in dialogue in a classroom setting where all ideas were valid. Instead of seeing their world from only one angle, they began opening up to new perspectives and realized that they had choices in life. They could get out of the cycle of crime. Literature had become a road to insight.

Waxler and Kane realized that they were on to something although at this point, all outcomes were anecdotal:

- Manuel, a small-time drug dealer, stated that "reading opened his mind." He felt that he could relate to the character Wolf Larsen in *The Sea Wolf.* Manuel soon became drug free and a college student.
- Mark, a former drug abuser, became a full-time college student and credited CLTL with helping to change his outlook: "I learned that Wayne St. Pierre is more than my probation officer—he is a human being. Judge Kane is a human being. They cared about me. That made me care about me and start making the right choices."

❑ Walter, who had spent two of his nineteen years in prison, af-
firmed that the program helped him return to school and want
to get his diploma.

Kane and Waxler realized that the Changing Lives program had a
powerful effect on the participants. Roles in the outside world were
less important in what became "a democratic classroom." All voices
added to understanding the literature, and both felt renewed in their
professional life. Judge Kane said, "Any professional, be he or she doctor, social worker, teacher, or judge, is only a complete professional
when the knowledge of scholarship is combined with the understanding of practice."

A year later, Jean Trounstine, a professor of Humanities at Middlesex
Community College, heard about the program from a talk by Judge
Kane at Framingham Women's Prison. Trounstine had been working
at the prison part-time since 1987, teaching college classes and direct-
ing plays, and immediately investigated starting a women's program
with Judge Joseph Dever and PO Valrie Ashford Harris from the Lynn
District Court.

Sue, one graduate of the Lynn-Lowell Women's Program, made a
list of her accomplishments after completing the program:

1. Read and completed a book
2. Comprehended others' point of view on same literature
3. Read books with uncomfortable subject matter
4. Related to characters in book
5. Read for pleasure
6. Expressed my opinions with less fear each time
7. Learned how to take time to focus
8. Different way of life other than AA program and parenting

Success came quickly: By the summer of 1993, with support from
the Gardiner Howland Shaw Foundation, forty men had completed
the New Bedford course with negligible recidivism and a women's

program had been added using a combination of the Lynn and Lowell District Courts. In addition, a graduation ceremony had been held in front of a full courtroom. Probationers who had finished a set of CLTL sessions received certificates of completion and praise from the judge, probation officer, and professor. This ceremony, one of the early traditions of CLTL, was symbolic: Success was showered on students in a courtroom, the very same place where they had been sentenced.

The CLTL program received nationwide publicity and program assistance from the Massachusetts Foundation for the Humanities (MFH) in 1994. An early study of the program had indicated it was worth the investment. Comparing thirty-two participants in CLTL with thirty-two similar offenders not in the program, the study found the recidivism rate for CLTL was 19 percent, and for the other group 45 percent. The statistics simply provided hard data for what we had suspected: Engaging in deep discussions about stories can enrich lives, arouse voices, and create change.

In 1994, CLTL received funding from the State Legislature of Massachusetts to expand into courts throughout the state, and in 1996, Texas came on board, as well as Arizona (1998), Kansas (1999), New York (2000), Maine (2001), Rhode Island (2001), and Connecticut (2002). In addition, a version of CLTL has been running successfully in England since 2000. Florida and Indiana are interested in starting programs, and one may be underway soon in Canada. CLTL has won awards and has been featured in the *New York Times*, *Parade* magazine, *The Christian Science Monitor*, and on the *Today show*, as well as in newspapers and on radio and television shows throughout the world. In 2003, CLTL was awarded an Exemplary Education grant from the National Endowment for the Humanities to develop a website and training materials to expand its reach, and in that year, it also received support for books and transportation from the MFH. In 2004, the New England Board of Higher Education honored CLTL with its Higher Education Achievement Award.

OUR PHILOSOPHY

CLTL is based on the idea that literature has the power to transform. Although it sounds simple—essentially a book club or reading group that meets over a period of weeks and is attended by an instructor, probation officers, a judge, and students—CLTL allows us to make connections with the characters or ideas in a text and to rethink our own behavior. The phrase *changing lives* may sound grandiose. But this program can be the first step toward permanent change or an additional step on the path to a new way of being part of the world. CLTL contends that through literature we can more deeply understand ourselves and our human condition.

> *It also depends on the old-fashioned idea of a good story and whatever it is that happens to us when we read a worthwhile book or immerse ourselves in a piece of literature.*

But what is it about literature that allows this to occur? And why do many of us who are involved with CLTL feel that it is one of the most underutilized tools in the criminal justice system?

As Waxler says, when we talk about literature, we are not just talking about the words on a page or about a book sitting peacefully on a shelf. It is the material that engages us deeply and enables us to be part of the tale. This way of relating to literature is active. It takes imagination and a willingness to participate. But, it does not necessarily require advanced reading skills or a college degree. Many who have not finished high school have found success in CLTL programs. But for most participants, opening up the heart and mind is as difficult as anything they have ever accomplished. We believe that this is often the first step toward change and toward believing, as Kit, one ex-offender who worked with Trounstine said, "There are other ways of living than the streets."

This process, which often creates epiphany, depends on material that engages us at a deep level. It also depends on the old-fashioned idea of a good story and whatever it is that happens to us when we read a worthwhile book or immerse ourselves in a piece of literature. If we are lucky and have been blessed with caregivers who read to us when we were young, or if we were successful in school, we may easily find our way inside a story.

But for many who have never had this experience with a book, CLTL is new and sometimes accompanied by fear, revelations that surprise, or emotions beyond one's expectations. After completing the program, one student from the United Kingdom said:

> It has made me realize how I have made people feel by acting and commit-
> ting the crimes that I have during the past. And the pain I must have caused
> to all the people who have been affected through my criminal behavior.
> Not just my family or loved ones who share the pain right to the very end,
> but the victims as well. Sometimes I wonder at just how much pain I have
> caused people in my life and when will I finally get this right?

Because the power of transformation through literature can upend us, the group itself is crucial to the process. In a group, participants gain support as they reflect, have the opportunity to hear what others have to say, and ultimately feel less alone in their journey.

As the program developed, each of the CLTL groups throughout Massachusetts and throughout the country diversified, incorporating differences based on the needs of particular courts, student populations, or facilitators' styles. Practitioners each added their own stamp to CLTL. Some CLTL programs met weekly while others met every other week. Some were not able to meet on a college campus so they chose to meet in a library. In some cases, judges were supportive but did not attend classes. Although we originally insisted on all-male or all-female groups, others wanted to explore mixed groups. In spite of these differences, one thing was the same: Everyone saw changes in the participants. Literature was empowering. Discussion enhanced that power. The process of reading led to reflection. Reflection often led to change.

The momentum of the program, expressed in news articles and TV and radio shows, caught the public's attention. In 1998, the University of Notre Dame Press approached Waxler about doing an anthology of readings that were particularly significant for CLTLers. Waxler enlisted Trounstine to help choose sample stories and chapters from novels that were effective with CLTL groups. *Changing Lives Through Literature* (1999) was our response. The book organizes readings around subjects that often allow our students to delve more deeply into their own psyches through the safety of story. These selections span a range of thematic issues, touching on identity/voice, violence, love and friendship, and family. We discovered that we each saw things a bit differently in terms of readings and believed that our single-gendered groups would each respond somewhat differently to the selections included. Trounstine selected work by women authors, and Waxler chose selections by men. At the end of each selection in our book, we comment on these texts and offer written responses. As often occurs in a CLTL class, we wanted our responses to open the way for others to share their understandings and encourage their own ways of seeing.

> *Literature was empowering. Discussion enhanced that power. The process of reading led to reflection. Reflection often led to change.*

Since it is an anthology, this first book does not explore the ideas behind CLTL. As the program grew, more and more people became interested in understanding the inner workings of CLTL. Thus, *Finding a Voice* was born. Where we once gave readers a chance to enter texts and respond with us, we now explore how these voices are heard and how that empowerment helps to change lives. *Finding a Voice* lays out the why, what, and how, and shows you, in practical terms, methods as well as dreams and desires.

From the anthology we co-edited, Waxler touches on why story is so powerful and hints at what makes it so profound a tool:

When my son Jonathan was young, I would make up cowboy stories for him at bedtime. Cowboy Jonathan became a character of endless adventure, riding off to meet his next challenge, returning home weary, yet always ready for another journey out. We were never certain what would happen to Cowboy Jonathan when he set out on any particular night, but we cared about him, rooted for him, felt his danger, and celebrated his triumphs. He became part of our collective memory, and we carried traces of his story wherever we went.

That particular story provided a way for Waxler and Jonathan to dream together, to defeat enemies, and to be heroic. The story allowed father and son to live inside the imagination. It allows this for all of us.

But what of readers who have not read much, who have had their imaginations stifled, or have had poor experiences with school? Many CLTL students struggle through books and think they have retained little of the text. They often are the first ones to say the book had no meaning. But in our discussions, where we sit around the table talking about the text and together recreate the story, where we refashion its travails and its successes, where we look into why the

> *These readers often find that, far more than they ever imagined, they have heard something in the story and found that a book stays inside them.*

characters do what they do, and where we reconsider their actions, these readers often find that, far more than they ever imagined, they have heard something in the story and found that a book stays inside them. A character touches a familiar chord, or a story allows them to rethink their own experiences.

Through reading, we see; through discussion, we hear. The CLTL discussion is as important as the reading. Reading on our own, the imagination comes alive through an engagement with language. In the classroom, language can lead to improved verbal and listening skills. As we hear others talk about their experience with the text, and as we talk about the characters with those who may see the world far differently than we do, we experience a paradox: We begin to see perspectives other than our own and, at the same time, we realize that our lives have brought us unique insights. A good story not only calls on us to exercise our minds, it asks us to reach deep into our hearts and evoke compassion for the characters, for each other, and for ourselves.

Much has been written about how stepping inside another's shoes opens us up, even frees us. We are able to consider even the most awful human actions through a character and come to grips with our own most dreadful experiences through someone else's story. There is safety in the CLTL classroom precisely because the story seems to be about someone else. The word *seems* is important. Whether we identify fully or just see parts of ourselves and those we know in the characters we meet, the CLTL discussion enables us to process our own experiences without confessing. Another paradox: CLTL is not therapy, although the process of learning about our lives can be therapeutic. This is what we mean by *transformational:* CLTL is based on the idea that literature has the power to transform lives.

> *A good story not only calls on us to exercise our minds, it asks us to reach deep into our hearts and evoke compassion for the characters, for each other, and for ourselves.*

Every CLTL program is different, as you will discover browsing through this book, but all have this in common: literature, discussion, and a plurality of voices. The literature may be a stepping-off place, or it may be the meat and potatoes of the class. All of the programs are connected to the Socratic notion that "the unexamined life is not worth living. . . ." We reach out to offenders who have the motivation to change behavior that has caused them to end up as statistics in the criminal justice system. Through literature, we ask participants in CLTL to explore their identity, and the result is often their way out of crime.

I don't know if it's a turning point, but to read about Frederick Douglass and how a little thing like reading and writing can so profoundly change someone's life, and how I take it so much for granted, makes you wonder what else I'm taking for granted, things like freedom. It will make me think my decisions through before I act on them.

Student, Dorchester, Massachusetts Men's Program

THE TEAM CONCEPT

CLTL has as a premise a team of three who are behind every CLTL student: the facilitator, the probation officer, and the judge. The program is unique because there are four *equal* voices around the table.

The Student

I received a new path from this class, of thinking ability. The doom of embitterment is closed and a window of wisdom opened.

Student, Dorchester, Massachusetts Women's Program

The *student* is the lynchpin of CLTL. Without students, there would be no program. The students in CLTL classes can be sentenced from the bench by a judge or found among clients at a particular court by a probation officer. Many of our programs offer some time taken off the probation sentence, and some offer a fee reduction, but this all depends on each court's rules and sentencing guidelines.

We serve both men and women, most often in same-sex groups, and the students in our adult programs have been as young as seventeen and as old as seventy-five. Most of our students have prior records. Many have served jail time. What seems important for success in the program is the degree of willing participation in CLTL; while courts may strongly recommend CLTL, ultimately, participation is voluntary.

Many of our students have physical, emotional, and/or sexual abuse in their backgrounds. Most come from poor or working-class families and are struggling to make ends meet. Many students arrive as avid readers. Reading abilities and interest in reading vary enormously from town to town and within an individual program. Some programs serve towns with primarily African-American populations, whereas other programs are racially diverse or exist in primarily white communities. CLTL students are expected to treat each other civilly in the classroom and

> *Success means not bailing out when a book is hard to understand. Success means reading the book even if it seems irrelevant to one's life right now. Success means not giving up.*

respect the rights of all group members. The students often have many issues they must deal with while on probation, along with attending the CLTL program: jobs, housing, relationships, family, health, substance abuse, sexual orientation, stress, and, often, sheer survival. The classroom is expected to be a place where we all come together.

Students are expected to live by the rules of their probation officers and/or their facilitators. In most cases, they attend all classes and do all of the reading. Some students bring notes to class so that they can be more active in the discussion. Others reread parts of a book just before they come to class. Many share the books with family members and talk about them long after class. We expect that many of the characters in these texts will touch our readers and that many of the themes in the readings will have meaning for their lives. As one of the students from the Woburn, Massachusetts Men's Program said: "I am in a very labor-intensive job, and to have some intellectual stimulation to wind down the day, to say to myself I'm worth more than humping furniture and drinking with the guys sort of calms me and soothes the soul." In some programs, offenders are able to substitute CLTL discussion group meetings for meetings with their probation officer.

What is true for all students is that they need to be willing to assume some responsibility for their choices and to allow the program process to take hold. Success means not bailing out when a book is hard to understand. Success means reading the book even if it seems irrelevant to one's life right now. Success means not giving up.

Kim came to CLTL with a long record. She had done prison time. She had been strung out on drugs for longer than she wanted to remember. She could hold a job, but she was often secretive, got high at work, was engulfed in her own life and impervious to others, and couldn't manage a good relationship. Most of the men she was attracted to were abusive, abrasive, or not interested in much besides drinking and drugging. Kim had grown up in Lowell, Massachusetts, and had a tough demeanor. From the things she said during the CLTL classes, it was clear that her childhood had been rough, with a divorce and court involvement beginning in her teens.

After fourteen weeks (seven sessions of CLTL), Kim wrote about how she had changed as a result of the sessions:

> I've been able (to allow myself) to share my feelings—to be able to express them as they come up. . . . I've changed my personal attitude about expressing myself. I feel comfortable. I feel sincere. I feel and see myself changing. A lot of self-awareness—how opinionated, how extreme, how vulnerable.

After CLTL, Kim went on to Middlesex Community College and she graduated. She continued in a B.A. program in psychology at the University of Massachusetts, Lowell, and she kept up with Alcoholics Anonymous and Narcotics Anonymous. She met a man and fell in love, got married, bought a house, became a stepmother, and had her own children. None of these steps was easy for Kim. She struggled every inch of the way to stay off drugs and alcohol, to keep perspective, and to handle her emotions. She took some important steps in CLTL on her road to a better life.

First, she allowed herself to learn and to be open to the process of reading and reflecting during the sessions. This is no easy feat, for many come into the program ready to fight and others believe that everything they have to say is worthless. It is not easy to allow oneself to feel the small successes: a book read, an idea praised, or another class attended. Kim, like many of the women in CLTL, was a few months clean and sober at her inception, and she had an earnest desire to stay that way. As she says, she allowed herself to share. Trounstine remembers how surprised Kim was when Judge Dever, a man she never imagined would give her the time of day, actually listened to her intently as she discussed her reactions to Anne Tyler's character Pearl in *Dinner at the Homesick Restaurant*. Kim said she understood and admired Pearl. She was a woman who had raised her children by herself, in spite of a man who left her. Dever agreed. Perhaps Kim recognized something of her own mother in Pearl, but what seemed most important was Kim's demeanor—a broad smile, an almost shy "Yeah?"—as Dever nodded his head in recognition. Kim felt acknowledged. Another success.

Kim used CLTL in the best possible way and added Trounstine to the support group she was gathering around her. She already had found a counselor she turned to when she needed emotional support and a program administrator she had met at Framingham Prison. She always stayed in touch with her supporters, keeping it clear to herself that she was headed toward a healthy life. When she got married, she invited them all to her wedding, along with friends from AA. Part of Kim's success in CLTL was an understanding that she was part of a community and that she had the power to build that community.

Success in CLTL is not always as obvious as it is with Kim, who still writes an occasional letter or calls to keep in touch, to share news of a new baby or a new move. It is often in the smallest moments that someone has an epiphany: Reading begins with a paragraph and continues with one page and then five pages. Coming to class with notes taken can bring pride and engender the willingness to find another book by the same author from the library. Listening also takes willingness, and the result can be understanding someone else's perspective. Success is admitting that you hated the book but finished it anyway. Success is completing something you never believed you could complete: a book, a session, sharing a piece of yourself.

Failures often come amidst the successes. A woman fails to make a class, and she knows she could have come if only she'd pushed herself, but she just can't leave the house. Maybe she needed that day to recover from a loss or a child's illness. Certainly, if it is a pattern, it will keep her from completing CLTL. But maybe for this woman, the missed class is an anomaly. And maybe if she had come to class, she would have gone out and gotten high afterward.

Learning doesn't always come in a rush with success after success. It has ups and downs. Understanding this process can enable true success. There are times when failure can lead to a new awareness or a renewed sense of recommitment. Failure in CLTL can stem from simply not being ready to do the reflection required of students who stay in the program. But it can also begin a process of self-examination.

Although CLTL is for students who have had trouble with the law, many learners, like Kim, lost their way when they were young or have not flourished in traditional school settings. We recognize that this book will serve students who come from all walks of life and practitioners who aim to create reading programs for students in halfway house, juvenile settings, school programs, and book groups where performance is not measured by grades. If you want to learn to read more deeply, the techniques and ideas in *Finding a Voice* will enable reading to touch your heart, enliven your spirit, and educate you about your surroundings, yourself, and others.

The Facilitator

[The purpose of Changing Lives Through Literature] is to inspire others to re-create themselves in a way that is contributory to the human experience and, in that way, to be an inspiration.

Cherie Muehlenberg, facilitator, Kansas Program

The *facilitator* brings love of literature to the table, enables the discussion, provokes the discussion, sometimes structures the discussion and at other times allows it to flow freely. We chose the term *facilitator* because it does not imply a podium and, by discouraging a lecture format, it encourages equal participation among participants. While most of our facilitators are college professors, they do not impose an agenda on the classroom or insist on one meaning for a text. Facilitators are ready with questions and ways to stimulate conversation, but their goal is to find practices that engage students in the literature, characters, and themes and to uncover questions that come from the texts. While the methods and strategies vary from classroom to classroom and teacher to teacher, the emphasis on involving the student is the same and is key to success.

> *A passion for literature and discussion as well as a belief in language help to inspire the CLTL process, so it is important to find facilitators who exhibit that commitment and understand the CLTL population.*

Often the team member who has had the least contact with criminal offenders, the facilitator understands and appreciates the close ties between literature and life and can bring deep insights to the discussion table. He or she must also rely on the probation officer and the judge for information and guidance outside of the classroom.

In a sense, the facilitator represents the alternative being offered to the offender through the reading and discussions on the college campus. The responsibility for choosing the books, facilitating the literary discussions, determining an approach to meetings, and arranging the logistics on the campus falls to the instructor. A passion for literature and discussion as well as a belief in language help to inspire the CLTL process, so it is important to find facilitators who exhibit that commitment and understand the CLTL population.

Taylor Stoehr, facilitator of the Dorchester Men's Program, says that "the educational sorting and labeling system put its 'rejected' stamp on most of [the offenders] long ago, withholding the rewards that more docile pupils collect after investing twelve to twenty years in school. Although we might wish to solve their personal, social, and economic problems by trying once again to put them through the mill, like flawed products bumped off the conveyor belt, it's not going to happen." He calls this "the shadow of schooling" and says it's important for facilitators to recognize this as we make programmatic decisions.

The facilitator's role includes deciding on the logistics and rules with other team members, such as how many weeks the course will meet, where best to hold the class, and how to deal with tardiness or absence. Most facilitators have a college or university affiliation and arrange to have CLTL programs meet on campus. Unaffiliated instructors arrange for libraries or other non-court arenas to be settings for the course: Some classes are held in community corrections centers and a few in prisons. But, the important thing here is that the facilator should be involved in these decisions if possible because the more the instructor functions as part of a team, the more he or she will be invested in the program.

The number of sessions planned will be crucial in determining the kind of reading material. Some groups prefer six meetings over a period of twelve weeks; others meet seven or eight times over fourteen or sixteen weeks. Some meet every week for ten or twelve sessions; most groups, however, meet every other week. If you meet frequently, you'll want short stories; however, many groups use novels. Choosing the books also means thinking about goals for each class, choosing the ideas to focus on during those meetings and the issues that will grab the students during their week away. Most facilitators do not know the details of their students' crimes, but knowing some of the general characteristics of a group may help make better selections (see Chapter 7).

We recommend you choose texts that allow participants to reflect on their own experiences through the characters. This means you will pick texts that resonate with you, that have allowed you to think more deeply about yourself and your surroundings. Unless you are engaged in the literature you choose, you cannot engage others. We recognize that not all of our sample texts will be the best choices for your CLTL program, but we have an extensive list included on pages 152–55 and 186–89. Your excitement about the literature you have chosen will help you to get others involved in the reading.

A good instructor needs to be an improviser. When comments take you in a direction you weren't prepared for, when a student seems like he or she hasn't understood the book, or when the book you've chosen falls flat, you must make quick but thoughtful decisions on how to handle the situation. Your ability to bring ideas and feelings out of the group and to stimulate thinking is at the core of an effective CLTL session.

A CLTL facilitator understands he or she is teaching the piece from one or more perspectives but realizes that other voices in the room are valid and bring their own way of seeing the text. A successful instructor draws out this diversity, learns over time how to capitalize on it, and allows the text to be the teacher. One facilitator from the Maine program remarked:

> Few college courses have engaged my mind as compellingly as these discussion programs with these probationers. They have offered extraordinary insights into the powerful literature used in the program. I leave sessions excited about the transformative capacity of great writing.

CLTL is a way of looking at literature and listening to others' insights. It is choosing literature with themes that resonate for a group, and speaks to students' underlying issues. It is finding ways to engage the disengaged, give voice to those who feel unheard, and include those who have felt disenfranchised by our social system. CLTL is as much a way of approaching a discussion about literature as it is a list of texts; and its methods can be used with groups that have members from diverse cultures, opinions, and backgrounds.

You'll find many areas in this book that will help you more deeply understand the role of a CLTL instructor. The material in Teaching Specific Texts (Chapters 8 and 9) will be invaluable to you. There you'll find guides and lesson plans. Also consult Chapter 10, CLTL Teaching Strategies. Browse Chapter 7, Starting a Program, to get an understanding of the process and what to do if you need to get a program off the ground. Chapters 2 and 3 will help you understand different perspectives on some of the variety of issues you'll face and the range of perspectives from our facilitators. On our website, *http://cltl.umassd. edu,* you will also find a Discussion Forum where you can engage with others in topics or ask questions about CLTL. We hope this discussion board will reinforce CLTL's subtle insistence on looking at literature in more than one way.

There is nothing like learning from experience. Each of us brings our own personal experiences to a text and thus comes up with our own interpretations and methods of making that text come alive. Each of us can be a good instructor unique to the program. This is one of the founding principles of CLTL and a key to our success. As Trudy Schrandt, facilitator of the Wrentham, Massachusetts Program, says: "To see a person change [in CLTL] before my eyes is one of the most fulfilling things that has happened to me in my life."

The Probation Officer

Over the course of probation, a certain amount of trust is generated between the probationer and the probation officer. But for those who've been through the CLTL program, a much higher level of openness prevails. And it works both ways. Listening to each other talk about what they've read shows all the participants...that we're not so far apart.

PO Wayne St. Pierre, New Bedford, Massachusetts Program

In a CLTL program, the *probation officer (PO)* connects the court to the classroom. Most often, it is the probation officer who locates potential students or obtains referrals from fellow POs and who spends the most time getting to know each student's history and background. The probation officer determines if a potential student is appropriate for CLTL by asking a series of questions. Can the person understand the literature? Is she at a place in her sobriety that would make her able to participate in this program? Will there be job conflicts? Is the student motivated to take on CLTL? Does he have too many personal issues that will get in the way of participating in the program?

To answer the first question, many probation officers use a simple reading test to determine if the student is capable of digesting the material. This can be as easy as asking the client to read a magazine article or having a brief discussion as to what the student likes to read.

The probation officer also works with the judge in the courts, talks with prosecutors and defense attorneys about the CLTL candidates, makes recommendations to the bench, draws up appropriate contracts and rules for eligible offenders, and supervises program participants, offering encouragement and praise when appropriate and recommending sanctions when necessary.

Initially, the probation officer is the team member to whom the offender looks for advice and trust. She or he joins in the literature discussions each session. The facilitator looks to the PO for feedback on the reading and discussions; the judge looks to the PO for recommendations and guidance.

Once the sessions begin, the probation officer follows up with a student who misses a class and decides or advises on the student's continued participation in the program. Most probation officers set up rules for offenders' participation and maintain contracts and/or attendance logs.

The probation officer is the person most likely to know the story of the offender, and in this sense, is central to the team effort. He or she may be responsible for helping the offender with other aspects of life, such as job interviews, therapy, family issues, and applying for school programs. All of these commitments interact with the student's success, and no one knows this better than the probation officer. Many probation officers view the opportunity to participate in CLTL as a way to see their clients in a new light.

In some courts, probation officers also bring in members of the community to add to the voices around the table. Reverend Matt Gibson, a community support person in Dorchester, has testified on our website that CLTL can "bring people back into the community. There are a lot of men in the program with whom I've had the opportunity to work and who are in my neighborhood yet don't feel connected to it."

As a probation officer, your involvement in this program is central to its success. By attending sessions, reading all the selections, and participating in discussions, the probation officer serves as a role model in the best possible way. That is, by sharing what you see in a text, offenders look to you for your reactions concerning the texts and also to see how you

> *By attending sessions, reading all the selections, and participating in discussions, the probation officer serves as a role model in the best possible way.*

think. They want you to listen to them and to appreciate their ideas, insights, and reflections. It is important that you challenge ideas in the classroom with your honest assessment of the reading material. Often, it is the tension among ideas that initiates a discussion, and the probation officer can be effective in the role of initiator.

A probation officer may work with a judge to arrange for the graduation ceremony to take place in the courtroom. You may also receive program referrals from the bench. Some will perform follow-up studies to see how the participants are doing after the program. As PO Wayne St. Pierre has said, the probation officer's job can be difficult in terms of balancing the sometimes paradoxical requirements of the courtroom and the literature seminar.

Throughout this book, you'll find some useful materials. Go to Starting a Program (Chapter 7) to learn more about how to initiate a program. Two program prototypes are provided (Chapters 4 and 5). Sample forms, a Discussion Forum, and other materials from POs experienced in the CLTL program are available online at *http://cltl. umassd.edu.* Consider reading some of the essays under Key Issues.

> Changing Lives Through Literature is one of the best programs we have in Dorchester District Court, mainly because it changes everyone's lives. . . . It's a program where, through literature, people look at their behavior and sometimes, this may be for the first time.
>
> *PO John Christopher, Dorchester District Court*

The Judge

> You can either give someone a fish or you can teach them to fish on their own. With CLTL we are teaching them to fish.
>
> *The Honorable K. Randall Hufstetler, 300th District Court, Texas*

In CLTL, the judge gives judicial authorization, serves as a role model for the clients and, ideally, participates in the CLTL sessions as fully as his or her schedule allows.

Without the judge's approval, a traditional CLTL program (for offenders sentenced from the bench or referred by probation) cannot take place. Since the judge gives the CLTL process legitimacy within the judicial system, he or she must be willing to publicly sign on and support the CLTL effort. This takes courage, in part because other judges may not support the idea. Judges who participate in CLTL start out with the belief that literature can be a means to changing offenders' behaviors; they are important in supporting the probation officer's involvement. Judges also highlight the connection between the university and the courtroom.

> *Since the judge gives the CLTL process legitimacy within the judicial system, he or she must be willing to publicly sign on and support the CLTL effort.*

While the probation officer often chooses clients from a dossier of probationers, in many courts, the judge senses that a man or woman would be suitable for CLTL and then sentences this person to the program. Often a good CLTL candidate is recognized in the courtroom. As the Honorable Joseph Dever, Presiding Justice of the Lynn District Court in Massachusetts, says, a good candidate may be an offender with "a minimum degree of literacy and a maximum degree of motivation." On the bench, a judge may conclude that an effective sentence will involve CLTL.

Once the program is underway, the judge attends many of the CLTL sessions, and becomes a role model for the students by demonstrating a personal involvement with the literature. He or she is a regular member of the reading group, sharing insights and honestly depicting his or her appraisal of characters and themes. Many judges talk about how the program has affected their understanding of their own role or of the ability of literature and literature discussions to foster change in so many of the probationers. By listening to the ideas of the men or women on probation, many of whom feel ignored by authority or unable to believe in themselves, the judge gives credit to their opinions and, thus, to their lives. By sharing his or her views, the judge provokes discussion, enables thought, and helps facilitate the turnaround that occurs in many CLTL students. The judge "steps off the bench," as the Honorable Joseph Reardon, First Justice of Barnstable District Court in Barnstable, Massachusetts, says. He means that the judge becomes more than a symbol of authority; he becomes an equal group member. By participating in the program, each judge, says Reardon, is an "exemplar of justice, a proponent for personal growth and change."

The judge is encouraged to attend as many literature sessions as possible after sentencing has taken place, given his or her schedule restraints. Some judges attend all the sessions; others attend a few; still others attend sessions at which the judge's presence is deemed to be most important by the team. It is clear from the testimonials found throughout the book that the judge's involvement is key to program success. They also see their clients with more clarity after participating in CLTL, and they can help facilitators and probation officers with perspective:

> By reading great books and identifying with the characters in these books, for the first time in their lives, [probationers] begin to look at life objectively instead of subjectively.
>
> *The Honorable Joseph Dever, Lynn District Court*

Judges lead CLTL graduations, which are often a public recognition of the students' success in the judge's courtroom, and they may adjust sentencing for the offenders. Some judges feel a reduction of the probation sentence is appropriate for those who successfully complete the CLTL program, and some judges reduce court fees. Judges may decide that students who have not completed the program can retry later sessions of CLTL. Others see students who fail to live up to their CLTL probation contracts return to their courtroom to have reduced sentences revoked.

The judge also serves initially as a symbol of humane and just authority as the CLTL sessions move forward. In this sense, the judge should be someone who clearly projects power, but who also has a keen sense of justice and flexibility. Like good literature, the judge can be a continuous reminder of the importance of creating a meaningful community.

In general, the judge's commitment to the CLTL program and willingness to talk about it to other judges and court officials are important measures of future success for the CLTL start-up. The judge is central to the growth of the program and is often a strong CLTL advocate.

If you are considering initiating a program, you will discover the number of judges who are committed to CLTL and will read what other judges have to say about it. Most important to launching a program, talk to other judges through e-mail or during telephone conversations. Many judges are listed on the website at *http://cltl.umassd.edu*.

If you are a judge initiating the program, finding an instructor is relatively easy. Approach your local university or community college. Many teachers are looking for a chance to be involved in a program like CLTL. Finding the right probation officer means looking for someone who will appreciate literature. Possibly an instructor or probation officer has come to you. If you can, observe an existing CLTL program.

Chapters 2 and 3 will help you understand different perspectives on some of the variety of issues you'll face. Chapters 4, 5, and 6 will clarify the way CLTL interacts with the judiciary more clearly. For more information, browse our individual program homepages online. If you love to read and recognize how important it is to change thinking in order to change behavior, you may join the ranks of other judges who feel like Judge Dever: "Changing Lives Through Literature is the joy of my judgeship." Many find that CLTL has not only affected their clients' lives, but theirs as well.

> I . . . have become reinvigorated and vested with new zeal for our work in the trial court as we realize that we are part of a rebirth of critical thinking and decision making by our probationers.
>
> *The Honorable Joseph Reardon, First Justice*
> *Barnstable District Court*

AFTER CLTL

In this book you will also find more testimonials that show how so many who have been involved with CLTL find renewed enthusiasm and deeper connections with themselves. Teachers, probation officers, and judges—team members—all continue to talk about how much the program changes them. As a result, we have included many voices drawn from our website who bring their unique perspectives on issues, teaching techniques, and CLTL premises.

But finding one's own voice is most important for our students, who struggle to get beyond their own self-definitions and create meaningful lives. Among these pages we include participants with their ups and downs as they struggle and succeed in the program, to show you the longing most feel for better lives. Tapping into this longing is in many ways what CLTL is all about. We recognize that we are often just a beginning and that our students may not connect deeply to their experience in CLTL until years later. Our students are our most reliable voices. They show us where we triumph and where we falter. And when they stay in touch, go back to school, find work they are proud of, and create relationships they know aren't easy, years later they sometimes write to tell us about how in reflection, CLTL helped them find a voice. Here is a part of one such letter from Kim, the woman from the Lynn-Lowell Women's Program:

The class didn't mean much to me while I was attending. My reason for joining was a suggestion as a way of making my weekly probation appointments. I was working at the time and could not schedule the appointments during work hours. In retrospect, I'm glad I attended. I don't know how much the books, the reading, and the discussions benefited me. What I "took home" from the class was a sense of belonging, of fitting in, of not feeling so lonely and isolated in society. Being released from prison after eighteen months is very scary. Especially to someone who can't admit they have fears. Someone who has pretended to have confidence and courage for so long that the real insecure scared person can't admit it. This group was a connection. A bond with other women who all acted one way and felt totally another. I wasn't alone.

. . . After giving this some thought, I also realize there was another important aspect to this group. The judge, probation officer, and teacher—all authority figures to us—they were all there for us, to listen to us, guide us, and direct us. It was their belief in the program and us that helped me deal with a lot of shame. They respected me until I could learn to respect myself . . . never pushed me or directed me, but somehow . . . inspired me to return to school. To attend classes with people half my age who had no criminal background . . . inspired me to believe I could do it as well as them, if not better, and I did.

2 Can We Change Lives?

> *"Astounding was the revelation that came to me somewhere between* Macbeth *and* Sea Wolf, *that all human nature and behavior has significance and relevance to me."*
>
> —*Student, UK Program*

THE VISION OF THE CHANGING LIVES Through Literature (CLTL) program has attracted a large group of dedicated participants. By its very nature, CLTL fosters diversity in instructor approaches, student populations, class guidelines, sentencing, and other strategies. We don't always agree with each other, but we do listen to each other, respect our differences, and move forward, hoping to change lives in the process.

The variety of voices and approaches is captured, in part, by the conversations and debates we have about key issues related to CLTL, many of which are found on the website, *http://cltl.umassd.edu*, and many that are included here.

A central question we continually grapple with is: What do we mean when we use the phrase, *Changing Lives Through Literature?* So many people argue that literature lacks any utilitarian value. We disagree with those who deny the transformative power of literature. We have seen it happen.

Of course, not all of us are convinced. Some would argue that while the literature focuses the discussion, the conversation is what is crucial. We would agree that CLTL is not a silver bullet that promises success in every case; of course, there will be failures. But what do we mean by success, and what do we mean by failure?

Most of us involved in CLTL have always believed in literature, in its healing power, in its ability to change lives. By *literature* we mean something that makes us a part of the story we are reading, or discussing with others. Literature is always alive for us. It keeps us free.

When we sit around the table with criminal offenders, the probation officers and judges, colleagues and friends, we are all seduced by the plot and drawn in by the depth of the characters. The story challenges us and forces us to make choices.

Waxler, for example, has always argued that by reading and then talking to each other about any good story, we get to know our limitations. It is in meeting ourselves and hearing our voice through the voices of others that hope always arrives. As Waxler puts it: We are struck by the magic

> *Most of us involved in CLTL have always believed in literature, in its healing power, in its ability to change lives.*

of the encounter with ourselves, the moment of surprise, the opening for transformation. That is how the change begins, not just for the criminal offender, but for all of us.

Judges, probation officers, instructors, students—we all journey through the complexity and ambiguity of language and discover our identity reflected there. The ambiguity of language unsettles us; opens us to a larger world than we expected; demands that we listen; and insists that we respect diverse perspectives, new interpretations, and unanticipated experiences. The voice of the characters in the stories, together with the voices around the table, begin to reshape all of us.

For example, one evening in the New Bedford Program, Anthony, a rugged but distraught looking man with dark hair about 32 years old, had something important to say before the discussion began. The group had talked about Hemingway's *The Old Man and the Sea* in the previous session. They had exchanged ideas about the main character, Santiago, and had read passages about his struggle, pain, and heroic endurance.

Anthony recalled how Santiago had battled against his own depression in his lonely fisherman's shack on the coast of Cuba, how he had fought off failure and loss, and overcome the excruciating pain riddling his body. Then Anthony told the group how he had walked down the main street of New Bedford a few days earlier, near his old neighborhood, tormented by his own troubles, ready to recant a year-long vow to resist drugs. He could hear the old song of his buddies, drawing him off the main street like the voice of the Sirens.

But before he made the fatal turn that day, Anthony heard the voice of Santiago, the old man. It was as if Santiago had become his friend.

But before he made the fatal turn that day, Anthony heard the voice of Santiago, the old man. It was as if Santiago had become his friend, a voice from literature now whispering in his heart to walk straight and to endure. Anthony refused the call of his friends that day, choosing instead to saunter down the main street of that old New Bedford whaling town. There was no guarantee that Anthony would always do it that way. But for that day, Santiago, the fisherman, kept Anthony alive.

It is not always clear whether it is the literature or the conversation about it that makes the real difference and allows for change. Taylor Stoehr from the Dorchester Program, for example, always insists that the key is in the conversation, and that what is most important is that the probationers are talking to one another in earnest. For Stoehr, we are not engaged in a journey to salvation, but simply in small moments of hope when "around the room the voices rise and fall, and people begin looking each other in the eye."

One thing we do know for certain is that it is not only the probationers whose lives can be changed by the CLTL experience. We all change.

Take the example of Jean Flanagan, facilitator from the Roxbury Program. The group was reading the essay, "Giving Up the Gun" by Andre Dubus. On our website, she writes about how change affected her in many ways. She recalls how the students began to talk, shaping the essay with their own stories.

"I loved this essay," said Andrew, "because I love guns."

"I remember my first gun," Bill responded. "I found it in an abandoned building. It was shiny and it had a pearl handle. I remember how it gleamed and how happy I was that I found this small gun."

James then shared his experience: "I remember the first time I was shot and how frightened I was. When I was at the hospital I kept thinking, am I going to live?"

And then Richard said to Flanagan: "You seem surprised. You white liberals, you'd be walking through Roxbury with your jewelry on and not even realize how much danger you are in. You'd just be smiling."

Flanagan tried to be cool, but Omari looked at her with a smile: "Teach, you are getting an education, too."

Flanagan was. She was beginning to enter the world of the students, listening to their voices.

We often wonder who is the student and who is the professor in our program. Deep reading is never an easy and secure activity, nor is the discussion of the texts. It is an ongoing activity, never finished. As the plot unfolds, characters come alive and draw us in: Santiago, the old man in Hemingway's story of fishing in the deep water off of Cuba; Atticus Finch, the idealistic lawyer in Harper Lee's tale of justice in the deep depression of segregated Alabama; Wolf Larsen, the Darwinian captain in Jack London's sea story of survival in the deep abyss of ocean consciousness; Pecola, the young African-American girl desperate for the blue eyes of the white world in Toni Morrison's novel. They call to all of us.

> *We often wonder who is the student and who is the professor in our program.*

After a long career at the Massachusetts Institute of Technology in the Laboratory for Nuclear Science, it was only Flanagan's second year of teaching. Most of her work-life at MIT was spent with men so when she went into her first CLTL class at Roxbury District Court, she did not fear teaching men or being a white woman working with mostly African-American and Hispanic men.

However, during the first few classes, she was anxious because of her lack of teaching experience and her understandable fear of the unknown. Could she control the class? Would the men do the reading? What if no one spoke?

During one class, discussion turned to the theme of working and self-respect. Omari said he could not get a job at Burger King® because he would not be making enough money. He would rather not have a job because "I wouldn't look good to my boys if I had one like that."

Flanagan got angry at that remark. She'd work at Burger King or anywhere else to maintain self-respect, she claimed.

"I bet you didn't come from a single-parent home," Richard offered at the table.

"Yes, as a matter if fact, I did. My father died when I was seven," Flanagan quickly responded. "My mother struggled to hold our family together, but she had a very strong work ethic that she passed on to me. I went to Northeastern University nights when there were very few women, and so I can't understand why you can't go," she said, as if striking back.

Then Stephen expressed his view that in "white" schools only "white" history is taught. As an African-American man, Stephen said he would not enter a "white" school. It made Flanagan consider how difficult life must have been for Stephen. How privileged was she to grow up in a neighborhood where most people survived well beyond their 20s?

Like so many instructors, Flanagan was reexamining herself through discussion, but she also began to see significant changes in the men after a few classes: They waited until the other men finished before they started speaking, came on time, stood straighter, and dressed differently. Their sorrows and regrets were more evident, and they helped each other with their struggles.

This is exactly what happened in Brian Sullivan's group in Connecticut:

> In our first group, which ran at Tunxis Community College, Sullivan said one of our 16-year-old female students commented on the first day of class that she was "pure ghetto," the implication being that she did not belong on a college campus. This student brought a negative attitude and a vocabulary that was laced with obscenities. By the second or third session, she had a far more selective and appropriate use of the spoken word in the classroom setting. Additionally, her attitude was upbeat and she genuinely seemed to enjoy the group discussions. She is now considering college as a very real possibility after she completes high school.

But these students are not the only ones experiencing change.

"What did you learn this semester, Miss?" Richard asked Flanagan at their final session.

"I learned that Changing Lives Through Literature changes me, too, and that each week you challenge me and my way of thinking."

We are willing to learn from each other in the CLTL sessions. That is part of the process of change. Jane Hale, a professor at Brandeis and an instructor in the Framingham Program, explains it this way:

> Many of our CLTL students put forth a tough facade of knowing what's best for them and the world, though a little below the surface lie tremendous insecurity and self-doubt. Again, this description could apply to most of us. . . . We want our students to know these feelings are okay, and are in fact shared by all of us at times, as well as to give them a group environment where it's safe, and useful, to talk about their fears and shortcomings, as well as their dreams.

For Hale, as for many of us, the language of literature is rich in ambiguity, forcing us to tolerate that richness as we explore its implications from a variety of angles. Through the ambiguity of language and the complexity of character found in good literature, we find ourselves questioning more, achieving what the poet Keats once called "negative capability," that refusal to put a "palpable design" on others. We tolerate the ambiguity, enjoy it, refuse that irritable reaching for simple answers, embracing instead the complexity of the human heart.

As Edie Shillue, a writer now in Northern Ireland who has worked as a facilitator in our Dorchester Program, says:

> *Through the ambiguity of language and the complexity of character found in good literature, we find ourselves questioning more, achieving what the poet Keats once called "negative capability."*

It comes as a surprise to many, our CLTL students among them, that literature is a particularly powerful catalyst for transformation. In the subject matter of poetry and fiction, we find intensely personal experiences presented with just enough distance for students to talk openly about decision-making, but not so far removed that they feel unable to empathize and connect with characters. The distance of imagined experience can be essential. The classroom, then, is not a group therapy session, but an arena for thought, speculation, and open discussion of the elements of socially engaged living.

It is this too that hints at what we mean when we say that we are engaged in changing lives. As Shillue is quick to point out: "The model is not the linguistic professor Henry Higgins attempting to teach the cockney servant woman Liza Doolittle 'good English' in a revised version of *Pygmalion*, but rather a democratic conversation that respects the rich diversity of all voices around the table."

Shillue points to the complexity, the fact that we are not doing literacy education in the traditional sense:

> Teachers are most successful when freeing themselves and their students from the additional burden of "reform" when engaging in explorations of language and literature. The forced humiliation of Higgins' pronunciation exercises and the disdain that accompanies many types of educational "correction" are counterproductive practices, particularly in an environment such as Changing Lives Through Literature, where the political and personal intersect with the judicial.

It is a way of finding voice, recognizing human character where language intersects across lines of class, gender, and race. As Hale claims: "CLTL students need particularly to learn how to represent themselves, their experiences, thoughts, and aspirations, eloquently and positively. Teaching them both the power and the conventions of spoken and written discourse through discussing their own and others' lives is a way to directly empower them to see and live their lives as if they had all the options for change we know they do."

> *Teachers are most successful when freeing themselves and their students from the additional burden of "reform" when engaging in explorations of language and literature.*

> *It is not so much a struggle to get others to meet a prescribed standard, but rather to create the conditions for everyone to give voice to their ideas, to convince everyone that they can be part of civic life.*

When we talk about changing lives then, we are also talking about a vision of an inclusive society. For us, change has value along those lines. It is not so much a struggle to get others to meet a prescribed standard, but rather to create the conditions for everyone to give voice to their ideas, to convince everyone that they can be part of civic life.

As Taylor Stoehr eloquently suggests:

> The crucial lesson involves communication of an attitude toward ideas
> and experience, rather than pushing any predetermined level of knowl-
> edge or expertise. This means taking into
> account the ideals and aspirations as well as
> the intelligence of our students. And it also
> means a growing awareness that language,
> aesthetic taste, and practical ethics are not
> simply inherited from the culture you are
> raised in but are continually being created,
> negotiated, and revised in the public realm, wherever groups of people
> come together to use or question or affirm their attitudes and beliefs.

Success in CLTL is certainly
not about getting good grades;
it is about recognizing our
vulnerabilities and doing
what we can to heal our own
and one another's wounds.

For Stoehr, as for many of us, the classroom has become the primary
forum, the setting for such cultural work.

Often the success of this work is clear to us. The example of Kim
from Trounstine's sessions in the Lynn-Lowell Program discussed in
the previous chapter is a good model for what success can be. But the
difference between success and failure is often not so perfectly clear.
As Bert Stern, an instructor in the Dorchester Program, reminds us:

> Success in CLTL is certainly not about getting good grades; it is about
> recognizing our vulnerabilities and doing what we can to heal our own
> and one another's wounds. These may not be moments of salvation,
> certainly not moments of permanent conversion, but they allow us to
> transcend our isolated egos, and act instead through the community
> we help to create, briefly and tentatively, as we talk together in the
> classroom.

Stern reminds us of our failures as well as our successes. He doesn't
want us getting rigid in our righteousness. He wants us open and vulnerable, questioning what success and failure might really be. Perhaps

Bob Dylan was right. "There is no success like failure, and failure is no success at all."

Stern knows that for many of the probationers the discourse in the class is the only chance they have to think about virtue and values. Such an opportunity to reflect, to experience community and trust, doesn't come readily in the streets. It can make a difference, though. Even if they slip or fall again out there, Stern argues, these moments of reading and discussion will remain with them. Who then is to judge what was a failure or success?

In a piece for the website, called "Success and Failure," Stern writes about Don, a Guatemalan whose face looked like a "Mayan carving." Don would be "menacing if it weren't for his big smile, which is a kind of language in itself: a smile that speaks a sheepish, self-ironic 'am I hustling you or are you hustling me?' and is excessively self-forgiving and just plain warm." Don seemed adrift in the world. Stern said, "Don badly needed people like him" when he entered the CLTL program in 2001.

But as Stern watched Don interact in the class, Don seemed to have found the secret of courage and will from reading about Frederick Douglass. As Stern put it after reading one of Don's homework pieces, "What Don actually wrote was that people like Douglass stood on their conviction 'that what they say and do can change their lives in a split second. Not only their lives. But [the lives of other] people in their own time. It was a movement for years and generations to come.'"

At the time, Stern was caught up in the idea that many CLTL participants "lived much of their lives on reflex, without reflection" and that the sessions "offered them the opportunity to learn reflection and choice—freedom, if you will." Don's statement embodied that truth for Stern, "the truth connecting the individual to a sense of history and hope." For Stern, Don became "a poster boy" for CLTL. In Don's words, Stern saw a "glowing testimony to the power of CLTL to shift the student's mindset by showing him more options."

Don graduated from the program, and it was a year-and-a-half later before Stern saw him again. At first, it looked like his perfect example of success had failed: Don was on probation again. But Don was also back in CLTL. At the end of his first class back, Stern asked Don if he wanted to say anything about the course to the others. Stern doesn't quite remember Don's words that night but they were "simple and positive, despite the ironic fact that he was back in the class, on probation again. His message wasn't so much in what he said as in the fact that he said it. He invited others to lend trust to the course."

A few weeks or so later, Don told Stern he'd been busted again. He was headed back to prison.

Was the CLTL class a failure then? It might have appeared so. But who could answer that question except God? As Stern might have reminded us:

> Human beings are complicated, ready to blaze up or go dim as they dance on a razor's edge. Who can say what Don will do when he steps out onto the streets again in maybe a few years? For that matter, who can say that in prison he won't go to the library, continue his reading, maybe remember how Malcolm X first educated himself by memorizing the entire dictionary, page by page.

We believe Don just might.

We have discovered that the phrase *changing lives through literature* sometimes creates assumptions that often prove too limited and too simple. Conservative judges and liberal judges alike embrace CLTL for the following reason—it extends beyond simple categories to some deeper truth about all our lives. In the process, it encourages continued conversation, expanding understanding, fostering debate.

> *Conservative judges and liberal judges alike embrace CLTL for the following reason—it extends beyond simple categories to some deeper truth about all our lives.*

The probationers, for example, typically assume that all judges are strict authority figures. After they sit around the table in the CLTL sessions with judges, probationers begin to see them stripped of their robes and to see them as human beings. Judges too begin to see probationers from a different angle—often as bright and energetic women and men with plenty of talent and potential.

It is indeed a delicate balance between failure and success. How can it be otherwise as our perceptions continue to evolve and change? The challenge is to remain open and tolerant, and to refuse to impose a "palpable design" on the person standing before us.

> *In fact, for most of the women, it seems to me that the cause of many of their troubles had more to do with lousy childhoods, the presence of learning disabilities, and the product of both—low self-esteem.*

When Gail Mooney, a facilitator from the Concord-Woburn Program, first started with the program, she was understandably impressed by how insightful the women were and how they were similar to many of the women she knew. She also assumed that most of the students had gotten into trouble because of their bad choices in men.

"I'm not sure why I assumed that," Mooney said. "In fact, for most of the women, it seems to me that the cause of many of their troubles had more to do with lousy childhoods, the presence of learning disabilities, and the product of both—low self-esteem. . . . These were girls generally left on their own with no real sense of community or support."

For Mooney, a sense of community and a strong sense of self-reliance are the cornerstones of success for CLTL. She believes this accounts for the two most popular novels in her groups: *Plainsong* by Kent Haruf and *White Oleander* by Janet Fitch. The first is about the importance of community; the second is about self-reliance and the forces that help us to survive or succeed.

As Mooney explains it:

> The main character in *White Oleander* has the gift of artistic talent as a means to express herself and an avenue to pursue, and we've often

discussed how very important having an outlet would have been for all of us in our youth and even now. When a woman in the group says, as one or two invariably do, "Yeah, but I have no talents," always, another member will be quick with a response: "You said you're a great cook!" or "You said you like to [sew/act/sing/garden/write]!"

In Mooney's group, as in so many CLTL groups, that group becomes a small community. "The women are often disappointed when the group is done; they've come to look forward to it because it serves a little as a group therapy class, but much more than that, because they get to use their brains, to read and reflect, to feel a part of something larger . . . a community, a class."

For Mooney, the most important element of the CLTL program is this "offering of an intellectual community. It's enabling and powerful because it's not a group for victims but for winners; if we can see ourselves in literature, then we are all, truly, in this together. We are all made of the same stuff, the same needs."

Judge Robert May, one of the judges in our Texas program, once commented that what may seem small and almost insignificant to us can often be a gigantic step for a probationer. May has presided over more than a few capital cases. "When you read a book," he said, "it slides into your soul. It gives you a glimmer, a dream of something a little higher.

> *It's enabling and powerful because it's not a group for victims but for winners; if we can see ourselves in literature, then we are all, truly, in this together.*

Sometimes the margin of difference is slight. But that small advance can actually be a huge gain. It can make all the difference."

This is Mooney's thinking as well:

This small realization is gigantic to someone who's feeling alone or out of tune with the rest of the world. It's powerful to be in a group engagement, to pull the symbols out of art and to make them real . . . community, sustenance, self-reliance, the need for beauty. . . . These are all the abstractions for which we often have no voice other than that found in literature, but it is exactly these things that ennoble us and that, by their pursuit, make the women in my CLTL groups feel good about themselves. And feeling good is always the very first step toward positive, vital action.

Part of the meaning of success for us then has to do with making sure that we have not underestimated ourselves and have not allowed others to do so. The probationers, for example, often misjudge their own reading abilities, having internalized a sense of failure over many years. It is part of the CLTL program to help them reconsider themselves, stick with the process, and reclaim their ability.

Trounstine describes it this way on the CLTL website:

> In one class of mine, a new young white student got up and ran out of the room in tears after she was given the reading list for the semester. Her mother had always told her she couldn't read and she carried that fear of failure with her. We brought her back into the group, and we helped her figure out exactly how many pages she had to read a night in order to complete the novel by the next class. The PO also helped her plan to check in a few times each week. Pretty soon, she was coming to class with notes on the texts. She stuck it out, struggling with book after book, getting family members to help her by reading aloud, and when she got to the point where she could read a whole book on her own, she couldn't have been prouder.

Fearing failure, our probationers need to feel good about themselves, sometimes to overcome their anxiety and rage. By reading and discussing these stories with respect and a critical eye, they learn something important about trust and esteem.

"I was just like Wolf Larsen," a probationer said about the power-obsessed captain in Jack London's *The Sea Wolf.* "I had a father just like that," another student said about the violent and alcoholic old man in Russell Banks' *Affliction*. "Curly fears he'll be exposed for what he really is in all his impotence," another probationer said about the boss's son in John Steinbeck's *Of Mice and Men*. "I know the pain Sonny must feel sitting all alone in his jail cell," another reader said when talking about James Baldwin's "Sonny's Blues." And with each remark, the men around the table silently nod with mutual understanding.

Anthony Farley, a professor at Boston College Law School and a facilitator in the Dorchester Program, has noted that it is just this kind of success that stands in bold opposition to the institutional failures of the schools and prisons affecting the lives of so many of the CLTL probationers. Thinking in particular about people of color in the CLTL program, Farley sees their past experience in the culture as somewhat analogous to the experience of slavery itself. Success becomes a kind of liberation from hopelessness, a victory of endurance and provides the possibility of hope:

> *It is just this kind of success that stands in bold opposition to the institutional failures of the schools and prisons affecting the lives of so many of the CLTL probationers.*

Many of the participants experienced the program as the first time that they ever read a book from cover to cover. Many have confessed to me their late realization that reading could be liberating and enjoyable. They speak of joy in discovering the pleasures of the text and of anger because the doorway to the world's imagination, the book, was hidden from them in school. They look back in anger at the ways that their schools succeeded in causing them to fail themselves by producing failing grades. They realize, more importantly, that they can read and that they have ideas about great literature. And this causes them to look forward with hope.

> *They speak of joy in discovering the pleasures of the text and of anger because the doorway to the world's imagination, the book, was hidden from them in school.*

We believe that every story is our story if we are willing to listen to it, read it over, rewrite it for ourselves. And in this sense, every story is a success story if we dare to explore its implications, its dark side as well as its surface. But each human success story also implies failure, just as life implies death. We are reminded of our vulnerabilities and our strength every time we read a good story. That is perhaps one of the reasons that probationers in Texas put their names on long waiting lists to get into the CLTL program there. According to William R. Kelly at the University of Texas in Austin, those probationers see CLTL as significantly different from other probation programs. It increases the desire and motivation to read and learn.

"On a scale of 1 to 10, where 1 means poor and 10 means excellent, Kelly reported, "the overall program rated 9.4."

That, no doubt, is an important bit of quantitative data. But, for us, there are always other questions, ongoing conversations with a multitude of voices: We want people in the Changing Lives Through Literature program to be successful of course. But what do we really mean when we say that? Are we talking about reduced recidivism rates? Are we talking about enhanced reading skills? We have overwhelming evidence that suggests we have achieved that kind of success. But is that enough? In fact, is that kind of measurement what we really want to talk about when we talk about success in CLTL? Can you really measure such success? How can you quantify the human heart?

Every human story is a success story once you get inside it, once you fully understand it. Judgment may be necessary, but we prefer mercy and compassion.

3

Where Does Literacy Fit in, and What Does Gender Have to Do with it?

> *"All these years I've been thinking that I could not read or write. Here, look at me now!"*
> —Student, Dorchester Men's Program

AS A PROGRAM BASED ON THE DISCUSSION of literature, it's only natural that we talk about literacy. Reading has often been a source of failure for many who enter CLTL, as has school. Yet, our students are sentenced <u>to read.</u> They do not take a reading test before they enter our programs but probation officers make sure that the students have a certain degree of willingness and often ask them to read a magazine article to assess their confidence about comprehending and interpreting words on the page. But what else is involved in literacy? Should we include offenders with poor reading skills or reluctant readers? How do we make room for those who come to English as a second or third language and who struggle with English? The ways in which we define literacy within the program are crucial, as is our national dialogue on literacy. As with all of our controversial issues, we recognize the debate and instead of trying to solve it, allow questions to propel us.

Likewise, questions arise about how we handle gender in the CLTL classroom. In the beginning, classes were either all men or all women. It seemed apparent that the differences in social, political, and economic issues between men and women dictated such segregation. Although coed education is the norm across the nation and we include coed groups in CLTL, how do single-gender groups affect the learning in CLTL? What happens when a male probation officer is in an all-female group or a woman teaches men?

In this chapter we seek to look at both what defines literacy in our programs and the relationship of gender to the experience around the table. These perceptions come from a variety of practitioners, all of whom comment about the program in our *Key Issues* section on our website, *http://cltl.umassd.edu*, excerpts of which are included here.

WHY READ?

When explaining to students why reading has such prominence in the CLTL program, Waxler thinks about Alberto Manguel's description in *A History of Reading* of the first time he was able to read words by himself, without the help of another reader:

> And yet, all of a sudden, I knew what they were; I heard them in my head, they metamorphosed from black lines and white spaces into a solid, sonorous, meaningful reality. I had done all this by myself. No one had performed the magic for me. I and the shapes were alone together, revealing ourselves in a silently respectful dialogue. Since I could turn bare lines into living reality, I was all-powerful. I could read.

Reading is the beginning of a social contract, as Manguel explains, a covenant between the self and the world. Words on a page are gifts creating a communal threshold, inviting us to participate in an ongoing conversation set in motion before we arrived, taking us to our future, tempting us with revelation about the world and our relationship to it. Through reading, Manguel suggests, we glimpse what and where we are.

It is not quite true to say that we are what we read, but reading is always a social process, even when we read alone. It allows us to find ourselves through a common language, a set of symbols set before us by other human beings. When we read, we bring our language and our voice to the black marks and white spaces on the page, wrestle meaning from them, and recontextualize ourselves in relation to them.

As Mark Turner says in *The Literary Mind: The Origins of Thought and Language*: "Knowing how to inhabit stories is the essential requirement of mature life." Through reading, we break free from our solitary lives, as Turner suggests, from the linear and local perspective of ordinary existence. We emerge from single vision into the complexity of a multifaceted human experience.

> *It is not quite true to say that we are what we read, but reading is always a social process, even when we read alone.*

Judge Joseph Dever, judge in the Lynn-Lowell Program, says that reading is a way to address the paradox he finds in our population: self-absorption and low self-esteem. Reading allows our students to get inside and outside of themselves. C. S. Lewis said we read to know that we are not alone, but we also might say that the byproduct of reading is becoming more aware of our connection to others.

In *The Talking Cure*, Susan C. Vaughan argues that recent findings in neurobiology and cognitive science give biological weight to Freud's psychological ideas: Psychotherapy works at the cellular level. We want to suggest that "deep reading" in our CLTL program performs the same function. As Vaughan says, through the powerful emotional experience of our relationship with good literature, we can recognize the main patterns of our life and remake our views of ourselves and others in relationships. Reading, like psychotherapy, can become a habit—and that habit can help change lives and possibly even reshape brain cell patterns.

But if reading can do so much, why do so many have such difficulty with words on a page?

HOW DOES CLTL ADDRESS LITERACY?

Taylor Stoehr from the Dorchester program says that "there are kinds, as well as levels, of literacy, matters of cultural savvy as well as linguistic expertise—everything from being able to read street signs and fill out a job application to mastery of the specialized jargon of computer programming or the protocols of international diplomacy." In our program, "literacy is a cultural competency, broader than mere reading and writing," and he points out that "our students come with different literacy skills and needs, not always well served by traditional schooling practices."

Traditional schooling works for many. But in spite of their willingness to learn, our students often have failed in traditional school settings. Edie Shillue, former facilitator from the Dorchester women's program, says that CLTL urges us to explore literacy from this angle:

> Those who are frequently defined as "lacking" in schooling have a degree
> of literacy that must be recognized and utilized in order for students
> to have successful classroom experiences, but first, we must define, as
> instructors, our own understanding of literacy and discourse within our
> own lives. Examining the multiple arenas in which we read, speak, and
> listen, and our position(s) within those arenas—our authority or lack
> thereof—is a good place to start.

Shillue feels that "because literacy is such a complex arena," we must "encourage our students to embrace the reading of literature . . . to act as facilitator and director of the subsequent exploration." We need to recognize that we are asking much more of them than may have traditionally been asked. Shillue writes:

> My first CLTL class observation included a student complaint about
> being asked to read Sandra Cisneros' text *The House on Mango Street*.
> Written in an adolescent voice, the novel is often received by students

as a humiliatingly simple text and one that reveals a teacher's underlying assumptions about student interests and skills. Watching this student-teacher exchange, I realized that teachers may wish to consider what literacy skills they assume are prevalent within the student population when preparing materials. They may also consider finding more creative ways of addressing the inevitable diversity of skills that comes with adult education. Cisneros' novel, for example, can be utilized as part of an exercise for parents to critique adolescent literature. Similarly, a discussion about literary technique, and its success and failure, is not beyond the skills of our student body. Inviting students into the discourse of the classroom with explanation and definition of its parameters is a more fruitful exercise than the memorization and recitation associated with traditional learning.

Shillue calls CLTL "an education of engagement, an inherent responsibility of public institutions." Because inquiry in the CLTL classroom is based on experience, engagement is possible without the academic approach that may have stifled students in traditional settings.
Shillue describes her experience:

Some evenings it seemed impossible. Students were overwhelmed with all the hazards that go with urban life. . . . This one had to find her son, the other was delayed by a job she could barely hold on to, another was discouraged because she didn't know or understand many words in the reading. There were a multitude of things outside the room that blocked our path with a persistence and ominousness of the type you only find in a certain form of ghastly fairy tale. Our heroines advance just so far out of the dark, only to get smacked back by strange and difficult happenings. Step by step, they make their way—every moment a battle with internal and external negativity. This, of course, is the story of Zora Neale Hurston in *Dust Tracks on the Road* . . . informed by an unflagging persistence, an almost absurd optimism, and a full awareness of the dignity and power of her own humanity.

As our students struggle to overcome obstacles in their lives, it is obvious that understanding language on the page feels impossible at times. Shillue points out that "many students will have been taught reading and writing through an ideology that sees literacy as an autonomous skill." And she underscores that "much acquisition of language skills (at varying levels) is done in context." For many of our students, most who hail from poor socioeconomic settings, "print language is contained in the context of institutionalized documents and forms, while oral arenas provide richer, more meaningful communications."

She asks the important question: "How then do we engage students in an enjoyment of literary text while recognizing varied language skills?" Her answer: "The heart of the work must be a respectful recognition of the varied forms of oral and print discourse and an appreciative engagement of oral skills."

Shillue was one of the first to break away from using only stories and novels—the kinds of texts we began with in CLTL, because we believed, and many of us still do, that they are most engaging to our students because of the power of "story." But Shillue and others have found that poetry, autobiography, essays, and plays offer other types of introspection.

Jane Hale, facilitator from the Framingham, Massachusetts Program, believes that "students' own literacy tales must be drawn out, explored, listened to, written, and read as full texts in the curriculum." Hale says, "that way, students can experience their intellectual, emotional, and behavioral changes as free choices they make as individuals."

She is not alone in stressing writing in addition to reading. Although we hold that literature is at the core of our program, some facilitators use writing in the CLTL classroom. Tam Neville, facilitator in the Dorchester program, says it allows more "space for people whose lives have been narrowed by pain and violence." She reports that practitioners each choose to use writing in different ways: at the beginning of classes to anchor students and ease them into discussion and to help others express themselves; and at the end of class to help provide closure. Moses Glidden of the Arizona program says he asks students to write about the reading when they first enter the classroom:

> I ask them to write about one scene . . . to use . . . detail, description and dialogue. Then, the students read . . . aloud. After two or three classes the students look forward to this exchange and this builds connections. Writing is a great tool. It tells us who we are, where we're going, and why."

Discussion helps build literacy and it is where students find their own voices, as well as diverse ways of seeing the world. Carolyn Labun, facilitator from the Worcester, Massachusetts Program and a college professor, says she's found that after she discusses the reading in class, her students "invariably grasp it and enjoy it in ways beyond the reach of . . . younger, academically more advanced, students." The students, she says, bring much to the table: "a real desire to connect with the texts and each other; an appreciation of the academic setting; a willingness to let the words of the text touch them and to share their responses."

Although we hold that literature is at the core of our program, some facilitators use writing in the CLTL classroom.

Hale writes about an experience she had in the classroom that taught her about discussion. On her first night of teaching in CLTL,

> I walked into class with a lesson plan for discussion of "Greasy Lake" by T. C. Boyle. It had been fun to go through this story about teenage male drinking, peer influence, violence, and poor choices, thinking up questions to ask that would teach my students how drinking can make us use poor judgment, how physical violence can get out of hand before you know it, and how one should always keep in mind what the right thing to do is. Boy, was I naive! We ran through the list of my carefully

prepared questions in under 10 minutes. . . . The real question here was: Did the teacher learn anything from the experience? And the answer is yes. I learned that the course would not be about teaching some poor ignorant criminals what most of them already knew: how to tell people in authority what they want to hear. It would rather be about modeling, for a heterogeneous group of young people, ways to read, write, and discuss literature so it has meaning to their own lives. It would also be about teaching them to tell and write the texts of their own lives, so they could feel how much personal power lies in the telling.

"Greasy Lake" remains on Hale's CLTL syllabus, even though her method of approaching it in class has evolved as has her understanding that her students have their own degree of literacy, perhaps different from what many of us have traditionally labeled the term. They can teach us as we can teach them.

One student from Bert Stern's class in Dorchester offered this insight at the end of a course, illustrating another kind of literacy that speaks not only to engagement but to perspective:

I [learned to look] at the white man differently. I thought they were racist, but the way everybody in my class acted and responded to questions, they answered the questions like any normal human being would respond. I also hear the things my classmates have been through, even the teacher. We all go through things but yet we go forward. I think we all have encouraged ourselves no matter what, to love ourselves and cherish life, no matter what color we are or how we look.

In his CLTL Dorchester Program, Taylor Stoehr is "more concerned with how students perceive their abilities than with assessing or upgrading them." While many of us pride ourselves on getting students to return to school, get their GEDs, or take college classes, Stoehr holds a somewhat different view based on his experiences with probationers:

Rather than setting out with an agenda that assumes lack of competence, let us begin by giving as much scope and play as possible to the powers of speech our students already have and encourage them to exercise these powers with more self-conscious confidence, in the circumstances where they actually find themselves, before asking them to think about their weaknesses or what more schooling might do for them.

But from Hale's perspective, "CLTL endeavors to motivate and prepare young people on the margins of society to claim and exercise full membership within it." Her view is somewhat different from Stoehr's:

In asking students to learn, we are fundamentally asking them to change their ideas, their skills, their attitudes, their behavior, their values. Since change means going from one state to another, students whose present lives are not centered on literacy can feel an understandable reluctance to leave the only life they know behind.

Here she uses the term *literacy* in its more traditional sense, but many of us would agree that our understanding of literacy in CLTL is deepened by our students' perspectives. Literacy for CLTL often means a willingness to read, to think, and to speak out. As we continue to evolve, our appreciation of different points of view enriches us and informs the program. (Also see Chapter 7.)

It is important to remember, as Shillue says, "We are not so much encouraging others up a ladder as making our way up one ourselves."

GENDER ISSUES

We have often discussed how men and women entering our programs have different perspectives and thus often wrestle with different issues and problems, and so there is value in forming groups with gender in mind. Most CLTL groups are same-sex for this reason, although some practitioners hold that mixed-sex groups work well. In fact, many single-gender CLTL groups actually have some mix (e.g., a male judge for a women's group, a female facilitator for a men's group).

Waxler began the first program with the notion that choosing the right books was key in a single-gender group. If the texts were those that men related to, they could encourage conversation about male identity, confrontation with mainstream authority, violence, and power—issues about which many men are conflicted. Conversation about these matters proved to allow for self-reflection, recognition of alternatives, and opportunity for new possibilities. And conversation around our CLTL table continues to be a safe place for such inquiry.

The men are often unsure of themselves, although they would never admit it. Many of them have a record of violence. Many suffer from low self-esteem, poverty, family breakdown, alcohol and drug abuse—all typical causes of violent behavior. They are also usually uncertain about how the reading of literature, not a particularly male activity as far as they're concerned, can possibly help them.

Women who are part of the court system are in some ways different from their male counterparts. They often have more sexual abuse and mental illness issues; suffer without financial resources and partners; and consistently have drug and alcohol issues that impair their abilities to mother. Trounstine, who taught women in prison for ten years, finds that success in CLTL comes by understanding and accepting those differences.

> *They are also usually uncertain about how the reading of literature, not a particularly male activity as far as they're concerned, can possibly help them.*

With single-gender groups, women also feel freer to express themselves, and as they report, safer.

Jill Carroll, facilitator from the Texas program, says that "gender difference in the classroom potentially undermines the power of the personal inquiry the program seeks to facilitate. The kinds of issues we tackled in our women-only classes were issues that many of the women would not have engaged in had there been men in the room with them."

Trounstine feels that this safety does not necessarily mean that men cannot participate in the CLTL women's groups. Men can add diverse perspectives, which is a fundamental tenet of CLTL. But it seems important to let the women dominate the conversation, to allow the CLTL session to be a place where they read about and tell their stories. The fact that the classroom essentially belongs to them creates this safety.

Gender plays a part in book choices and how we direct discussion, but even more important, in the behavior of participants and their attitudes toward learning and change. Keeping the stakes high is important for women because they have often been underestimated and infantilized. At the same time, it is essential to avoid minimizing their difficulties when they "can't understand" a text, have nothing to say, or even when they try to fake their way through a discussion.

> *But it seems important to let the women dominate the conversation, to allow the CLTL session to be a place where they read about and tell their stories.*

Much has been written about women's issues and about women's success or lack of it because of societal forces: the need to be nurturers; the fear of failure; the pressure to live the American dream and have 2.5 children, a husband, a happy home, and a white picket fence; the responsibilities of family and homemaking that fall to females; the fact that women make less money in their careers than their male counterparts. Some of these insecurities and attitudes are culturally based. Helping women understand how to change their thinking often means coming to grips with what our society inculcates into and expects of them.

Women and men of color face even more pressures than whites as they struggle with the higher incarceration rates of their family members and larger issues of poverty and societal racism. CLTL can address some of these issues through the texts chosen and through the way discussions are run, but the agenda must never be to force opinions on the probationers. Instructors need to allow students to see where we are coming from and to acknowledge that we don't necessarily understand their life experiences. We need to encourage them to make choices that allow them to lead productive, healthy, and satisfying lives but always with an eye to what they want.

One way low self-esteem expresses itself with women is that, across the board—African-American, white, or Latino—women will underestimate their reading abilities. Ways to bypass these anxieties include using short stories, assigning books over a longer period (one book in two sessions), and reading aloud in the classroom. Kelly DeSouza, who founded a program in the women's jail in Dartmouth, Massachusetts, says:

> The first story we ever read was "Everyday Use" by Alice Walker. . . . At one point, there was an older woman in the group who was of Native American and African-American descent. I remember how fond she was of the story. She mentioned how she had items that were handed down to her and how even though she did use them, she still cherished them . . . she actually had a quilt from her grandmother, made from old skirts and dresses, just like in the story.

This woman may not have tackled the story if it were more than its twenty pages. She may have needed to be eased into the program, not because of her abilities but because of her insecurity. Lack of confidence can show up in early meetings, perhaps in part because the students are not used to being asked for their opinions. Some probationers are at first afraid to talk in the discussion, certain that their ideas are wrong or that they don't matter. This fear disappears as they begin to feel listened to by the group, by the males in the group, as well as by the females. They begin to feel a sense of their own power.

> *One way low self-esteem expresses itself with women is that, across the board—African-American, white, or Latino—women will underestimate their reading abilities.*

At first, power manifests itself differently in these women, many of whom have never learned to be assertive but have relied on being passive-aggressive or outright aggressive. They blurt out things; they put themselves down; they say, "I agree with her," and stop talking. Once we draw these women out, we see the kind of power that comes from contributing, taking a stand, and engaging in an idea.

But men too feel a power in the classroom when they understand that their opinions are actually being listened to by a judge. They can be "smart" in the face of authority. Judge Robert Kane, co-founder with Waxler of the original men's program in Dartmouth, used to say how many men seemed to find excitement in the classroom when they took on a judge, the same excitement they might have found on the streets. What he meant is that there is energy in discussion and a need that develops to grapple with ideas. The men try to get attention to prove themselves, to question authority. He maintained that the energy around the table created a challenge for the probationers and could actually replace some of the challenges on the street.

Theresa Owens, probation officer for the Taunton, Massachusetts District Court, points to how this challenge manifests itself in the classroom: "Probationers see that there's a different means to deal with [their issues], different actions that may be able to be taken down the road." Conversation can lead to better choices.

Speaking out is something we value highly, and it needs to be modeled. Although we don't force people to have opinions, we try to accentuate the fact that allowing different voices in the room is positive and a way to combat both male and female stereotyping.

Having some men in the class—judges or probation officers—can be helpful for the women probationers, but the Dorchester Women's Program prefers otherwise. Their program has a female judge, Chief Justice Sydney Hanlon, who recognizes the value of the all-women's group in the discussions:

Many of the women speak about their own victimization and experiences with violence, about serious mental and physical illness and disability, about awesome responsibilities for children, and of unthinkable family tragedies. I have come to understand what a little part of them and their lives I see in the courtroom.

This promotes the idea of single-gender groups. However, Trounstine recalls one session on Barbara Kingsolver's *The Bean Trees*. The main character, Taylor, has a crush on Estevan, a married man, and one scene involves a night they almost sleep together. Judge Dever of the Lynn program said that he felt it was "noble" for Estevan not to succumb to his passions. One of the women, who had been shy early on, and timid in discussions, told him politely but firmly that the only reason the man didn't give in was because Taylor was too tired and "didn't let it happen." It didn't, she said, have anything to do with "nobility." They batted ideas back and forth, didn't agree, but accepted their differences. Most of the women looked at the judge kindly, but there was a sense in the room that the women, not the judge, were the straight thinkers on this point. It was an empowering moment for them, the realization that they had more insight into women's lives than someone who was universally considered a symbol of authority.

This would not have happened if a judge had not come from his male perspective or if the women did not have a chance to engage with his point of view. This kind of discussion cannot always be planned, but if we as instructors are aware of our group dynamics and make use of the voices, there is value in all the different configurations of gender around the table.

Learning to express oneself appropriately in the face of authority is important for both men and women. Our women come from histories of violence, where authority has meant domination. Men too have seen yelling, physical abuse, sexual abuse, rape, and, in some cases, murder. Men and women both are victims of violence, but some are also perpetrators and have abused their children or partners. A few associate vigorous discussions with forcing others to see things from one angle and only one angle. These participants, mostly women, can be afraid that assertiveness means force. Touching upon these intense issues in the classroom undoubtedly differs depending upon who takes part in the discussion.

Waxler says that many male participants involve their partners in the learning process and that, on occasion, have brought girlfriends to class that have participated with the probationers. This can be a powerful reinforcement for all involved. Not only do many female CLTL students not get support from their boyfriends, but some men resent their partners' participation in the program and have trouble with their empowerment through education.

> *Learning to express oneself appropriately in the face of authority is important for both men and women. Our women come from histories of violence, where authority has meant domination.*

As one female probationer said about herself while examining Zora Neale Hurston's *Their Eyes Were Watching God:*

> Like Janie, I don't want to be anyone's slave or servant, nor do I want to be someone who's just around for convenience. I want to be treated as an equal. I've had too many experiences already where guys want you for your money, car, or sex and only treat you nicely when you're providing them with those things. As Janie said, there are two things everyone has to do for themselves, and that's go to God and find out about living on their own.

Hale began her Framingham, Massachusetts Program with a different idea than many of us. She is in the forefront of mixed-gender groups and found her first class set-up enriched the conversation:

> It hadn't been my experience at all that the women in my groups were particularly inhibited by the presence of men. Furthermore, it seemed to me all the more necessary that men and women learn ways of interacting with one another, in which frank discussions and even disagreements

about gender roles and assumptions could be handled in an intellectual, rather than physical or emotional, atmosphere.

Since our initial programs began, practitioners continue to change the original paradigm, adding their own voices to the choir. Mary Stephenson, from the UK group in Sussex (see Chapter 6), says that both she and her male students have grown from their participation in a group behind bars. "There is a danger," she says, "in a same-sex group that they will support each other in stereotypical views or reassure themselves that a man would never behave like that:

> This was particularly strong in discussions of both "Greasy Lake" by T. Coraghessan Boyle and "Where Are You Going, Where Have You Been" by Joyce Carol Oates. The prisoners' reaction to the young men's near rape of the girl in "Greasy Lake" ("We were on her like Bergman's deranged brothers—see no evil, hear none, speak none—panting, wheezing, tearing at her clothes, grabbing for flesh") was shock and disgust. They even claimed it could never happen like that. Again, in "Where Are You Going, Where Have You Been," which describes in horrifying detail how an innocent teenage girl is lured by a predatory male hell bent on sex and brutality with her, the prisoners were quick to claim no identification with the male character. They even got angry with us for making them read such work. Here we were, in a room full of convicted prisoners, some of whom were serving time for rape, many of whom had been guilty of violence towards their girlfriends and wives, all of whom I suspect had at one time or another manipulated, cajoled, or coerced a woman to have sex with them, and they were behaving like a room full of celibate priests.

Stephenson believes her female presence in an all-male group allowed her to say that she had "suffered considerable force, both mental and physical," from many men in her life, "some of whom normally appeared to be the gentlest of characters." She added, "it was a rare man who didn't try some sort of pressure for sex in my experience." Once the prisoners got over their "outrage," an honest discussion followed.

Stephenson says that "having a strong maternal instinct" also allowed her to relate to the prisoners as a mother, and they treated her with the same respect and affection they would show a mother (or even a grandmother). "Opening their hearts and displaying emotions were safe with me, it was what I expected them to do. . . . On the occasions when they locked antlers, the presence of women often brought order back to an otherwise explosive situation." She says that being female also allowed her to

> speak as a mother myself, assuring them that a mother doesn't prefer lies to the uncomfortable truth and that mothers can see through their letters home saying that they were having a great time. I could speak as a loving daughter who had benefited enormously from a father who had been there for me, showing his pride in me and all that I achieved. I could assure them that a father's love means more to a daughter than his career or wealth. And, of course, I could identify with their wives and girlfriends, acting as a kind of sounding board to help them unravel the mysteries of the female mind. In turn, I found myself pleasantly delighted to hear a group of "tough" men talking about love and vulnerability and fear.

It may feel safer to be in a room exclusively with your own sex, but Stephenson raises the question: Is "safe" what we're seeking in our work?

In the Barnstable, Massachusetts Program, the team has been experimenting with all-male groups, all-female groups, and mixed-gender groups. Perhaps the composition of the groups is less important than what goes on around the table, they say. Judge Joseph Reardon, who initiated that program, says that this "process" inevitably leads one on a "journey of self-discovery and the realization that these characters are not unlike ourselves."

Whatever the group's composition, our approach suggests an old-fashioned commitment to literature and identity that embraces the notion that human beings have depth, imagination, passion, and an interior self. Too often, both men and women in our culture have refused such insight, and we aim to get it back.

4 The New Bedford Men's Program

> *"Professional wholeness requires that the master of scholarship enter the murky ground of practice and reflect on how his or her acquired intellectual knowledge can provide health and justice to the people who are being served. "*
>
> —*Judge Robert Kane,*
> *New Bedford Men's Program*

THE BEGINNING

IN THE EARLY 1980s Waxler received a National Endowment for the Humanities Summer Grant to participate in a seminar at Princeton University on the topic of literature and society. Much of the discussion that summer focused on the role of literature in a society that was becoming increasingly fascinated by technology and the business of science. Was literature doomed to a place, at best, on the margins of this society? Had the power of numbers, of binary codes, and of quantitative analysis become so seductive that a belief in literature was now as remote from the center of our consciousness as a faith in an ancient religion?

Almost a decade later, Waxler sought to answer this question, one that had a practical application. One day after a tennis match with his friend Robert Kane, who was then a district court judge in New Bedford, Massachusetts, Waxler issued Kane a challenge: "Bob, if you're willing to take eight or ten criminal offenders, tough guys, who are coming before your bench and are headed to jail, and instead sentence them to a literature seminar at the university, I would be willing to set the course up, get the room, choose the books, and facilitate the discussions."

Despite the signs of the times, Waxler held firm to the notion that literature was still the most important tool we had to humanize ourselves and our society. Why shouldn't we think about literature when we wrestle with difficult public policy issues? Why shouldn't literature remain central to our lives?

Waxler knew that Kane had been concerned about the "turnstile justice" he had seen in his courtroom—offenders who were sentenced to jail, and after serving their term, were out the door and then back in the courtroom. So Waxler's proposed literature program made sense to Kane. Why not try it?

Waxler gives Kane a lot of credit for this. It takes considerable courage and determination—commitment to human justice—for a judge to agree to become involved in a literature program like CLTL. Kane had been a feared prosecutor in an earlier phase of his career and to assent to what must have seemed at first to be a soft idea could not have been easy. Of course, over the years the CLTL program has proved to be not at all soft but as tough as the probationers participating in it.

Waxler and Kane began to map out this idea they considered an experiment in justice and literature but had no clear idea how or even if it would work. However, given Waxler's passion for and deep belief in literature and Kane's commitment, it seemed certain that CLTL could make a difference in the lives of the offenders. After exploring the idea further, the realization came that the role of sentencing, the moral value of reading, and the interplay of men of privilege with men of little power were also important.

Kane immediately enlisted Wayne St. Pierre, an energetic and sensitive probation officer in New Bedford, who understood the vision and appreciated literature. Although Wayne had serious doubts about high expectations, he wanted to be involved. His role would be to help screen potential students for the literary discussions, supervise the group, and participate in the discussions. Wayne became the third vital member of the three-person team—a judge, a probation officer, and an instructor—that would eventually serve as a model for the CLTL program.

HOW WOULD IT WORK?

How would program participants be chosen from the large pool of criminal offenders passing through the district court each day?

Waxler asked Kane to choose "tough guys" with significant criminal histories so that if the experiment did work, critics could not easily claim that the program had stacked the deck with non-violent offenders. As it turned out, the average number of convictions for those entering the first two CLTL groups, for example, was 18.4 per person. There was no doubt these were tough guys. Their offenses commonly included drug and alcohol use, community disruption, and assaults. But the program has had a wide variety of offensives represented, including armed robbery with a mask, substance abuse, erratic employment, and unstable domestic relationships. These men, on the whole, are lacking confidence in their abilities. They generally feel they have no voice in the mainstream culture. They are alienated, dispossessed, and in need of self-reflection and human community.

As Kane says: "Their alienation manifests itself episodically in courtroom behavior and in the form of smoldering rage. These offenders, though, appear to possess internal control capacities suggesting that confinement does not represent the only reasonable response to their criminal behavior." Waxler, Kane, and St. Pierre needed to help these men find their voices through literature, find a way of giving shape, through language, to their rage and intelligence.

Some general guidelines were established for this first group in New Bedford. To qualify, an offender had to not be actively addicted, had to be capable of reading at an eighth-grade level, and had to have not committed criminal acts of rape or murder. But these guidelines would be flexible, depending on the individual situation. Waxler believed from the beginning that almost anyone could benefit from this program, and over the years that has proven to be the case.

> *The CLTL program works as well for violent offenders as for non-violent ones.*

The CLTL program works as well for violent offenders as for non-violent ones. In our program we see batterers, bank robbers, and drug dealers who have committed assaults, as well as first-time offenders. Reading good literature and exposure to language through discussion of books seem to mitigate violence, according to formal studies conducted at universities (the Jarjoura Study and the Kelly Study, for examples, cited in Chapter 3) and informal studies conducted by local probation officers. Not only are recidivism rates lowered through CLTL, but those offenders committing a crime again tend to target property rather than other human beings, the studies indicate.

And although Wayne St. Pierre screens for reading ability—by simply asking the offender to read a paragraph or two from a popular magazine—there are no formal tests to determine reading skill levels. We have discovered that those apparent levels seem to rise significantly in a few weeks, once the participant gains confidence around the table and begins to discover his voice and recognize himself. Those struggling with "Greasy Lake" the first week often seem to be able to master the longer stories—*Deliverance* and *The Sea Wolf,* for example—before the end of the seminar series.

As the New Bedford Program developed, Waxler and Kane began to sense that in part it offered what great literature has always offered readers: an exploration into the complexity and challenges of human character and conscience, a way to connect with the human community, a way to engage deeply in language and conversation, and a way to make us more self-reflective. As Kane put it: "These offenders commit criminal acts, in part, because they operate from a belief system that privileges appetites and instincts over reason and thoughtful choice and that insists that authority is by its very nature a victimizing position. The program challenges this belief."

HOW DOES THE SENTENCING PROCESS WORK IN THE COURT?

The original plan was for St. Pierre to screen potential candidates for the program, make appropriate referrals, and check with defense counsel and prosecutors. If there was agreement on the defendant's interest and willingness to work for a change in perspective, the prosecutor and defense counsel would then usually search for common ground on a disposition that included the CLTL program. After agreement on a recommended disposition to be made to the court, Kane would consider the eligibility of the offender: his genuine interest, the source and method of the referral, the risk level, his criminal history, etc.

No doubt the interaction between the probation officer and the judge is central to this early process; in fact, the judge often gives considerable weight to the probation officer's evaluation. Where the judge finds the referral appropriate, and that is usually the case, the sentencing process proceeds to an agreement formed between the court and the defendant.

FORMING THE AGREEMENT

Originally, the New Bedford Program was established as an alternative sentencing program for offenders headed to jail, but the agreement model here is highly flexible and subject to change according to the group, the court, state guidelines, etc. For New Bedford, the overall process for forming an agreement could be divided into a few related parts, but it is the idea of the agreement that needs special consideration, regardless of the form it takes. The agreement is a metaphor, a covenant that helps build community and responsibility. The defendant agrees to enter into a contract with the court and must appreciate the full weight and responsibility that he is assuming. That responsibility is also a privilege. It offers the defendant an opportunity to be free as a citizen in the community.

The ritual of agreement conducted through the court gives meaning and purpose to the participants in terms of their engagement with the CLTL program. It calls for commitment, and it allows rewards for meeting goals. The agreement suggests that the CLTL program is a challenge: It is tough but worthwhile. And the agreement reminds all the parties that they are in this together and are all responsible for the program's success.

How did this agreement process work in New Bedford?

The defendant chosen for CLTL would appear before the judge's bench, listening carefully as Kane defined the sentence. Working within the guidelines of the district courts in Massachusetts, Kane might determine that the defendant serve a partially executed sentence (split sentence), or consecutive suspended sentences, or be put directly on probation. Kane would formally announce his decision and make it clear that any violations of the agreed-upon terms could be converted into a fully executed sentence. If there were violations, the defendant's opportunity to participate in the CLTL program would be revoked, and he would be put back into jail.

Kane would next explain that if the offender successfully completed the CLTL program, his sentence would be shortened by six months. This was part of the incentive and the reward for participation. Then Kane would describe, in general terms, the program's purposes, format, and expectations, emphasizing that this was a tough program and a genuine challenge. Discussing the program publicly from the bench gave it an additional formal and communal value.

During this process, Kane would purposely pause a number of times to ask the offender if he understood everything that was being said, emphasizing the importance of listening and understanding. Once the program was explained, Kane would give the offender another opportunity to think about his choices, his commitment and responsibility, and to consider their meaning and full implications.

Almost all offenders choose the literature program, but of course they are not required to. When they formally announce their choice, they are told that it represents a conscious and considered commitment of effort and loyalty to the justice system and to the community. In this regard, their agreement takes on genuinely symbolic implications, making the process part of the overall ritual structure of the justice system and the CLTL program.

JUSTICE AND LANGUAGE

As Kane and Waxler developed ideas about this process and its meaning, they also underscored the importance of language and communication. Kane suggested that the selection process transformed the judge and probation officer into communicators who enhanced the role of justice by emphasizing the use and meaning of the probation relationship. By thinking about the

> *The process became an important way of humanizing judicial authority, of restoring genuine justice. It was a type of ritual that gave special meaning to the connection between the courts and the community.*

defendants as individuals and addressing them through this type of alternative agreement, the relationship could, as Kane said, "startle some offenders into suspending cynicism about the value of the probation relationship."

Kane was right. The process became an important way of humanizing judicial authority, of restoring genuine justice. It was a type of ritual that gave special meaning to the connection between the courts and the community. It demonstrated, in public, a clear sense of confidence in the offender by certifying his ability as a citizen.

THE FIRST LITERATURE SEMINAR

Waxler had offered the challenge of CLTL to Kane because of the power of literature to transform lives. So, the central focus of this program had to be the literature seminars. Thinking back to those discussions at Princeton University about the marginalization of literature within our society, Waxler hoped that CLTL could restore the recognition of the importance of literature. The program was an opportunity to think again about the significance of good literature. Even English departments were often spending too much time talking to themselves about abstract theory, overrationalizing the meaning of literature. Instead, according to Waxler, the program of CLTL needed to explore and celebrate the relationship between literature and the human heart.

As the literature seminar was planned, Waxler and Kane agreed to small groups for discussion with the ideal being eight or so offenders together with the three team members. Waxler wanted to create an open and democratic space for full participation, and that number seemed about right. Kane anticipated they might lose one or two offenders along the way, so it would be better, for example, to start with a group of ten, imagining it would be down to eight after a short time. This turned out to be right. Most groups tend to lose one or two at the very beginning of the series of seminars, before people have settled in.

> *Kane and Waxler knew old habits and stereotypes about schooling, literature, teachers, judges, and authority in general would have to change.*

Kane and Waxler also thought it was important for the seminars to take place, if possible, on a college campus to underscore the importance and dignity of the program, wanting these men to feel special, to feel they had been chosen, and to understand the privilege and the responsibility they were taking on. The key was for the men to benefit from the opportunity as well and to enjoy the pleasure of being on a college campus.

There were several other considerations before CLTL got underway. The program needed time to get the probationers excited about literature, time for the group to feel like a community and to trust each other, time for the books to make a difference in the participants' lives. Kane and Waxler knew old habits and stereotypes about schooling, literature, teachers, judges, and authority in general would have to change. Although these goals were ambitious, Waxler and Kane recognized human limitations. In the simplest terms though, Waxler wanted to give the offenders what good literature offers—a glimpse of another life, a new way of seeing, and a surprise that shocks us into a deeper recognition of our humanity.

"How long should we make this first series of literature discussions?" Waxler wondered. The decision was two-hour sessions that would meet every two weeks for twelve weeks. This would allow everyone an opportunity to read the books carefully, but only in six sessions. This was not a lot of time, but perhaps it would be enough to get the students thinking about change and even get them interested and excited about a different life.

The offenders would be expected to attend all sessions, to have read the assigned stories, and to take an active role in the discussions. They would have to analyze the characters in the stories and offer their perspectives on them by answering such questions as: *What kind of people are these characters? Why do they do what they do? Do they change during the story? If they do change, why do they and how?* Although the plot of the stories would engage these readers, it would be the characters and the themes, the hidden depths and surprises of the stories, that would offer the most intrigue as they moved through the discussions. Each book and discussion would be a journey of discovery.

Waxler chose stories from modern American literature that dealt with issues of male identity and violence, with relationships between an individual and the society, and with the problems of facing authority. Works by writers such as T. Coraghessan Boyle, Raymond Carver, James Baldwin, Richard Wright, James Dickey, Jack London, Ken Kesey, John Steinbeck, Ernest Hemingway, and Norman Mailer seemed worth trying.

Waxler wanted the emotional intensity of the works to help promote discussions and believed that these modern American stories would help get the participants to the topics they might be wrestling with in their own lives. Several years later at a panel discussion, Kane reflected on just this. Telling a group of judges how reading and violence intersected in the CLTL program, Kane recalled a moment in a discussion of a Raymond Carver story when Waxler had asked the offenders why the main character had taken a boulder to the head of a young woman. The offender "looked up with his eyes filled with knowledge," Kane reported. It was as if the story, his own experience, and the question had suddenly come together bringing a new understanding of himself, a moment of surprise. "Rage," the offender responded to Waxler's question. It was rage.

> *Waxler wanted the emotional intensity of the works to help promote discussions and believed that these modern American stories would help get the participants to the topics they might be wrestling with in their own lives.*

Waxler and Kane could have chosen other books, of course, and as the CLTL program began to grow, other groups would use very different books to address different issues. But at the beginning, these writers seemed central to their vision and purpose.

The group consisted of male participants, and this too made a difference. The books chosen and the issues raised in discussion should be determined by the makeup of the group. If the discussions worked well, they might serve as mirrors to the inner consciousness of the participants and to the deep patterns of the culture itself. Such a process could help change lives.

One goal though was to avoid discussion of personal lives. Kane and Waxler did not want these sessions to become group therapy; rather they let the men talk about the universal issues and the fictional characters in the stories. The discovery was that the discussions allowed participants to protect their private selves, yet reveal their deepest selves.

For the first two sessions, Waxler and St. Pierre would join the offenders in these discussions on the campus. Kane would join the group in the third and subsequent sessions, once the group had begun to bond. Almost immediately though, people began to hear about the energy and intensity of these literary discussions, and they wanted to join in. The girlfriends of the offenders began to read the books at home. Professors at the university wanted to join the discussions. Other court officials wondered at what they were hearing about these sessions. Waxler and Kane wanted to preserve the core group and the idea of a single-gender discussion, but they also began to believe that they should allow others to participate as well. So after a few sessions, visitors were permitted—ranging from other instructors to court officials and lawyers, to friends of the offenders—to participate. There was one rule all were required to follow: Everyone had to read the assigned book for that night. Kane and Waxler didn't want tourists; all were to be serious participants who would be treated like everyone else around the table.

> *Almost immediately though, people began to hear about the energy and intensity of these literary discussions, and they wanted to join in.*

Through this reading and discussion process, the offenders would have an opportunity to widen and deepen their confidence and trust, exercise their growing communication skills, sharpen their analytic abilities, and expand their imaginations. As the facilitator, Waxler was not there to teach lessons on morality but to enhance the conversation, offer his perspectives, and encourage everyone to use their empathetic imagination to enter the depth of the story. The purpose of the journey was not primarily to learn about moral commandments, but to discover the core of the human heart.

The First Group

That first group at the University of Massachusetts, Dartmouth, in the fall of 1991 was remarkable, but also typical, with members ranging in age from 19 to 44. Some had little schooling, not even high school, and others had some college education. There were eight male offenders, with 148 convictions among them.

The first night, Jeff, an offender, came with his father, a man in his early fifties, who had spent several years in Walpole, the toughest prison in the state. He was dropping his son off; he wanted him to succeed. Jeff's stepmother stayed out in the parking lot for more than two hours, seated in the front of the paneled truck, waiting for him to return.

A drug dealer who knew the streets and loved the excitement, Jeff had quit school after eighth grade. He had made more money than most college graduates, but at 22, with a young daughter and dedicated girlfriend, he wanted to change his life. It would have to be the life of the mind that hooked him to that change, though, not an argument about how education could lead to financial gain. Jeff had made enough money with his eighth-grade education to know that if education meant anything, it had to mean more than cold cash. If the CLTL program were to work, it would have to convince probationers that there was something exciting and interesting about reading and talking about stories. The pleasure and meaning of it were not means to a commercial end, but an end in itself. Great literature could enrich lives.

After a few sessions, Jeff would say that Waxler looked anxious that first night, that he had noticeably sweaty palms. Waxler would jokingly respond that it was Jeff who looked befuddled. But the truth was that all shared in that initial anxiety until it gave way to a kind of magic as "Greasy Lake" by T. Coraghessan Boyle was read and discussed.

The participants sat around the long wooden table, listened to each other, amazed by the variety of perspectives. "How do I stack up against your college students?" Jeff wanted to know. He was doing very well; they were all doing very well. In fact, it seemed that they were teaching the facilitators more than they could have imagined. At first, Waxler had thought each one of them was the student and he was the professor, but he now wondered if it was the other way around.

"Greasy Lake"

Waxler decided to use "Greasy Lake" the opening night because it could be read silently in about half an hour, and because it seemed like a story all had experienced in their own lives. In addition, it resonated with the issues men were struggling with: male identity, violence, and confronting authority.

"Greasy Lake" is about three 19-year-old men (the unnamed narrator, Jeff, and Digby) who drive up to a local hangout looking for adventure before they head home for the night. They find much more excitement than they anticipated. They journey to the dark side, forcing readers to move with them, beyond the boundaries of acceptable behavior. They are fascinated and fearful, attracted and repulsed by the transgressions and violations.

These boys want to be "bad," but they are typical middle-class, suburban guys going to college, driving their mother's Bel Air, and living at home for the summer. Their usual idea of excitement is to play a practical joke—throwing eggs at mailboxes, for example—and then to go home satisfied. When they get to the hangout this particular night, though, their practical joke turns into a nightmare. They lose their car keys in the dark and find themselves in unknown territory, frightened and exhilarated at the same time.

Eventually the boys get into a fight and almost kill their antagonist ("a bad greasy character") with a tire iron—and, pumped with primal instinct, they attack his girlfriend, almost raping her. When a second group of young men (fraternity boys) pull up in their Trans Am, the narrator flees into the lake where he seems to wrestle with his own darkness and mortality (as well as with a corpse floating in the water). His friends head into the woods. At the end, the three return to their car, find the keys with the light of dawn, engage in one further encounter with two older girls before they take off, and drive home.

"Greasy Lake" worked perfectly that first night; it has been used ever since to open a CLTL series. The offenders almost always seem to enjoy the story and to identify with it. They often say that it is their story. And when they leave after that first discussion, they seem energized. They understand what will occur in the sessions, and they seem interested.

Waxler starts the first session by asking about the three boys: *What kind of people are they? Are they really 'bad'? What privileges do they have? How do they compare with the other characters—the greaser, the girlfriend, the second group of boys, the older girls, and the corpse?*

As the group gains an understanding of these characters through the opening discussion, the focus widens with larger questions concerned with issues of male identity and human emotions. These three young men, like all of us, are on a journey not only to Greasy Lake, but into their own selves. When they lose their keys, they seem to enter a different world that they know little about, but one that is exciting and taps into their primal energy.

Then Waxler might ask: *What do you think the narrator feels when he attacks the greaser with the tire iron? How do these feelings relate to the subsequent attack on the girl?*

Such questions help focus the discussion on a pattern common in the reading and throughout the CLTL sessions—a pattern that suggests the seduction and thrill of adventure and violence but also the destructive force within, that of unleashed instinct and raw energy. We have all felt that force and sensed its power, so the discussion about the story inevitably shapes itself along these lines. We want to recognize what this force does to our human con-

> *The result of the discussion is the beginning of recognition that we have choices, and that human experience is always complex, ambiguous, and shared.*

nectivity and, ultimately, to ourselves. "It's like taking drugs," offenders will often say as the conversation gets fully underway. They are beginning a self-reflective journey into their own experiences.

By the middle of the discussion, the group is often talking about the beating of "the greaser" and the potential rape of the girlfriend. Waxler will ask: *How do these moments connect with the narrator's encounter with the corpse? What do you think he feels when he first touches that corpse? What is he thinking about?*

The perspectives and responses reflect the diversity of experience among the group members. "He must be thinking he went too far." "He must be thinking about his own death, his own mortality." "He must be thinking about how he almost killed the guy up on land." "He must be wondering how he ever got in this mess." "He must be hoping somehow he will make it home."

As the meaning and implications of the event are explored, it becomes the group's story as they feel the intoxication and power of the adrenalin rush. The result of the discussion is the beginning of recognition that we have choices, and that human experience is always complex, ambiguous, and shared.

The three boys head home, but before the group ends that night, Waxler asks another series of questions: *How do these young men feel as they head home? How will they feel in the future? Will they return to their local hangout? Will they pursue new excitement, eager for the next thrill?* The men are often uncertain whether these three 19 year-olds have experienced enough during this one night to change their lives, but they are interested enough to think about the next reading assignment and to anticipate the next discussion.

Deliverance

The stories become longer and more challenging as participants move through the program and begin to gain confidence and trust. A few weeks into the program, *Deliverance* by James Dickey is discussed.

It is a story about four suburban men who decide to take a white-water canoe trip down a raging river in rural Georgia. At first it might seem that such a story and setting would have little interest for primarily white working-class criminal offenders coming out of the inner cities of New Bedford and Fall River, but like "Greasy Lake," *Deliverance* cuts close to the core as a journey into the primal self. Before it's over, one man is dead and the other characters are permanently changed.

Lewis, one of the main characters (the one Burt Reynolds played in the film version), is the macho man in the group, a leader, but flawed and filled with confidence, perhaps too much. Participants talk about Lewis and begin to appreciate the complexity, as they always do, of the human character.

His bravado inspires action, but he seems too caught up in himself. He strikes out without thinking, so he never learns from his mistakes. He is intuitive, and his friends seem to count on him, but he is not rational, and his friends seem not to be able to depend on themselves. If his buddies have been too comfortable in their suburban homes, though, Lewis is too self-centered and driven. In the end, it is Ed, Lewis's closest friend, and not Lewis, who will deliver the men from the primal rage of the river.

"As I was reading the story," John, one of the offenders, said one night, "I was trying to picture myself in the roles of the various characters." At first, John might have thought about identifying with Lewis, but finally, perhaps surprisingly, he felt closest to Ed. "Ed was laid back, wasn't the leader type," John said. "But when he had to, he took over. That's how I am. I procrastinate, but I can do what has to be done."

The Sea Wolf

Near the end of the twelve weeks, the group talks about *The Sea Wolf* by Jack London. This is a story seemingly about a rugged sea captain, Wolf Larsen, a man of considerable passion and rage. He is a monomaniac who believes that might makes right. For him, power defines all relationships. Once you meet him, you will never forget him. Larsen is contrasted with Humphrey Van Weyden, a wealthy literary critic, who at first cannot stand on his own two feet. Unlike Larsen, Van Weyden believes in immortality and the value of the human spirit.

Like Ed in *Deliverance* though, Humphrey eventually gains independence and confidence and surpasses the more limited Larsen who does not grasp the nature of compassion and love. Like Ed, who seems to move beyond the limits of Lewis, Humphrey expands his own boundaries of self, stretching beyond the powerful and impressive Wolf.

"I used to be like Wolf Larsen," one of the men in the group claimed. "I thought I could manipulate everyone. I was stupid then."

The offenders are often filled with rage that over the years they have externalized, often turning it against others. For them the passive and dependent Van Weyden seems such a wimp at first, a literary teacher connected to their own previous failures in the classroom. But as they move through the reading and the discussions, they change as Van Weyden changes and as the ocean itself changes.

Over and over again, the CLTL program reminds us that our lives are stories that we can create and shape. Waxler recalls Mark M., who had spent one-third of his life in jail before entering the program. He was a heroin addict infected with HIV. Coming through the program, he decided to rewrite his story despite the death sentence looming over him. After CLTL, he began to take courses at the university, dreaming about a college diploma. He died of throat cancer before he completed his heroic journey, but he transformed his life by changing his story through the reading and discussions in CLTL.

Completing the First Group Experience

At the conclusion of the first series of seminars, Kane, St. Pierre, and Waxler agreed that this experiment in reading and in justice, Changing

Lives Through Literature, needed to continue. It offered an opportunity for powerful transformation.

On the whole, the offenders agreed they had never experienced anything quite like it before. Jeff, the drug dealer with an eighth-grade education, for example, was now reading to his daughter. As he said, he now believed that the challenge of walking into a classroom where his opinions were valued by college teachers and judges was superior to the challenge he found on the streets. Other offenders were reconnecting with family. Many planned to pursue further education. No one really wanted the program to end.

> *Other offenders were reconnecting with family. Many planned to pursue further education. No one really wanted the program to end.*

Area businessmen were invited to share their stories with the group, in part to try to effect a smooth transition from the world of novels to the world of work, in part to let community leaders know about the success. In addition, Waxler arranged for each student to receive a framed certificate with his name and the official university seal on it.

A graduation ceremony was conducted on the last night of class and then in a more formal setting in the district court the next day. Family members and friends came to the public ceremony in the courtroom. St. Pierre petitioned the bench, and the judge responded by acknowledging each offender's success and by praising him for his efforts and accomplishments, reducing his sentence accordingly.

After the program, each probationer was also required to work with St. Pierre on his own story—a "Plan for Success" as St. Pierre called it—a story incorporating job skills, educational background, financial obligations, and career and personal goals. It was part of the contract, part of the ongoing story, providing a context for the future.

HOW WE CONTINUED

The Gardner Howland Shaw Foundation Funding and Evaluation

To keep the CLTL program running, it received limited funding from the Gardner Howland Shaw Foundation, a small non-profit agency in Boston that was committed to innovative criminal justice programs.

After the first four groups were completed, in 1993, the Foundation commissioned an independent evaluation to analyze the outcomes. The researchers, Drs. Roger Jarjoura and Susan Krumholz, set up a formal longitudinal study, mainly to evaluate recidivism, supplemented by case studies and interviews with the offenders. This study is mentioned in Chapter 1 (see page 4).

The results were heartening, although not unexpected. According to the Jarjoura final report, 45 percent of the comparison group—the group that had not gone through the CLTL program—had been convicted of new crimes. The researchers indicated this was about average given the makeup of the group and a result they would have expected before starting the evaluation. A little less than half of the criminal offenders in the comparison group had reoffended.

By contrast, the researchers reported that only 18.75 percent of the CLTL group had been convicted of new crimes during the same period. This was clearly a remarkable statistic, the researchers suggested. It was unexpected, if not off the charts. The results indicated that the CLTL program was clearly making a difference and could, in fact, cut recidivism by more than half.

Furthermore, the report indicated that only one of the CLTL students who had re-offended had committed a violent crime after attending the program. Considering the violent history of the group as a whole, this too was worthy of special note. And it was consistent with our general belief that language and literature could be a significant way to fight crime and help stop violence. Later, less formal studies of the CLTL program would reinforce these notions.

In the Jarjoura report, the role of the judge was also noted as a significant factor in the process. His obvious respect for the offenders in the court and his participation in the seminar discussions made them feel important, the study noted. According to the report, the CLTL students also admired the professor, specifically his ability to understand human nature and to offer revealing insights through the readings. He cared deeply, the participants said.

In addition, the researchers concluded that the public ceremony in the courtroom as part of the graduation at the end of the literature series was an important ritual enabling "a successful transition to a conventional, non-offending lifestyle." There was validation that the CLTL program helped create good citizens, giving the participants the social verification and legitimization leading to reform and redemption.

REFLECTIONS

The probationers in the New Bedford Program had too long felt isolated, as if they were caught in an enormous present without escape. They had been marginalized and pushed aside by the mainstream. In essence, they had been silenced. Language—reading and discussion—became a social force for these men, an enabling power that bound them together and allowed them to recognize that they were

> *They now know that walking into a classroom where their opinion matters can be more exciting than all the challenges they have found on the street.*

capable of humanizing the world that surrounds them. It is true not only for them, but for all of us. Literature can lead us to such recognition. And with that recognition, we can make choices, create a future, and build a story for ourselves.

The men in CLTL are smart. They have often survived brutal family histories, drug and alcohol addiction, and their own pent-up rage. In New Bedford, they range in age from 18 to 45 or so. Some are married;

some are not. Some have children—a future they want to connect with, even nurture. They now know that walking into a classroom where their opinion matters can be more exciting than all the challenges they have found on the street.

Language and literature can deter violence and crime. They can add meaning to manhood. These men know that now.

5 The Lynn-Lowell Women's Program

> *"I never liked to pick up a book and read and now I do. I feel better about myself. I expected the program to be bad and it wasn't a piece of cake but it really helped me understand a lot of things. I liked how we all talked about the books together. It was great; everybody had their own thoughts about a book. . . . Now I want to go for my GED. Before I used to say it but now I am really ready."*
>
> —Allie, Lynn-Lowell Program

HISTORY OF THE PROGRAM

THE LYNN-LOWELL WOMEN'S PROGRAM was the first CLTL program founded for women and the second program begun in Massachusetts. It serves female offenders requiring maximum supervision, those primarily sentenced from the Lynn or Lowell district courts, but it also handles referrals from nearby communities. While it is a voluntary program, it is a condition of probation, and sentencing can be initiated from the bench. The program often offers students time off probation or, in some cases, fee reduction upon completion.

Almost from its inception, the program served two jurisdictions in order to make sure there were enough women for a group of seven to eight students. Both Lynn and Lowell are urban cities outside of Boston, about thirty miles apart, and because the program meets at Middlesex Community College (MCC) in Lowell, the women from Lynn take a van to Lowell, accompanied by the judge and the Lynn probation officer. The college provides the van, and it has become one of the unique factors of the program. Lynn-Lowell also has consistently involved a student intern from MCC who reads with the participants and currently both drives the van and takes part in the program.

The program meets twice a year for seven meetings each session; the 90-minute seminars run every other week for fourteen weeks. They are held around a table in President Carole Cowan's office at MCC, followed by a graduation ceremony at the Lynn District Court.

FINDING CLTL

In 1986, Trounstine was teaching high school in an upper-middle-class town in Massachusetts where most students were white and Protestant and most families expected their children to go to college. But when offered the chance to teach behind bars, Trounstine found a community of women who had limited schooling. Some came to class to find solace from the restrictions of prison life, others out of boredom or for a good time or as a way to get time off their sentence, but most of all, they came with a desire to learn: CLTL offers such students access to literature, and, ultimately, access to a world most have not experienced. These women had street smarts, talent, minds that needed challenge, and lives far richer than most of us imagine. Sometimes, Trounstine felt she was living with a secret that the rest of the world did not know. Women behind bars were a community with hopes, dreams, insights, and humor. They wrote poetry, short stories, and essays, and they appeared in eight plays Trounstine directed at the women's prison.

In 1991, a few years after teaching full time at MCC, Trounstine learned about CLTL from a teacher at Framingham Prison. She had attended a talk by Judge Robert Kane, then a District Court judge, during which he mentioned the program in the southern part of Massachusetts begun by him and co-founder Robert Waxler. CLTL was dramatically different from most programs. It offered moderately literate offenders probation and a reading seminar instead of jail. It promised to work on the thinking skills of a person, getting each to look differently at his or her life. Instead of concentrating on the text for its pure literary value, CLTL encouraged readers to focus primarily on themes and characters. Thus, a text became a way into a person's psyche rather than a purely fictional piece.

Alternative sentencing ideas advocating literacy were not new, but there was a fascination with CLTL due to its unusual make-up: student-offenders, the judge who sentenced them to the program, and one or more of their probation officers as well as instructors. Literature discussion groups with offenders on the same playing field as judges and probation officers seemed unheard of in our criminal justice system. The notion that everyone's opinion about the story mattered, and no one had the final say, democratized the conversation. This might bring new ideas about choosing literature for a particular group, new ways of leading literature discussions, and a deeper understanding of how literature has the power to influence one's thinking.

At the time, the only CLTL program that existed was for men. The first group had a good success rate, according to conversations Trounstine had with Kane and Waxler. Waxler and Trounstine had similar views about the potential healing power of the humanities and arts. Trounstine was interested in expanding the current curriculum to include women's concerns and saw this as imperative to CLTL program development. Also, most female offenders had read few books by female authors and often had less con-

> *Most female offenders had read few books by female authors and often had less confidence than their male counterparts about their reading abilities.*

fidence than their male counterparts about their reading abilities. They were used to identifying with the male hero because they didn't have a great deal of experience with readings about women. Women behind bars had often been silent in class discussions in school, and they historically discounted their own opinions. Some had never finished a book, yet, almost all wanted their children to learn to read.

After getting the okay from Kane and Waxler to initiate the first women's program, Trounstine wanted to begin the group in Lowell at Middlesex. The only problem was that there was not a judge sitting at Lowell District Court who could be passionate about the program, good for a women's group, and a willing participant in classes.

The Judge's Perspective

Kane knew Judge Joseph Dever, Chief Justice of the Lynn District Court, from his participation in a reading seminar for judges at Brandeis University. Dever has always been an avid reader and performed in community theatre productions, plus he comes from a long line of lawyers concerned with humanity as well as the law. He says he eagerly accepted the opportunity to be the first judge in the women's CLTL program, believing that women deserved the same opportunities as men, and he felt ready to prove that "great literature can influence lives." At the time (1992), Dever regularly began volunteering in CLTL.

Because it was important to hold CLTL classes at a college, Dever agreed to ride in the van provided by MCC to the college, along with the sentenced women and the Lynn probation officer (PO). He has continued this practice for more than twelve years and enjoys the process. The women, he says, may be silent on the way to Lowell but vociferous on the way back, often continuing the book discussion group in the van. Dever doesn't just sit in on each discussion group. He participates fully without dominating the discussion, allowing the facilitator to lead the group and allowing the women to control where the conversation and texts take them.

Dever is a good listener, a caring but firm person, and he does not allow the women to talk about their personal court matters in the reading group. Although there may be some benefits in having a female judge in a women's group, because of the power issues involved with men (see Gender Issues in Chapter 3), Dever's contributions have been invaluable. His attitude is that all opinions are to be respected.

From the onset of the program, Dever looked for participants from the bench and continues to find himself drawn to the "human story" in each defendant's face. He may invite them to participate in the program during the course of hearing their cases, or the participants may be selected by the Probation Department. Dever often takes six months off their terms of probation, waives some fees, and may divert some from going to prison if they participate in CLTL.

The Probation Officer's Perspective

The first program in 1992 began with Lynn participants, a Lynn judge, and a Lynn probation officer, Valrie Ashford-Harris. Soon after, the group combined women from the Lynn and Lowell courts, due to the fact that there were not enough sentenced women in one district court for a program (eight is the optimum number). The program was then joined by Assistant Chief of Probation from Lowell, Richard White. While Dever and Trounstine have been continuing participants, Probation has brought in new CLTL personnel over the years, including Assistant Chief of Probation Robert Hassett from Lowell, and PO Michelle Carter-Donahue, who rides the van from Lynn with Dever.

Hassett says that reading has always been important to him. He has felt that his work should be about affecting change, but in his regular court work, he found that the relationship between clients and Probation was far too often adversarial. In addition, he points out that a typical probation visit can last ten minutes, during which the offender comes into the office, fills out forms, verifies his or her current address, gives proof of employment, and proof of visits with counselors or proof of participation in programs like Alcoholics Anonymous or Narcotics Anonymous. Hassett heard his friend and colleague White talking about CLTL, and he felt it might give him the "human side of things." What attracted him was the notion of change.

Hassett, who has been in the field of Probation for more than thirty years, has been the Lowell probation officer involved with the CLTL program for almost ten years. He says that getting involved in the program immediately gave him more insight into where his clients were coming from. "I've always been interested in the whys," he says, "and how we can change the whys." He points out that the average probation officer has 100 cases, and CLTL allows for a much greater chance for interaction with clients.

Hassett, who also rarely misses a CLTL meeting, enjoys reading the books and discussing them with participants, even if he's read them before. He gets referrals from other probation officers and sometimes from other courts. At the college, outside the classroom, he has participants fill out contracts and attendance forms at each two-hour CLTL meeting every other week. Hassett also conducted his own informal recidivist study and found that out of 100 CLTL participants versus non-participants, a greater percentage of women who completed CLTL, although they may have returned to crime, had fewer crimes against humanity.

Becoming a Facilitator

Trounstine says that the first session—whether six, seven, eight, or ten classes—is always the most astonishing for the facilitator. It's in the first session that facilitators begin to realize the power of CLTL as they observe the students' potential and hear their voices, however strong or weak, and the yearnings underneath.

Theresa, a former addict and alcoholic, in a baseball cap, was an unlikely person to be sitting in the MCC president's office, in the very first CLTL women's class. When Trounstine asked her what she liked about the stories, her insightful response was, "Those women. I'm surprised that I liked them because they're like me."

Besides Theresa, in that first class, was Addie, a waitress who had dropped out of school in ninth grade and had no support from the father of her child. Devora, a woman with AIDS whose record spanned several pages, had earned her GED behind bars. Jesse was twenty, a young mother with three children, unemployed, and living in a local shelter. Nina, a Latina woman with nine brothers and eight sisters, had never held a job or completed high school. Bonnie was a forty-three-year-old single mother and former prostitute with a history of childhood sexual abuse. Two of the women had bounced back to the streets before the first session ever began.

They all had done prison time, having served sentences for crimes such as possession of drugs, prostitution, assault and battery, shoplifting, and theft. But unlike their male counterparts, they had no support from worried wives or girlfriends and no encouragement to find jobs. Their drinking and drugging had often brought them abusive boyfriends who threatened their lives and parents who kicked them out of the house. Some were single mothers. They all had lives of failed commitments, longings, and unfulfilled dreams. They all had ceased to believe in themselves.

But Trounstine says it took a while to see these things. At first, the women struggled as they read Tillie Olsen's "I Stand Here Ironing." Olsen's narrator struggles, too, to make ends meet. She is deserted by her husband and has to make choices that are heartbreaking: putting her child, Emily, in an institution; going to work and leaving Emily with the lady in the downstairs apartment; bringing her home sick to a house full of other children. The daughter eventually finds some fulfillment on stage but does poorly in school.

Some were sympathetic with the mother, and some rejected her, feeling she'd mistreated the daughter. Others were angry at the fact that the narrator was abandoned by her husband. The intensity of response by the women was an eye-opener for all of the participants.

Other books that were read during that first session also brought strong reactions. When the women returned after two weeks, without homework, knowing they would not have quizzes or tests, they were encouraged to bring their notes and to think about the family in Anne Tyler's *Dinner at the Homesick Restaurant*. This novel emphasizes relationships among several members of a family, all who see the world from different points of view.

Bonnie arrived late, her son having been in an accident. She talked about how hard it was to read the book while working two jobs, going to school, and raising her children. Not surprisingly, she had mixed reactions about the mother, Pearl Tull, a cold but feisty lady who raises three kids in an unsympathetic world.

"That's my family," exclaimed Jesse, who looked like a typical college student and, in spite of her homeless status, loved to read. She had dropped out of school in the eleventh grade after having a baby and saw CLTL as a lifeline. "I understand my mother more after reading this book. Just like Pearl, you couldn't love her but you couldn't hate her. Every so often, she'd yell and scream, but you couldn't blame her, raising three kids all by herself."

The group knew she was talking about herself as well as about her own mother, without directly discussing her own issues. She had seen into her own life by understanding Pearl.

The women attended the group every two weeks. In between they had to live their lives without drugs and alcohol, attending other programs required of their probation, and dealing with more stress, it seems, than the average student.

"Where is the hope in this book?" Trounstine asked the evening the group was discussing Toni Morrison's *The Bluest Eye*. Nina sat twirling her dark hair around a pencil. She looked up: "There is no hope. It's awful what happens to Pecola." Pecola, the sad African-American girl who wants desperately to have blue eyes so she will fit into the white world, is raped by her father.

Bonnie agreed, saying she hated reading the book. Her repeated battles with alcoholism and drugs had landed her in prison, which she called "a better place than home," where she, like Pecola, had dealt with incest.

But Theresa, an African-American, heatedly began to argue with them, pointing out how Claudia, the narrator, survives to tell the story of her growing-up, with wisdom and insight into her community. "I think Claudia is the hope," said Theresa, defending a book she had read twice because she understood the world Morrison describes. The group then discussed how they could all identify with Claudia, the survivor who lives to tell the story.

Nina, who admitted she was struggling with her own memories of abuse, seemed unsure. Trounstine and the group members felt they might lose her after that class.

But it is not just the texts that empower these women. A healing happens in the discussions as they seek to understand together how characters get through their struggles. The class allows them to hear each other's perspectives, to share their ideas, and to see that their opinions are valued. Thus, by class three, the women had formed a bond, nodding at each other's comments, taking cigarette breaks together, laughing, and telling stories.

Nina came back, and with the others delighted in Sandra Cisneros's *House on Mango Street*, the poetic tale of a Mexican-American girl who grows up in a poor Chicano neighborhood in Chicago and dreams about having a home. Nina saw herself in Esperanza, whose name means "hope" in Spanish. She talked about her favorite part, when Louie

> *But it is not just the texts that empower these women.*

stole a yellow Cadillac and flew down the street, followed by cops, with Esperanza waving at him. She talked animatedly about Esperanza's ability to survive with so little.

Other texts read during that first session gained mixed responses. The women loved Barbara Kingsolver's *Animal Dreams* but had trouble with Sylvia Plath's *The Bell Jar*. Still, the conversation was charged, and the graduation in the Lynn courtroom just as powerful. The judge saluted the graduates. All of the staff and students felt changed by the experience.

"This is just the beginning for me," said Theresa the day of graduation. And, as she walked out of the courtroom, it was clear she was carrying her books.

That first session hooks us all.

PLANNING FOR THE GROUP

Who They Are

While the facilitator determines what will be read for each CLTL program, the probation officer and judge determine who will participate. Most facilitators do not find it useful to know particulars about the offenders because such information usually gets in the way of teaching with a clean slate, so they leave the casework to the probation officers.

From working in prison for ten years and from experience with CLTL, Trounstine makes certain assumptions about who the participants are before choosing the books. Many of the women will be unmarried single mothers. Many will have a drug or alcohol problem and will have been prostitutes. Most will not have finished high school, although some will have a GED and a few will have started college. The majority of the Lynn-Lowell participants will be white, commonly of Irish or Italian descent; some will be Latino or Black; only a few will be Asian. Quite a few will have a history of abuse—domestic violence or sexual abuse. Some will have been perpetrators, as well as victims, and some will have problems with anger. Almost all will have a checkered job history. In each group, there is often someone who has done time, and many of the women have been arrested over and over again.

That said, the assumption can also be made that almost all yearn for a better life, want to be good mothers, seek to understand why their relationships aren't working or haven't worked in the past, are looking for something to keep them out of crime, and struggle with their needs for a quick fix when things don't go their way.

In terms of reading abilities, they vary. Some women love to read while others claim they never read a book in school. Those who take on CLTL may never have had success in school with reading and need to be coaxed by Trounstine and by their probation officers into believing they can read. Success often depends on a willingness to take on the task.

Choosing the Books for Lynn-Lowell

One of the most interesting aspects of facilitating a CLTL program is choosing the reading material. It is also an awesome responsibility because characters can affect us. Trounstine uses the example of *To Kill a Mockingbird.* When we read that book, many of us identify with Atticus Finch, the wise father who teaches us about moral values without preaching, a white man who stands up for a black man, in spite of danger. No preaching is necessary when you have a role model through a piece of literature. But likewise, exposing the women to Cholly's abuse in *The Bluest Eye* allows us to question that abuse.

Program facilitators get material from stumbling upon it, but sometimes the probation officer or the judge suggests a book. The groups primarily read short stories and novels, with an occasional memoir and a few poems thrown in for good measure. From the beginning of CLTL, the belief has been that story is most accessible to the readers, and facilitators seek to engage them with narrative that is compelling. Although poetry, drama, and essays have much to offer, a story seems to creep inside us. We imagine ourselves somewhere in the story or see its characters in relation to people we know.

Novels are most effective. But a character in a short story can resonate for weeks with the women. And short stories, precisely because
they are short, are very useful for the first class, if the group needs
less of a challenge, or if the group needs to meet two weeks in a row.
Memoir often gives the women a chance to say, "I really like true
stories." They begin to understand that fiction is often based on truth
and memoir often involves imagination.

Trounstine designs a CLTL program around themes and around
the difficulty of the reading material. Subjects that the texts
explore may include self-discovery, self-image, relationships with
family, relationships with lovers, friendship, love, abuse and violence, work in the world, motherhood, raising a child alone, racism,
politics, and human freedom. Reading about survivors who struggle to keep a family together, make
their way out of poverty, or become
their own person can inspire us to
succeed in our lives. By observing
what characters do, how they solve
problems, confront issues, and succeed or fail, we can learn to change
our thinking and our behavior. By voicing our opinions and listening
to those of others, we can begin to change our way of being in the
world.

> *Reading about survivors who struggle to keep a family together, make their way out of poverty, or become their own person can inspire us to succeed in our lives.*

Of course, it's not always that simple. Raising issues in a group means
that a variety of responses will come forth. If we are not moved by a
character or provoked by an idea, we won't use the book.

Sometimes, it's not the main character who is compelling but a
supporting character. Dorothy Allison's *Bastard Out of Carolina* is a
good example. Bone's Aunt Raylene, the openly gay character, is ap-
pealing to the participants because she helps Bone survive unspeak-
able brutality. For the women in CLTL classes, her actions may or may
not sink in as much as Bone's. Sometimes the women say they hate
the book, but what they mean is that they hate abuse. The program
continues to use Allison's text because it offers so much material for

discussion, because Raylene deserves our consideration, and because Bone is a survivor.

Trounstine most often uses work by women because many students have not read female authors, and this seems empowering for them. Trounstine will also add a book by a male author because the theme might be relevant or to show that men can write sympathetic female characters. For example, in *Night*, Elie Wiesel's gripping account of his experiences as a child during the Holocaust, the women were most touched by imagining their own child going through something "like that." Also, some of them had had no exposure to that period of history, and the book served as a way of opening their eyes.

Likewise, with Barbara Kingsolver's *Animal Dreams*, the women usually learn about America's involvement in Nicaragua, and some find it fascinating that Codi's sister Hallie has a passion to help others with farming in a country that's "down there." This provides the opportunity for a geography lesson, but more important, for raising problematic questions like, "Why would someone leave America?" or "What is it like to risk your life for something you believe in?" As long as we don't try to force a political point of view on them, and allow them to explore issues that the author raises, the women are usually willing to consider things from a point of view other than their own.

Occasionally, the women's fear of difference or their unwillingness to move past stereotypes affects book choices. When Lynn-Lowell once read Esmerelda Santiago's *When I Was Puerto Rican*, several students proclaimed that if Santiago didn't like the continent (which she discusses in all its glory and not-so-glory), "she should go back to Puerto Rico." One probationer decided she was just like "all those Spanish types" and refused to accept any of Santiago's perceptions of feeling like an outsider in her own country. Trounstine was careful not to tell her she was wrong and asked her to think about how she might feel moving to another country. Although the conversation left many important issues hanging in the air, it was difficult to hear some of the students' prejudices. When a book provides too many obstacles, Trounstine does not use that text again.

Still, that happens rarely. A book usually deserves a second chance. The women respond well to books about female identity. And even if the book is tough, like Allison's *Bastard Out of Carolina*, it provides much to think about. Quests for identity seem to be different when presented from a female point of view. Women do not sail with Odysseus or look for the great white whale as much as they seek to understand their troubled fathers or find the strength to get out of a no-good relationship. Just as in Tillie Olsen's "I Stand Here Ironing," an epiphany can occur over an ironing board.

When including a work by a male author, Trounstine often structures the discussion to get at ideas about the text that women would relate to. For example, Lynn-Lowell has used "Greasy Lake," the short story discussed in Chapter 3 that includes male violence against a woman. It takes a distinct turn when we consider the potential for violence in the male characters rather than solely discussing the text as a journey for male identity. Thus, a story by a male author that is read in an all-female group opens us up to the different ways we come at a text, and thus, perhaps, helps us see some of the different ways we come at life. What is most important is that characters go through a struggle and that we see them dealing with painful and powerful human issues; that we are left with some hope.

> *Women do not sail with Odysseus or look for the great white whale as much as they seek to understand their troubled fathers or find the strength to get out of a no-good relationship.*

Trounstine often varies the texts, trying with each session to add a new book so that the probation officers and judge have something to look forward to as well. Lynn-Lowell tends to use modern American fiction because it seems most accessible, but this is not an absolute. For example, the group has read British authors and is considering a New Zealand author. The texts themselves are the teachers, and Trounstine chooses books that give the reader the chance to get lost in a character and become affected by themes.

Different groups like different material, and we've come to understand that choosing the reading is only one part of the process. Material that Trounstine has used over the years includes the following books and short stories. A more complete list of CLTL texts can be found in Chapters 8 and 9.

James Agee, *A Death in the Family*
Dorothy Allison, *Bastard Out of Carolina*
Maya Angelou, *I Know Why the Caged Bird Sings*
Margaret Atwood, *Alias Grace*
Dee Axelrod, "River"
James Baldwin, "Sonny's Blues"
Toni Cade Bambara, "Gorilla, My Love"
Russell Banks, *Rule of the Bone*
T. Coraghessan Boyle, "Greasy Lake"
Marta Brunet, "Solitude of Blood"
Sandra Cisneros, *The House on Mango Street*
E. L. Doctorow, "Jolene: A Life"
Janet Fitch, *White Oleander*
Jane Hamilton, *Map of the World*
Zora Neale Hurston, *Their Eyes Were Watching God*
Mary Karr, *The Liars' Club*
Sue Monk Kidd, *The Secret Life of Bees*
Barbara Kingsolver, *Animal Dreams*
Barbara Kingsolver, *The Bean Trees*
Barbara Kingsolver, *Pigs in Heaven*
Harper Lee, *To Kill a Mockingbird*
Ursula Leguin, "The Wife's Story"
Doris Lessing, "Woman on a Roof"
Bobbie Ann Mason, *In Country*
Toni Morrison, *The Bluest Eye*
Alice Munro, "Boys and Girls"
Gloria Naylor, *The Women of Brewster Place*

Rita Marie Nibasa, "A Line of Cutting Women"

Joyce Carol Oates, "Where Are You Going? Where Have You Been?"

Tillie Olsen, "I Stand Here Ironing"

Tillie Olsen, *Tell Me a Riddle*

Sylvia Plath, *The Bell Jar*

Annie Proulx, *The Shipping News*

Esmerelda Santiago, *When I Was Puerto Rican*

Alice Sebold, *The Lovely Bones*

Anita Shreve, *Strange Fits of Passion*

Anne Tyler, *Dinner at the Homesick Restaurant*

Alice Walker, "Everyday Use"

Elie Wiesel, *Night*

Gender Issues and Success

We have written extensively about gender in Chapter 3, but it is important to note that as women start to feel successful in CLTL, we have found they have to deal with people who don't want them to succeed. Sometimes this is the controlling or abusive boyfriend. Trounstine remembers how one woman from Lynn asked the van driver to drop her off at the end of the class, a street or two away from the Lynn Court. She didn't want her boyfriend to see her in a van driven by a man because she knew the boyfriend would be jealous. Partners of our women are in many cases disparaging of the women's success. Early on, one woman wrote a letter about how difficult it was for her to be in the program because of her abusive boyfriend. Trounstine remembers seeing his car when he drove up to the college to pick her up after class. When she got in the car, he raised his voice at her about making him wait, and Trounstine could see her sitting sullenly and staring straight ahead, hardly the lively woman who had blossomed in discussions.

Not only do female CLTL students in the Lynn-Lowell Program lack their boyfriends' support, many have to fit reading in between taking care of kids and looking for work. Some have jobs they hold on to that pay minimum wage. Others can't find work. Some are on welfare. Most have not had the luxury of thinking about what they want to do with their lives. "What do you want to do with your one wild and precious life?" asks Mary Oliver in her poem "Summer," and to many of the women, this question is new. When Dever and the probation officers meet with them at graduation and when Trounstine talks about continuing their education, students begin to get an idea about lifelong learning. Learning that they have choices is a first for them because they tend to see themselves moving through life on a conveyor belt.

Where Lynn-Lowell Holds Classes and Why

Trounstine followed the lead of the first men's program and decided to hold sessions at an institution of higher learning. There's a different feeling at a college campus than in a room at a courthouse. Whereas courts stand for justice, colleges stand for academic freedom. At MCC, the president gave the program her office for a classroom—a room on the top floor, overlooking Lowell, with an oblong table able to sit twelve in cushioned chairs. The women are always a bit in awe the first time they come together, up the elevator, and find that they are treated "specially." They are not used to such treatment, don't expect it and, in fact, mostly feel they don't deserve it. To distinguish between their crimes and their humanity is a way to show them that this program is addressing a part of themselves that they often ignore.

The environment of a college campus has proven over and over again to have an effect on the probationers. Many have negative experiences with school but want to belong and fit in. The first time the program met during a warm September, several of the women came up the stairs of the building and into the lobby of City Campus dressed in tight shorts, heels, and tops that were revealing. No one else on campus was dressed that way, and it was interesting to watch probationers check out other students who passed them by on their way up the elevator to classes. Without anyone saying a word, the women came dressed a little differently the next week, and soon, you couldn't have distinguished them from any other students. The environment affected their behavior.

Likewise, as they hang around a college, they start to think about getting back into college, getting their GEDs, or starting college for the first time. From every program, at least one or two enroll in college classes after they complete CLTL.

REFLECTIONS

The program aims students toward education as well as toward a better frame of mind; more self-esteem; clearer thinking; more options in the workplace; deepened understandings of self and others; reading, discussion, and social skills improvement; and deepened awareness of social environment.

Students say it best:

> Before I started this class I was about six months sober, working and going to GED prep and doing counseling but running with a warrant. I'm very grateful to be in this class. It was a wonderful change not to run scared and be here. . . . I had to push myself into reading, but what I found out is that I like to read and how reading strengthens your mind and helps you build confidence. I enjoyed these classes and still am continuing school so that I can start college soon for physical therapy, which I'm excited to do. It's six years and I'm willing to try my hardest and do my best.
>
> —Danielle, Lynn-Lowell Progam

6 Other CLTL Programs: We Keep Growing

> *"Often, the human condition of these offenders has stopped their growth. Alcohol, drugs, and violence harden people. They are locked in. This becomes their fixed identity. The CLTL program can break up that hard ground, soften it."*
>
> —*Judge Robert May,*
> *149th District Court, Texas*

SINCE CLTL BEGAN IN NEW BEDFORD, Massachusetts, with the Lynn-Lowell Program following close behind, we have graduated more than 4,000 students in twelve years and run programs in Massachusetts, Texas, Kansas, Arizona, Rhode Island, New York, Maine, Connecticut, and in the United Kingdom. Most of our programs are for adults, but some are for juveniles. Included here is a brief look at many of the programs to underscore the different ways we approach CLTL, depending on the jurisdiction and class makeup.

There are differences from court to court and state to state, but what is important to remember is that everyone has the ability to adapt the principles of CLTL to their own needs. It is part of what makes up the "democratic" nature of the program. By the time this book reaches you, there will be more CLTL programs on the way and existing programs will find more creative ways to use the principles of CLTL. These profiles have been modified from our website, *http://cltl.umassd.edu.* Programs are listed in order of their inception.

DORCHESTER, MASSACHUSETTS

Dorchester has both a men's and a women's program, each founded in 1994 by Presiding Justice Sydney Hanlon, along with Probation Officers Deirdre Kennedy, Theresa Owens, John Christopher, John Owens, and James "Bobby" Spencer; and Professors Taylor Stoehr (men's program) and Ann Brian Murphy and Anthony Farley (women's program). Except for one year, the programs have operated continuously since 1994.

A large majority of the students have been African-American or Hispanic, reflecting the demographics of the jurisdiction. Students are recruited by probation officers (POs) from their caseloads, and not by judges or other court officers. Participation is voluntary. Students successfully completing the course receive a six-month reduction of their probation sentence. Classes are held on the campus of the University of Massachusetts, Boston. Graduation ceremonies are held twice a year at the Dorchester Courthouse, with Hanlon presiding and other justices sitting with her in a full courtroom.

The Dorchester Men's Program has the following characteristics:

❏ It features a staff of about five—probation officers, facilitators, judges, and community volunteers, along with visitors (district attorneys, public defenders, and a few representatives from programs in other countries).
❏ It meets for ten weekly sessions, ninety minutes each, on weekday evenings.

- ❑ A primary text, Frederick Douglass's *Narrative of the Life of an American Slave*, with shorter readings by a number of other writers from Richard Wright to Leo Tolstoy, are chosen to take the class through a progressively more intense series of discussions on "life crisis" themes.
- ❑ Writing assignments accompany the reading assignments, and each class begins with an opening writing exercise on the topic for the night, followed by small-group discussions of the readings and the answers to the exercise.
- ❑ Discussion groups typically have four or five members, including a facilitator (who might be a professor, a probation officer, community volunteer, or a judge).
- ❑ General discussions involving the entire class are conducted on an ad hoc basis, depending on the issues that come to the fore in small-group work.
- ❑ All writing is then typed by the instructors, along with brief feedback, and returned to the authors. Each week, copies of a few especially interesting papers are distributed to the entire class—typically read avidly during the period while early arrivals are waiting for class to begin.

For a variety of reasons, the Dorchester Women's Program classes tend to be much smaller, averaging between five to seven students a semester. Perhaps because of this smaller size, however, the class often becomes a cohesive whole because most of the discussion is done as a class, not with small groups. Certainly the women in the program show remarkable dedication to the class, and a large majority complete the class and graduate each semester. Indeed, in the second year of the program students in the last class asked, "So what do we do now?" and expressed an interest in writing. So in the following semester, one teacher met with three returning students at the Dorchester Public Library and worked with them on their writing, while another teacher met with a new class of students at the University of Massachusetts.

The women's program has had numerous teachers, each of whom has brought her own interests and experimented with her own approaches to the class. About five years ago, for example, facilitators began using writing in the classroom, but each has used it in different ways. Some occasionally ask the students to write poetry, and others ask them to write their thoughts and feelings each week on the themes and ideas touched on by the readings. While there is no set format for the women's program, and classes continue to change from year to year and teacher to teacher, most classes share some or all of the following characteristics:

- A staff of about three—one or two probation officers and a judge, in addition to the instructor.
- Ten weekly sessions, ninety minutes each, on weekday evenings.
- Readings including a collection of short stories, essays, poems, and occasionally a novel; writing assignments that accompany the reading assignments, often at the beginning or ending of the class, related to the topic for the night.
- Readings and discussion focusing on themes, sometimes in the form of issues such as substance abuse, domestic violence, and love, and sometimes more general categories such as change, work, family, children, and life choices.
- Student writings typed by the instructor each week, and the students' original writing returned to the authors the following week with feedback from the facilitator.
- Printing and binding of a booklet of the students' writings as part of the graduation ceremony.

One Dorchester male student wrote:

Through the course of this program I've learned how to communicate with people a little better. It seems like before I came to this program I was going numb. I can't remember the last time I picked up a book to read it or even skim through it. I also have a better relationship with my girlfriend. I try to think about other people's feelings now. It just isn't about me anymore. (Spring 2002)

BARNSTABLE, MASSACHUSETTS

The Barnstable Program was founded in 1995 by the Hon. Joseph Reardon; Dr. Laurie DeBower, Chair of the Language and Literacy Department at Cape Cod Community College; Henry Burke, PO Barnstable District Court; and George Albert, Adjunct Instructor at Cape Cod Community College. They have operated continuously since 1995.

Students are African-American, Latino, Cape Verdean, and Anglo-American. Ages range from 20 to 66. Probationers are recruited by judges, probation officers, and counselors. Each student may receive from two to six months off their probation, depending on variables such as the offenses, student's history, and performance in class.

Classes are held at Cape Cod Community College. Graduation takes place at Barnstable District Court before a full audience of judges, court personnel, and the public. Reardon is the presiding judge.

Classes meet for seven weekly sessions of two and one-half hours each. Of twenty-three cycles, twenty have been all men, two have been coed, and one has been all women. Barnstable plans another all-women cycle for the future.

Two anthologies of short stories have been popular: *The Hudson Book of Fiction* and *The Best American Short Stories of Our Century.* They have used *To Kill a Mockingbird* (Lee), *Black and Blue* (Quindlen), and *The Old Man and the Sea* (Hemingway) as novels. Writing assignments are completed in class.

Examples of what students have said about Barnstable:

"The program gives you a chance to get a positive attitude about life. It gets you going in the right direction."

"The program opened up my mind. I plan to go on to Cape Cod Community College."

Reardon noticed after eight years that with recidivism, there is, "a very substantial diminution in the severity of any new offense," what he calls "a confirmation of the efficacy of the program." Whenever he decides to sentence men or women to the program, he looks for the type of offender who is "chronically before the court, charged with misdemeanor offenses resulting in incarceration. His CORI (Criminal Offender Record Information) will indicate that the House of Corrections is a revolving door for this offender." Reardon has always believed that "loss of freedom is not the key to motivating a change in lifestyle." He says:

> *We have repeatedly seen men blossom into more thoughtful human beings who learn to respond to situations instead of reacting in the usual manner.*

> Since incarceration did not effect change, I wanted to know why. In my discussions with clinical personnel, I was told that people will not change unless they internalize the messages they want to send and adopt as new ways of looking at their lives. CLTL accomplishes this end result. We have repeatedly seen men blossom into more thoughtful human beings who learn to respond to situations instead of reacting in the usual manner. I am convinced beyond any reasonable doubt that the roundtable literature discussions evoke dormant concepts and surface long forgotten thoughts of morality, ethics, conscience, duty, and responsibility.

Reardon believes strongly that judges and probation officers can influence the offenders by their participation in CLTL. He also says that he became "reinvigorated and vested with new zeal . . . as we realize that we are part of a rebirth of critical thinking and decision-making by our probationers."

ROXBURY, MASSACHUSETTS

The Roxbury Program has operated continuously since 1996. It draws mainly African-American students from the community. They range in age from 19 to 60. Students are recruited by the probation officers, and participation is voluntary. Each student receives three months off their probation, and sometimes the payments for probation are reduced. Classes are held at Roxbury District Court, and graduation also takes place at the Courthouse.

A staff of one facilitator, two probation officers and one judge meets for ten weekly sessions, from 5:30 to 7:00 PM weekday evenings with probationers. At present the class is all men but occasional coed classes have been held.

Roxbury is one of the court programs that added writing as a way to get students more engaged. Facilitator Jean Flanagan initiated the idea that students are required to keep a journal in which they write about the texts that they read. For homework, they answer questions relating to the material that are often factual but always help them stay focused on the reading. After students answer and discuss these questions in the classroom, the class moves on to discuss broader, more experiential subjects.

An insight from one student: "I saw my life under a different light, but I also have learned from others through their life experiences."

BRAZORIA COUNTY, TEXAS

In January 1997 the first Texas CLTL Men's Program began, based on the Massachusetts model. The group met for two hours each week for six sessions, started with the short story "Greasy Lake" (Boyle), and then moved to longer works, primarily novels. Carolyn Huff, a retired English teacher, facilitated the discussions with Dr. Lawrence

Jablecki, the Chief Probation Officer of Brazoria County at the time, and Judge Robert E. May.

The sessions were held in the President's Seminar Room at Brazoport Community College in Lake Jackson. Each student was charged a $10 fee to participate but had to purchase his own books. Later that rule would change: $35 per student, including the books.

The success of that initial program encouraged further interest and participation in Brazoria County. Other facilitators joined in: Richard Wilcher in the summer of 1997, for example, and Bill Lockett at Alvin Community College shortly after Wilcher. Dr. Jill Carroll also began classes for women at both Brazoport and Alvin based on the Massachusetts model. All facilitators, it was agreed, would be paid between $1,200 and $1,500 per cycle out of the budget of the Adult Probation Department in Brazoria County. This was similar to what we pay facilitators in Massachusetts.

The probationers enjoyed the classes and found them, on the whole, meaningful and energizing—better than watching television, they said. Word began to spread about this unique humanities program for criminal offenders. The judges and probation officers began to comment on what they observed: a positive repetitive pattern, probationers returning for their GED, less violence against wives and girlfriends, and enhanced verbal skills. Such results inspired and reinforced genuine interest in the CLTL program.

Jablecki was invited to give a talk about CLTL to the prestigious Houston Philosophical Society. The CLTL classes had triggered the attention of Dr. Chuck Henry, one of the Vice Presidents of Rice University, and thus, the CLTL program expanded rapidly in Brazoria County.

It was nearly impossible to get other counties in Texas involved. Carroll began to teach courses on the Rice campus as did Henry. Jablecki published an article based on his lecture about CLTL at Rice in the well-respected journal *Federal Probation*, further boosting the CLTL effort.

Probationers actually began to put their names on waiting lists hoping to get into the program. Jablecki put his unique stamp on CLTL when he decided to facilitate his own version of the program, using classic philosophic texts that he had found most important to him personally. While others continued the traditional literature focus, Jablecki, teaching several cycles each year with about fifteen students per class, used his favorite texts from John Stuart Mill, Plato, and Epictetus because he found they addressed the great questions of life.

Jablecki set the rules at the beginning. No visitors were allowed in these all-male sessions. It was "their private time," as Jablecki said. He wanted to be tough but fair. If the probationers missed one class for any reason, they lost fifteen hours from the seventy-five hours of reduced community service. If they missed a second class, they were out. He made it clear that he would use his own discretion in terms of sanctions if anyone was "late" or had not done the reading.

His approach in class was, in essence, Socratic. He asked the probationers to read passages from the assigned texts each week and then he would begin the dialogue by firing questions to bring the philosophic texts together with personal experience. For Jablecki, reading these important philosophic texts and the discussion that followed allowed probationers to locate themselves in relation to the world around them. It offered what he felt was the opportunity to engage in genuine education "to know thyself." As he insisted: "The issue here is self-reflection. The texts evoked discussion, and the discussion inevitably led to stories of their own lives, their own stories as examples of the conceptual frame for philosophic ideas."

When Carroll began the Texas Women's Program she held classes at the university or the community college, believing that "great literature . . . makes us reflect on what matters in life and on how we are living our own particular lives, and such reflection is what makes us human, perhaps even divine." Borrowing from the Lynn-Lowell Women's Program, a typical syllabus included "I Stand Here Ironing" by Tillie Olsen, "The Yellow Wallpaper" by Charlotte Perkins Gilman, *The House on Mango Street* by Sandra Cisneros, *Their Eyes Were Watching God* by Zora Neale Hurston, and *The Bluest Eye* by Toni Morrison.

A key strategy of Carroll's course involved homework discussion questions. At the end of every session, students took with them a set of ten discussion questions for that week's reading. They were to bring completed questions with them and be ready to talk about both the text and their answers to the questions at the next session. Carroll says that this strategy worked for several reasons. It provided the participants a structure of access to the texts, and as we've seen in other programs, the questions focused students on certain issues, themes, or characters. Second, the questions—more specifically, the various answers to the questions—gave a starting point for discussion in the class.

In February 2001, Dr. William R. Kelly at the University of Texas in Austin submitted an independent evaluation of the CLTL program in Brazoria County. On a scale of 1 to 10, where 1 means "poor" and 10 means "excellent," Kelly reported "the overall program" rated 9.4.

As Kelly wrote in his final report: "One might speculate that the primary reason for the program's popularity is because it is an easy 75 hours of community service ('sure beats pickin' up trash'). In fact, the appeal of the community service hours is an important incentive for initially agreeing to participate. However there are a number of very consistent and important advantages and benefits that the research participants reported:

- ❏ the CLTL Program is perceived to be significantly different from other probation programs because respondents believe it is designed to help offenders; they view it as positive and constructive rather than just punishment or lacking a purpose
- ❏ increased desire/motivation to read and learn
- ❏ positive psychological impacts such as increased tolerance, enhanced self-esteem, and a sense of accomplishment
- ❏ anti-criminologic effects such as better control over impulsive behavior and increased awareness/understanding of the consequences of behavior."

As of 2004, more than 600 probationers had successfully completed the Brazoria County Program.

PHOENIX AND PRESCOTT, ARIZONA

In the late 1990s, two programs were established in Arizona, one a traditional and dynamic program in Phoenix with the participation of judges, probation officers, and facilitators, and the other, an energetic non-traditional program in Prescott at Yavapai College through the commitment and vision of Professor Moses Glidden.

Unfortunately, the Phoenix Program lost its funding and is currently not running, although it still has its supporters and there is hope that it will be revived.

The Prescott Program continues to run on a limited basis as English 118, a two-credit literature-based class with a minimum of 3,500 words of written text throughout the ten-week, three-hour class course. The class is taught by Glidden, who was the first to arrange college credit for participation in CLTL. Each semester, there are approximately four college students in the class along with about fifteen students referred by the courts, a mix that allows for important interaction for all the students.

A major purpose of class is recognizing how our daily lives are made up of little human stories. Glidden feels such recognition opens every-one to recognition of our common humanity and provides building blocks for developing character. Students see and appreciate that the choices they make create their stories. By offering them choices, they can begin to change their lives.

As Professor Glidden explains:

> By recognizing the types of choices, attitudes, and conclusions that occur in these stories, students should be able to better recognize and develop their own character. By writing comparisons between literary stories and their own life stories, there is an extra bonus of authoritative examples to follow or reject.

Glidden has noticed that after a few weeks, students become aware that they can move in the direction that they choose, and that "If I go to jail, jail is my choice. If I am successful, success is my choice."

> *After a few weeks, students become aware that they can move in the direction that they choose, and that "If I go to jail, jail is my choice. If I am successful, success is my choice."*

CONCORD/WOBURN, MASSACHUSETTS

The Concord Men's Program was founded by Probation's Ed Gaffey in 1997. Students are predominantly Caucasian, recruited by the probation officers, and their participation is voluntary. Judges often remit some of the probation fees when the CLTL course is successfully completed. Classes are held at Middlesex Community College (MCC) in Bedford. Graduation takes place at the Concord Court. There is a staff of two facilitators, two or three probation officers, and one judge. It meets for six sessions of two hours each, every other week.

Some of the short stories that have piqued student interest and provoked interesting discussion are "The Swimmer" by John Cheever, "Where I'm Calling From" and "Cathedral" by Raymond Carver, and "Hunters in the Snow" by Tobias Wolff. Some of the novels that have been used successfully are *Montana 1948* by Larry Watson, *The Sea-Wolf* by Jack London, *Affliction* and *The Sweet Hereafter* by Russell Banks, and *The Things They Carried* by Tim O'Brien.

Writing assignments are completed during class time and are anonymous. Students write to respond to the text and to make connections with their own lives. Discussion takes place with the whole group followed by small-group discussion questions.

One of the more interesting elements of the Concord program is that it has been taught by a husband-and-wife team, Sandi Albertson-Shea and Ray Shea, who "publish" the writing of their students for the class to have at their completion of CLTL.

One of the probation officers in the program said, "This class is what I value most about being a probation officer. It's about learning, growing, healing through insight and education. It is 'the court' respecting the group, wanting to hear what they have to say, acknowledging that they have something important to offer. Also that we are all human beings figuring life out as we live it."

The Woburn Men's Program also meets at MCC and began when Judge Marie Jackson contacted MCC Professor Orian Greene to see if she would be interested in starting a program. The first session was in 2001, and the program has continued to spark interest.

Most of the men are from Woburn, although some occasionally come through the Concord Court. The majority of the men are Caucasian, with a few African-American and Hispanic members from time to time. Ages run from 17 to 79. Students are recruited by probation officers. Participation is voluntary. The compensation varies, but most receive six months off their probation and may be released from probation service fees. Classes are held at the Middlesex Bedford campus, and graduation takes place at Woburn District Court with Judge Marie Jackson presiding.

The Woburn Program has a staff of two judges, two probation officers, and one facilitator, and it meets for six sessions of two hours each, every other week.

Some of the texts that Greene finds absorbing to the students include these short stories: "Greasy Lake" by T. Coraghessan Boyle, "Giving Up the Gun" by Andre Dubus, "The Five Forty-Eight" by John Cheever, and "Cathedral" by Raymond Carver. Novels that students respond to are *Night* by Elie Wiesel, *The Barracks Thief* by Tobias Wolff, *Of Mice and Men* by John Steinbeck, and *The Old Man and the Sea* by Ernest Hemingway.

Before the beginning of each session the students answer short concise questions to get them warmed up for discussion. At the end of class they write again. These are both short writings on a 4 × 6 card.

About the program, Jackson says: "CLTL has made a difference to everyone who has had contact with it, the probationers, their family, and the staff at the court as well as myself."

Concord District Court in conjunction with Woburn's District Court, began a Concord Women's Program in 2001. The students are also predominantly Caucasian, ranging in age from 17 to 62. Classes are held at Middlesex on the Bedford campus. The staff includes one probation officer and one facilitator who meet with probationers every other week for two hours.

Some of the texts that have had the most impact include the following: "Woman on a Roof" by Doris Lessing, "The Chrysanthemums" by John Steinbeck, "The Lottery" by Shirley Jackson, *White Oleander* by Janet Fitch, *Ethan Frome* by Edith Wharton, as well as the memoir *The Liar's Club* by Mary Karr.

The class is conducted as a seminar with the facilitator posing some questions and keeping the discussion focused on the text. Writing assignments are used in the beginning of the course as an aid to discussion, but according to Gail Mooney, facilitator, the women's classes have no trouble engaging in lively discussions and after the first few classes a writing assignment isn't necessary.

Mooney enjoys the women and finds that they learn to see themselves in a better light through the session. "Community, sustenance, self-reliance, the need for beauty . . . are all the abstractions for which we often have no voice other than that found in literature," says Mooney, "but it is exactly these things that ennoble us and that, by their pursuit, make the women in my CLTL groups feel good about themselves. And feeling good is always the very first step toward positive, vital action."

JOHNSON COUNTY, KANSAS

The CLTL Kansas Program began in 1999. The program's inaugu-
ral advocate was Melanie Fenske, a public information officer with
Johnson County Corrections. Having heard Robert Waxler speak
of the program's effectiveness, Fenske spoke with attorney Greg
Kincaid, the juvenile representative to the courts at that time, and Judge
William Cleaver of the District Court about starting a CLTL program
in Johnson County. All three founding members have a profound belief
in the power of literature to effect change.

The Kansas program is a series of weekly or bi-monthly workshops
composed of two-hour sessions, and each workshop lasts seven weeks.
Male groups and female groups are separate. The adult groups meet at
Johnson County Community College, and the juvenile groups meet at a
library branch. There has also been a CLTL program held at a Johnson
County Corrections male residential center. A judge, probation officer,
and facilitator are present at all literature sessions. The facilitator leads
discussion with all those in attendance expected to participate. In the
literature sessions, participants read and discuss a variety of short
stories and novels. Film has also been used to collaborate on ideas and
stimulate discussion. The groups are deliberately small, numbering
between eight and twelve people.

A unique feature of the program is that after each literature discussion a short evaluation is given to provide feedback. At the end of the
seven-session workshop, a participation evaluation is given.

Members of the Kansas Program believe in providing the best possible environment in which to conduct thoughtful discussion of literature. Johnson County Community College and the Johnson County
Library System have provided rooms. The facilitators further believe
in personal ownership of books as concrete evidence of participation,
a way to revisit ideas and the possibility of reaching others through
reading. Consequently, books used for the CLTL are provided for

those participating. Snacks may also be provided at each session with a culminating pizza party upon completion of the program.

The Kansas Program has been funded by community donations; a grant from Alcohol Tax Fund (ATF) through United Community Services; Johnson County Library Staff for in-kind services; Johnson County Corrections for in-kind services; and bookstores giving book discounts.

The Kansas Program was one of the first to add a juvenile program to its male and female adult programs. Their reading list includes *Touching Spirit Bear* by Ben Mikaelsen, *Hero* by S. L. Rottman, *Breathing Underwater* by Alexandra Flinn, *Swallowing Stones* by Joyce McDonald, *Hole in My Life* by Jack Gantos, and *The Giver* by Lois Lowry.

Facilitator Kathy McLellan talks about how rewarding it is to work with juveniles:

> We begin as strangers, but immediately the literature gives us something in common. We come to know each other rather well, and the connection we make with these teens extends beyond their probation period. We see them in grocery stores, restaurants, and believe it or not—in the library! And we can always ask that question that gets right to the point, "What are you reading?"

In 2004, we held a training for CLTL in Massachusetts, as we do every year, and we looked at the successes and difficulties of running CLTL juvenile programs. As Dorchester facilitator Taylor Stoehr commented on our website at *http://cltl.umassd.edu*, "How can a 'literature' program succeed with juveniles who, by the very nature of their cases, are completely absorbed in their own crisis situations, impatient with anything they don't immediately understand—including their thoughts and feelings!—and . . . as one of the panelists from Kansas put it, how can we avoid ruining the book for them, the way school so often does?"

Kansas CLTL is hoping to answer that question.

SUFFOLK COUNTY, NEW YORK

The New York Program began in September 2000 after Waxler and Trounstine presented a workshop at Suffolk County Day Reporting Center to the entire staff, including psychologists, probation officers, and teachers. The program has run continuously since then, with classes sometimes held daily. The team concept continues, with counselors and support groups often following up on issues raised during CLTL classes.

CLTL classes at the center show how fruitfully the program can be adapted for various populations and settings. Reading Specialist Linda Jacino pioneered the program, facilitating twice-weekly classes as part of a constellation of services offered to clientele. Jacino often also has a co-teacher help her. CLTL seminars typically include up to twenty-two men and women from the ages of 16 to 65. The group atmosphere is as therapeutic here as elsewhere in the center. Jacino says: "Sometimes we have guys who are almost illiterate sitting in the class. Many people will take risks and read out loud."

The program uses a variety of texts, primarily short stories, novels, and plays. When Jacino can, she takes her students to see live performances. She also has used many classic pieces of literature, including *The Diary of Anne Frank* by Anne Frank, *The Miracle Worker* by William Gibson, *As You Like It* by William Shakespeare, and *The Crucible* and *Death of a Salesman* by Arthur Miller.

Jacino often chooses texts and plays that mirror present-day political issues. The group has read books such as *The Things They Carried* by Tim O'Brien and a piece about a zoo in World War II Japan. They've read about school violence in the play, *"Bang, Bang, You're Dead"* by William Mastrosimone. After reading that play, the group saw the movie *Bowling for Columbine.* Jacino also has had participants research federal and state gun laws and write their congressional representatives about their views on gun violence.

She reports that the center's program is a "model program. People from all over the world come to see us." Clientele are sentenced by a judge either through drug court or as an early-release option. All have been involved with substance abuse. The center also offers health care services, substance abuse counseling, tutoring, remedial education, high school equivalency, consumer economics, English as a Second Language, art, vocational training, and career/life planning.

FRAMINGHAM, MASSACHUSETTS

The Framingham Program, the first coed group, was founded in 2001 by POs Charles Ashe, Ann Schneider, and Lenny McLean; Judge Robert Greco; and facilitator Jane Hale. Students range in age from 17 to 40. They are of mixed ethnicity and, as in most CLTL programs, from a variety of backgrounds. They are at fairly high levels of education on average (it's rare for them not to have completed high school and some are even in or have completed college). Participants are referred by a probation officer and enter the course voluntarily. Upon completion of the program, each participant will either have probation monthly fees waived for the period of the program and, if the participant has only a few months until scheduled termination, in some instances probation can be terminated if the participant satisfactorily completes the course.

Unlike most Massachusetts programs that are held in colleges, this program is held at The Law Library, Framingham District Court. Graduation takes place at court with the presiding judge, Greco. They have a staff of three probation officers, the judge, and one facilitator, and they meet for seven to eight sessions of two hours each. Depending on court or vacation schedules, they meet either weekly or every two weeks. They have been coed since inception. Hale, the facilitator, says that the CLTL classroom provides "an exceptional model and opportunity in their lives to have a sustained, respectful, non-sexually charged relationship between men and women."

Framingham has used the many texts successfully. Says Hale,

> The texts deal with such topics as love, work, family, sex, crime, illness, violence, and alcohol and other drugs. The list could continue indefinitely, for that's what literature is: a record of what people have felt and experienced and of how they have acted in their lives. In CLTL, we look at how our lives intersect—or don't—with those of the people we read about, and discuss what we might have to learn from their experiences. We emphasize the choices and decisions available to fictional characters who find themselves in various problematic situations, and try to connect our own life experiences and options to the ones we read about.

She recommends "Greasy Lake" by T. Coraghessan Boyle, "Sonny's Blues" by James Baldwin, "On the Rainy River" by Tim O'Brien, *Of Mice and Men* by John Steinbeck, and the autobiography *Brothers and Keepers* by John Edgar Wideman.

Ten-minute writing assignments are done in each class. Students have a choice of questions to answer: They can respond directly to a text, speak about their personal experiences, or connect both. Participants sometimes read answers aloud or share them with a partner. Selections from the assignments are compiled into a course booklet, similar to the Concord Men's Program, which is given to everyone at graduation.

Discussions are conducted in varied ways: The facilitator leads off with prepared questions. Students are asked to write two questions for discussion as they read the text. The facilitator gives students a written list of questions to prepare orally for the next class discussion. The facilitator prepares a list of questions to be used in class, among small groups, each of which chooses two or three questions to answer and then bring back to the group for discussion. The students are each asked to be responsible for introducing the reading one night with a brief reaction statement and then a discussion question.

One student said: "I came here kicking and screaming it would be a waste of time. I was completely wrong. I enjoyed it and learned from it."

MAINE

Changing Lives has inspired two multi-faceted programs in the state of Maine: one sponsored by a Native American Tribal Court and another through the Maine Humanities Council.

The first, a collaboration among the University of Maine, the Penobscot Tribal Court, and the Bangor Court System, was created after court officials saw a presentation by Waxler at a conference. The second, Stories for Life, under the direction of Julia Walkling, is one of a cornucopia of programs sponsored by the Maine Humanities Council.

"When people ask me what I do, I tell them I organize book discussion groups in places where you wouldn't expect people to be talking abut books," says Walkling. "When you hold a discussion with a 69-year old man who is just learning to read, you learn that that person can focus ideas just as well as any of us and that's what it's all about."

Stories for Life is a reading and discussion program for probationers co-sponsored by the Maine Humanities Council and the Maine Department of Corrections. Scholar-led discussions of short stories provide participants an opportunity to reflect on their own lives and the choices they have made. Probation officers work with scholars to co-facilitate the group sessions. Since the program's inception in 2001, forty-four Stories for Life programs have been held in eight locations around Maine. In each site, a lead probation officer gathers a group from

> *People don't know how to start a conversation about themselves, particularly with a person in authority. They feel too vulnerable. But the readings serve as a change agent that starts to break down the barriers that limit communication.*

among his caseload and those of colleagues working out of the same office. Each group participates in five discussion sessions led by a facilitator. Participants may or may not continue on to further sessions.

Maine CLTL uses short stories because of their accessibility for participants who may not read very well or who are generally not in the habit of reading. Participants receive two books of stories to keep, in the hope that they will continue to read after the program is over. So far, Raymond Carver has been the most popular, discussible, author; but they have also used books of stories by Tobias Wolff, Annie Proulx, and John Steinbeck.

"The power relationship often inhibits probationers from saying what's really on their minds," explains Nancy Bouchard, associate director for adult services, Maine Department of Corrections. "What the book program offers is a neutral ground in which both parties can discuss a reading experience they have in common. And the stories often reflect the life situation of the probationers." Bouchard says the pilot program has already opened many doors, "People don't know how to start a conversation about themselves, particularly with a person in authority. They feel too vulnerable. But the readings serve as a change agent that starts to break down the barriers that limit communication."

RHODE ISLAND

Serious discussion about establishing CLTL began at the University of Rhode Island in 2001 with Dr. Dorothy Donnelly, English Department Chair at the time; Dr. Bernard Lafayette, the Director of the URI Center for Nonviolence; and Susan Peterson, a graduate student. (Peterson is now a professor at Curry College.) Shortly after those discussions, Patty Fairweather, who had served as a facilitator in Massachusetts while a law student at Boston College, joined the ad hoc group.

Since 2001, there have been various attempts to organize CLTL both as an alternative sentencing program through the state courts and as a prison program through the Department of Corrections. Pilot classes have been conducted most recently in the minimum security branch of the Adult Correction Institution. These classes emphasize an approach that includes a significant emphasis on nonviolence in the context of the fundamental CLTL vision.

In June 2004, Fairweather moderated a panel discussion about CLTL at the Rhode Island Bar Association Annual Meeting in Providence that drew attention to the program from a number of judges and other important figures in the legal community.

Currently, the Department of Corrections is helping to provide administrative support for the classes, and the President of the Rhode Island Bar Association also plans to lend support. While the Rhode Island Program is focused on work within the State Adult Corrections Institution they also continue to develop a second track for CLTL as an alternative sentencing program.

WRENTHAM, MASSACHUSETTS

Wrentham CLTL is a small suburban program serving the towns of Foxboro, Franklin, Medway, Millis, Plainville, Walpole, and Wrentham. At the present time, the program involves a judge, probation officer, and instructor; however, with the arrival of a new presiding judge, the program is hopeful it will be able to grow its staff and client base.

The Wrentham Program offered its first classes in 2002 when the first nine participants were recruited. Classes have run continuously each fall and winter/spring since that time. The driving force was Judge John Connors who saw the merits of the program and recruited probation officer Gayle Weinberg-Krause and instructor Trudy Schrandt to facilitate the program in early 2001. With the aid of Chief Probation Officer Al Pizzi, a site for the program was established one year later.

By the second session a contract came into being. In effect, each probationer agrees to attend all classes, read all materials in full prior to each session, and miss no more than one class to graduate. By the second session all participants must present a valid library card.

Until recently all participants have been male and volunteers. Beginning with the winter/spring session in 2004, female participants also became involved.

Following the completion of the program, each probationer must write a letter to the court stating what he or she has gained from the program and justify what remission of probation sentence would be appropriate, up to a period of six months. Probationers who fail to meet the terms of their contract may repeat the program if it is felt they will benefit from the second session.

This concept of second enrollment is allowed and encouraged in Wrentham. Currently probationers cannot receive more than six months off their probation sentence. However, probationers who do not receive a maximum sentence remission may re-attend the program to gain up to the reduction. Others may choose to participate in a second session if there is room available. To date, three graduated probationers have repeated the program with extraordinary success in their level of involvement, participation, and leadership.

The suburban setting, lack of a state college campus in the vicinity, and the lack of public transportation caused the group to look for a meeting place outside the college system. The Tri-County Vocational High School in Franklin, Massachusetts, is at a central location. Participants without licenses are encouraged to attend the first class and make car-pool arrangements with others in the program.

The program meets every other week for eight weeks in the fall and spring of each year. Each meeting is two hours in length. A ninth meeting is scheduled for a graduation ceremony and social gathering for the participants and their guests. Classes are small and average seven to eight participants.

The literature selections for the course are made up of five short stories and five novels. Poetry is selected to enhance themes within the readings. Authors included to date are Eudora Welty, Alice Walker,

T. Coraghessan Boyle, John Cheever, Paul Bowles, John Steinbeck, Ernest Hemingway, Chaim Potok, William Golding, Elie Wiesel, Larry Watson, Victor Hugo, Richard Carver, and Harper Lee, to name only a few. Discussions are roundtable and include the entire class, facilitator, probation officer, and judge. The focus is on understanding the material with special attention paid to the decisions and the outcomes.

CONNECTICUT

The Connecticut CLTL Program was started at Tunxis Community College in Farmington, Connecticut, in the fall of 2002 through the New Britain Alternative Incarceration Center (AIC). Brian Sullivan, a retired probation officer working at the AIC, and Filomena Aresco, a college intern at the AIC at that time, approached Professor Francena Dwyer at Tunxis Community College with the idea of starting a program. Dwyer embraced the concept and the first class was born. Community Partners in Action, the agency that funds and manages the New Britain AIC, has been extremely supportive of the reading groups since they began in 2002.

In the fall of 2003, Joseph Wickliffe started a CLTL program at Yale University in New Haven through the New Haven AIC, known as Project More. The program was planned to benefit the AIC clients from Bridgeport and New Haven. The participants included the clients, Yale students, the Bridgeport AIC supervisor, a school liaison, and a Yale professor who facilitated the sessions. The course responsibilities included regular meetings, attendance, participation in discussions, reading homework, and writing assignments.

The clients always looked forward to attending the CLTL meetings. They identified with the literature assigned and, as the discussion developed, connected with it and reflected on experiences they'd had in their lives. They started talking and came to realize, as well as analyze, some of their past misconducts and judgment failures.

Groups typically meet for eight sessions of ninety minutes per session. The group rules are stated in a "do and don't list." All issues discussed during group sessions are confidential, and clients are advised to respect the feelings of others around the table and treat their issues as important and relevant. Anyone who violates these rules is dismissed immediately. Students sign a form agreeing to the group rules.

As a facilitator of the program, Wickliffe said he learned a great deal. Most of the literature selected for the fall of 2003 connected with real-life experiences, such as decision-making techniques and issues resulting from poor judgment, flawed thinking, and inappropriate reactions. The reading list has included poetry by Maya Angelou and Langston Hughes, short stories by Shirley Jackson and T. Coraghessan Boyle, and novels by James McBride and Rodney J. Carroll.

CLTL at Yale has been a particularly heart-warming experience for those involved. One client said, "I love the adventure of coming from Bridgeport to Yale. The environment makes me want to come more and more."

Plans are underway to expand the CLTL program to other communities in Connecticut, such as Manchester, Hartford, and Middletown.

OTHER POSSIBILITIES WITH CLTL

Juvenile Programs

An exciting development taking place over the past few years is the application of the CLTL model with juvenile probationers. This is happening in Kansas. Massachusetts also has juvenile programs in New Bedford and Dorchester. Other states are considering beginning such programs.

The New Bedford Juvenile Court began the first juvenile program in Massachusetts in 2001. Judge Bettina Borders came aboard soon after. For each of the ten to twelve classes, male students are bused from the New Bedford Police Station to the University of Massachusetts in the company of PO Stella Rebeiro. During the two-hour classes, they read aloud around the table. This avoids the problem of students not doing homework and losing books at home, thus ensuring a way to keep students from failing.

The novels used successfully include those dealing with gang violence, such as *The Outsiders* by S. E. Hinton, and those dealing with growing up, such as *The Rules of the Road* by Joan Bauer. Interspersed with reading is discussion of the texts and the issues they raise. These discussions are lively and often heated, and range in topic from personal to larger societal issues. The group has tackled educational ideas like Ebonics and community learning, and discussed ways that students can present themselves to get jobs. They might discuss the morality of drug laws or why we get angry when we are not listened to.

In Dorchester, Massachsetts, there are programs for boys and girls. The girls program began in 2004 when Juvenile Court Judge Marjory A. German enlisted POs Idella Carter and Barbara Anne Loftus, and instructor Anne-Marie Kent, from the University of Massachusetts. The class began with eight teenage girls and graduated three, others having dropped out for a number of reasons, mainly non-attendance.

Stoehr, Dorchester Men's Program facilitator, wrote up notes from our training. He reports that female students "respond to the readings with their own writings, sometimes in dialogue with the authors, sometimes creating their own poems, which they share with each other. Much of the writing is done in class." He also says that "the focus of the course has been the preparation of a kind of 'personal journal' prepared by each girl, filled with self-defining writing, drawing, photos, and other material that is chosen to represent the author's true self."

Juvenile Court Judge Marjory A. German, with the help of Dorchester juvenile probation officer Robert Nagle and instructor Rev. Matt Gibson from the Ella J. Baker House, began a program for boys in 2004. The spring class began with ten boys and ended by graduating seven in ceremonies conducted at the courthouse.

The boy's session met weekly, for ninety minutes after school hours, over a period of ten weeks. Most of the reading material consisted of poems, which were chosen for their relevance to the students. Students also worked on projects involving their own lives and "stories." One class involved a joint excursion with the girls program to visit the University of Massachusetts Boston campus and meet with the head of Admissions and the Vice Chancellor for Student Affairs.

Stoehr reports that all our juvenile program participants agreed that "the most important ingredient in their success recipe is . . . that these children need to be taken seriously by adults, and especially by adults who represent authority, like a judge."

At the Dorchester graduation, one female student read a poem she had written. At our training, German said, speaking of the low attendance and the new sense of self-worth for the graduates:

> We at Juvenile Court try to make a difference every day, with the 30 to 40 cases that come before me, but we don't make a difference every day—or even every week. If once a month, it's a big success. But last Tuesday at our graduation, I can name ten children that—maybe—we did make a difference to.

United Kingdom CLTL behind Bars

While the Changing Lives concept is ideal for people on probation, several very successful programs are running behind bars. At the Dartmouth Women's Center of the Bristol County Prison in Massachusetts, Kelly DeSouza started a program for female prisoners that is based on the CLTL premise.

In the United Kingdom, a dedicated core group has worked to bring CLTL into prisons. Following a meeting with us during a visit to the United Kingdom in 1999, the Writers in Prison Network Ltd. brought the Changing Lives Through Literature program to the notice of its members at their annual conference. Writers in Prison Network is a not-for-profit organization dedicated entirely to promoting and encouraging the creative arts in prisons, with ex-offenders, and with those at risk of offending. The Connections Program is now offered in several prisons in the United Kingdom.

Two early programs were then adapted for use within the prison system. One was attempted for young offenders but received little support. The other was designed primarily for a twelve-month stretch, exclusively using novels.

Following these programs, Mary Stephenson next applied for funding for the literature programs. A Writer in Residence at HMP (Her Majesty's Prison) Channings Wood, a medium-security prison for adult men in Devon, Stephenson believed that although CLTL had been run in the United States as an alternative to custodial sentences, it was possible to adapt the main concept to run as a program behind bars.

In 2000, Stephenson received funding from Arts Council England to develop her work at Channings Wood with the adapted version of CLTL as one of the main initiatives. She also re-named the program "Connections" because she believed that the word *literature* could act as a deterrent to the men and that *connections* would reinforce a primary aim of the program: To help the prisoners make the connection between the experiences and actions of fictional characters and of themselves.

With the help of her colleague, Neil Galbraith, who taught English at Channings Wood, Stephenson set up the program with similarities to CLTL in the United States, in terms of frequency of meetings and texts, and with a few differences:

- Prisoners were encouraged to write draft notes after each session.
- Prisoners wrote final essays in week nine, drawing on their notes and reactions to the texts and discussion. The essay was to take the form of a "plan for the future," based on what had been learned from the texts and discussions. Final essays were to be circulated among group members prior to the final session (ten), during which each essay would be discussed in turn.

❑ A simple "How I See Myself" form would be filled in by prisoners in session one. At the final session, prisoners would again be asked to fill out a blank "How I See Myself" form, with the same questions as before. Once they had filled out this second form, their original forms would be returned to them so they could see what changes had been made. If prisoners wished, copies of these forms would be put with their files in Probation.

❑ A copy of the final essay would also be sent to Probation to be put in the prisoners' files as evidence of their work on the program and their future intention. Over the three-year funded period, nine groups would be run.

❑ Sessions were voluntary and run during prisoners' free association time in the evening.

By week ten, members of the group frequently asked if they might continue the course. Although this wasn't possible, it was decided to run a Graduates Course in which prisoners from previous groups were invited to an intensive three-day examination of one text, in this case, William Shakespeare's *Othello*, presented on video in the original version and a modern adaptation. Instead of allowing discussions to flow in whatever direction the prisoners took them, on this occasion, Galbraith and Stephenson drew up specific topics for the discussion to focus on, using excerpt from both versions to illustrate a particular issue.

This experiment proved very successful and demonstrated the flexible nature of CLTL work.

In October 2002, the Paul Hamlyn Foundation in England agreed to fund five new pilots based on their commitment to literacy and their belief that the program was innovative and interesting. Writers in Prison Network, together with Stephenson and Galbraith, have also prepared a comprehensive "How To" guide in running the Connections course, building on the experience of the Channings Wood program and the five new pilots. The guide will be modeled on the *Success Stories* booklet that Waxler and Trounstine helped to write in 1997 for the U.S. Department of Education when CLTL was in its beginnings. The booklet gave very practical advice for how to run a program, and we have built on that model here in the second half of this book where we discuss teaching strategies, texts, and other "nuts and bolts" of CLTL.

Some guidelines that Connections follows in prisons: In setting up the group, they maintain a continuity and consistency among group membership. The ideal group size is between eight and twelve. Venue for group sessions is non-educational—that is, soft chairs, carpets, etc. They provide each group member with a Compact/Guidelines in session 1, explaining what is expected from participants. They also plan sessions with a mix of activities, varying the approach through discussion, drama, writing, etc. They provide follow-up support between sessions.

It is generally agreed that prisoners too need some form of celebration to mark the achievement of successful completion of the program. And in addition to certificates of completion and books, they provide each group member with a list of recommended further reading. She says, "Never forget that stories change lives—and this can sometimes be painful."

Some of the texts used in these programs include: *Of Mice and Men* by John Steinbeck; *Angela's Ashes* by Frank McCourt; *A Child Called It* by Dave Pelzer; *One Flew Over the Cuckoo's Nest* by Ken Kesey; *The Diary of Anne Frank* by Anne Frank; *Loon Boy* by Kathleen McDonnell; *Made in Britain*, Alan Clarke and David Leland's film collaboration; "A Jury of Her Peers" by Susan Glaspell; "Greasy Lake" by T. Coraghessan Boyle; "Sonny's Blues" by James Baldwin; and poems such as "From Mother to Son" and "Still I Rise" by Maya Angelou.

Further information on all these programs and their personnel is available on the website at *http://cltl.umassd.edu*.

7 Starting a Program: The Nuts and Bolts

"When I returned to Texas after hearing about Changing Lives Through Literature in Massachusetts, I realized that those New Englanders had started another revolution."

Dr. Lawrence Jablecki,
Chief Probation Officer, Texas Program

IN MANY WAYS, CLTL IS A MAVERICK PROGRAM, outside the usual boundaries of court-mandated activities. That is part of its strength. Like good literature, it is filled with surprises. It stands as a proven partnership between higher education and the trial court, reflecting the importance of the humanities in our common struggle for justice and democracy. But since it

> *It stands as a proven partnership between higher education and the trial court, reflecting the importance of the humanities in our common struggle for justice and democracy.*

is not like most other alternative sentencing programs, it is often regarded with a very skeptical eye, especially by court officials who often find it difficult to believe that literature can make a difference and should serve as an alternative to jail. Thus, starting a program requires endurance and dedication to the concept that literature can change people's lives.

The wonder of CLTL is that programs may differ from court to court in their approaches, and they still work. The procedures and suggestions offered here will orient you to the things you'll want to consider before initiating a CLTL program. We do not offer them as hard and fast rules. This section is for enthusiasts who want to know how to make CLTL happen and for those who want to borrow some of our ideas to work with their own population. Anyone can work toward making the CLTL vision a practical reality.

THINKING ABOUT THE TEAM APPROACH

As we have suggested throughout this book, the democratic vision of the CLTL program is central to our success and reinforces the idea that each member of the team (see Chapter 1) enriches the others' experiences. To start a CLTL program, your first consideration should be this team (judge, probation officer, instructor)—what kind of people you are looking for and how will you find them.

All members of the team should embrace the possibility that literature can make a difference in people's lives, and they should be committed to a belief in justice. You want people who seek meaning in their own lives. If the CLTL program proves rewarding to the team members, as it often does, that reward usually comes from an engagement with a process that makes people feel they are doing something valuable and worthwhile: They are involved in a program that transcends any simple sense that this is just another job to be done. You want people who can appreciate that kind of reward.

You also need to consider how each member's perspectives on justice and the humanities will reflect their contribution and commitment to the program. Since the team is the core of each individual program, it determines the success or failure of the program. Consider carefully how each member contributes to the whole, and how much time and commitment each can offer to fulfill his or her obligation.

Each individual CLTL program grows and shapes its specific identity from the particular interests and perspectives of the team members as those interests and perspectives interact with the particular group of offenders being served.

JUDICIAL AUTHORIZATION

If possible, get the support of a judge early on. That is not always possible, but the judge can be very helpful in getting the program started. CLTL programs can work successfully without a judge. We know of several programs that have been launched without one—in community day centers, under probation, or in jails—and at times, this seems the most reasonable way to make progress if you are having a problem finding a judge. A probation officer or other official connected with the criminal justice system can start a program with an instructor on a college campus if there are no objections from judges or supervisors. This has happened in a number of CLTL cases.

Arrangements can be made, for example, to send a selected group of probationers to a program started by a court official (other than a judge) and an instructor. The challenge here is to put together a group and to establish a team composed of an instructor and a court official. Over time, this kind of program, meaningful in itself, can attract judges as well.

We have always urged people to get a program started as quickly as possible and not to worry too much about detailed planning. The best evidence inevitably is in the success of the discussions, the energy of the group, and the changes in the probationers that can often be noticed almost immediately.

But please keep in mind that in its ideal form, CLTL is an alternative sentencing program with a team made up of a judge, probation officer, and instructor. The judge's authorization of the program can be very helpful. Once the judge agrees to validate the process, he or she has officially begun "the story" of the CLTL program, and, in the process, the probation officers are also validated.

Even in cases in which the judge cannot consistently participate in the program, his or her authorization resonates throughout the court and the general community, and so contributes substantially to the ongoing success of the program. In addition, one judge talking to other judges about the CLTL Program—whether informally in the corridors or lobby, at conferences, or on panels—opens the possibility of getting additional courts interested. In this sense, it is very helpful to have a judge support the program at least in principle.

How Do You Get a Judge to Agree to Start a Program?

Look for a judge who believes in literature and is committed to community justice. Judges are often attracted to the CLTL program because they have a passion for reading and a belief that part of their role is to help strengthen all members of the community. Such judges often look forward to participating in a good literature program, and the CLTL discussions around the table become valuable for them as well as for the others.

When talking to a judge about starting a program, emphasize that CLTL has a clear record, dramatic at times, with regard to changing lives—reducing recidivism rates, putting people back on the education track, and enlightening folks.

Invite the judge to an ongoing CLTL program if you can arrange for that. Some judges from other states have visited our Massachusetts programs, for example. We have discovered that if the judge actively joins the literary discussions around the CLTL table, he or she will be convinced of the program's merits.

If a visit to an ongoing program is impossible, you can put the judge in contact with other judges who have participated in CLTL (see *cltl.umassd.edu* for names and locations of some judges). Judges talking to other judges about CLTL can often be persuasive. Probation officers and lawyers, including the District Attorney, can also be helpful in persuading the judge that this is a program worth trying.

WHAT ABOUT FUNDING AT THE START?

It costs very little to run a CLTL program, and almost everyone who participates seems to get the greatest reward from the meaning and joy of the program itself. Nevertheless, funding is a legitimate issue to consider when starting a program. Judges and probation officers rarely, if ever, receive financial compensation for their participation. In Massachusetts, instructors usually receive a small honorarium of $1,500 for each series of seminars. In such cases, though, it is not unreasonable to ask the instructors to contribute their time for at least the pilot cycle to demonstrate the value and success of the program. Once that pilot program is underway, it is easier to find further support.

Currently, no national funding is available for the CLTL program, so programs often must find their own ways of generating funds. In the past, programs have been funded in a variety of ways: through small grants from private and public agencies, small gifts from private donors, donations from college funds, or state budgets.

Budgets are always tight, of course, and budgets often come with turf battles. We do not believe that CLTL is just another program, nor should it be considered as one of the hundred programs the court happens to be running this particular season. But because of so many demands, CLTL needs to be spelled out to funders as unusual.

CLTL costs very little, but it is obviously helpful to have some money to pay instructors and administrative assistants and to cover other minimum costs such as books and transportation. Unless a group has financial support, books and vans are impossible to provide. Naturally, libraries are a meeting option for some, and, in some groups, students give rides to each other.

The success of the program in terms of life changes, and the clear fact that it saves government a great deal of money in potential incarceration costs, should count in convincing people to give what they can; some will give time and expertise, while others, we hope, will give material support.

CHOOSING THE FIRST GROUP

CLTL is first and foremost an alternative sentencing program. The offenders, upon successful completion of the CLTL course, are often rewarded by a reduction in their probation sentences. In some cases the offenders are actually given the opportunity to join the program by a judge who sentences them; in other cases probation officers identify persons on their case loads who seem likely to benefit from the CLTL experience, and offer them

> *CLTL costs very little, but it is obviously helpful to have some money to pay instructors and administrative assistants and to cover other minimum costs such as books and transportation.*

the opportunity to join. As suggested in our chapters on specific CLTL programs, different courts have found advantages in various methods of recruiting students.

We suggest that you try to get a single program going as a pilot. A successful model can lead to long-term success. Our experience suggests that the quicker a program gets up and running as a test case, the greater the chance of long-term success. The magic of the actual experience around the discussion table is usually the most persuasive argument we have for continued success of the program.

When forming a group, whether directly from the judge's bench or from the probation pool, we recommend that it be single-sex, with a range in age if possible, and with eight to ten offenders to start. Although individual programs have proven very successful with more than ten students (often breaking into smaller groups for discussion) and with as few as four students, we believe that a group of eight to ten works well for discussion and seems to be the standard. Keep in mind that in addition to the eight to ten offenders, you will often have three team members as well as visitors around that table participating in the literature discussions.

Between the time of putting offenders in the group and the beginning of the discussion on the campus, it is not unusual for two or more offenders to experience difficulties (returning to jail, violation of probation, etc.) that prevent them from joining the group. If the goal is to start with eight students, for example, it is best to recommend at least ten participants to start.

When forming a group, it is also worth noting that, in general, a men's group is usually larger than a women's group, and more women than men seem to leave the program before it is finished. On the whole, there seem to be more men than women coming into the courts for sentencing, and the women chosen for the program often have a more difficult time attending the program than the men because of the logistical and social problems they face, such as family commitments, abusive boyfriends, and lack of transportation.

We have not encouraged mixed-sex groups because we have generally believed that the choice of books and the topics for discussions often work best at the core with single-sex groups. We have run mixed-sex groups, however, and met with considerable success with those groups as well.

When the group is being formed through the judicial process, the team members also need to consider where the literary discussions will take place. We favor a seminar room on a college campus, if possible. The college environment provides an important, sometimes dramatic setting for the CLTL experience and signals a change from the courthouse, the neighborhood, and previous schooling. In addition to participating in a seminar discussion on a college campus, the criminal offenders mingle with the students in the corridors, feel as if they are part of the college experience, and often sense the privilege of being part of the college environment. In this context, a formal or informal agreement with a college to lend support to the program gives additional authority and value to the CLTL process and serves as a significant reminder of the partnership between the trial court and higher education. Some colleges now use CLTL as an opportunity for their own students to engage in community service.

If a room on a college campus cannot be found, we recommend a room in another intellectual environment, such as a public library filled with books.

GENERAL SUGGESTIONS ON FIRST CONSIDERING WAYS TO APPROACH THE DISCUSSIONS

Once the judge and the probation officer have chosen a group of offenders to participate in the CLTL program on a campus (or other location), the instructor needs to consider the approach he or she plans to use. Once the program actually begins, the approach will be adjusted, of course, but it is valuable to have an overall plan.

The approach is determined by the interests and perspective of the instructor as well as by the makeup and mix of the group chosen: Men or women? African-American, Caucasian, Hispanic, Native American? Suburban or inner city? Middle class or working class?

Whatever approach is chosen, the goal is to arrive through literature and language, through texts and discussions, at shared moments of self-realization and insight, at moments of surprise and of bonding with the group, at moments of communal working together around the table. That is the challenge, and it is not an easy one, although it is basic.

The instructor does not need to know the details of each offender's biography, but, together with the probation officer, he or she needs to think about the overall makeup of the group in the context of the demographics, such as gender, ethnicity, age range, etc. The instructor is not there to teach moral lessons, to impose a value system on the rest of the group, but to help evoke deep discussions about issues important to the group, issues the students are wrestling with, issues often blocked from awareness.

The instructor needs to consider an approach that will allow him or her to listen for opportunities to inspire further discussion and to validate the diverse voices (not only those of the offenders but those of the judges and probation officers) and the range of perspectives at the table. Through the reading and discussion of stories, each member of the group discovers himself or herself and the relationship to others, and the instructor needs to be ready to make connections and to help that process along.

The initial approach, then, must be flexible and subject to easy change as the literature sessions actually get underway. But once the group has been selected, these questions should be considered:

- ❑ Given what we know about the group, what themes and issues seem most relevant and important to consider with this group?
- ❑ What books will work best to help us wrestle with the issues and build a coherent series of discussions over time?
- ❑ Should we break into small groups regularly to give everyone the best opportunity to voice personal perspectives?
- ❑ In addition to reading, should we also use writing to help enhance the discussions?
- ❑ How often and how frequently should we meet? Every two weeks for twelve weeks? Once a week for ten weeks? Two hours each time?
- ❑ Should we use primarily short stories or complete novels? Should we assign complete novels for a single session or read and discuss a novel over several sessions?

(See Chapters 8, 9, and 10 for more details.)

Curriculum

The makeup of the selected group helps to shape the curriculum. We have found that stories about struggles for manhood, about violence, about individuals fighting for freedom against rigid authority often appeal to the men as they begin to encounter their own dark side. Women's lives are different, so they call for different stories. Women in our program often suffer from lack of support and encouragement, abusive boyfriends, or childhood rejection. Often they are single parents, alone and anxious about their children. (See Chapter 3 for more details on gender issues in relation to literacy.)

In the same context, different ethnic groups often profit from stories relevant to their interests and concerns, their particular struggles and desires.

Choosing books for discussion is obviously an important matter. The best books will provoke deep discussion; offer characters for self-reflection; and explore themes that disturb us, shock us, and remind us that we are not alone.

Many groups have found it important to start with books that are short and easy to read, progressing to more difficult and longer books in later sessions. This approach builds confidence because many offenders have never read a complete book. Once confidence is gained, though, the reading ability of the offenders seems to increase dramatically and quickly. (See Chapter 3.)

Many CLTL programs primarily use novels for discussions, believing that the sense of accomplishment that comes from reading a complete book significantly enhances the offenders' confidence and self-esteem. The length of a novel also lends itself to a full development of the complexity of plot and character, allowing for a rich range of perspectives and insights to emerge in discussion.

Many team members, though, favor short stories and poetry, arguing the merits of these shorter forms. Autobiography is also used at times, especially when relevant as a model for a particular group.

Some groups now structure the CLTL program as a twelve-week series of discussions, two hours each time, meeting every two weeks for a total of six sessions. Others meet for seven sessions over fourteen weeks. Still other groups prefer weekly meetings, sometimes extending over a ten-week period. Meeting every week over a longer period (ten meetings over ten weeks, rather than six meetings over twelve weeks) has proved valuable in some courts as a means of maintaining continuous involvement and deepening the sense of classroom community. Nevertheless, a twelve-week course, meeting every two weeks, for a total of six sessions, remains our standard.

The first session is particularly important in order to set the tone and indicate through example what the sessions are all about. We usually provide a syllabus the first night, with the complete schedule and list of books as well as a few generic questions about theme and character. But the syllabus always remains open to change and revision as we move through the sessions, the discussions shaping the reading as we go. (See examples of texts in Chapters 8 and 9 and examples of syllabi on *http://cltl.umassd.edu.*)

We recommend the use of one or two short stories the first evening (read silently or aloud around the table) followed by discussion demonstrating the relationship between the story in the text and life itself. As the plot unfolds, so does the interior self. A good discussion on that first night often ends with a recognition that the story we have explored—the issues raised, the themes discovered—are our own stories. We are all embarked on a journey that will take us in future weeks deeper into this interior terrain, mirroring our fears and desires.

As the reading continues from week to week, we begin to weave the themes and issues together into a rich tapestry of complex meaning, recognizing ourselves, not only in each story, but also in the connections made through discussion from one story to the next, from the interplay of literature and life.

Although not all groups use writing, we have found that writing used as a prompt for further discussion is very effective. Writing is closely connected to thinking, sharpens focus, and enhances the connection between personal revelation and the story under investigation.

Writing in small groups has proven particularly valuable. Not only does it allow each student to find his own expression and give voice to her thinking, but it serves as a useful springboard to enhance further discussion in the larger group sitting at the table. (See Chapter 10 for detailed discussion of teaching strategies.)

REALISTIC GOALS

From one perspective, as the name of our program suggests, our goals are bold and ambitious, if not presumptuous: Changing Lives Through Literature. We believe it. We have seen it happen again and again.

But from another perspective, CLTL is modest in its goals and expectations. We do not anticipate that criminal offenders coming through our program will become perfect citizens or wonderful students. They are often very bright and filled with important insights, but they will not necessarily become well-trained college students or model civic servants. Often they are not very good readers. Sometimes they are fearful and angry, unsure of themselves, and undisciplined in their approach to work and life. Nor do we claim that they will never commit another crime. The recidivism rates for CLTL are noteworthy, but some offenders no doubt will relapse; some will return to jail.

> *We do not anticipate that criminal offenders coming through our program will become perfect citizens or wonderful students.*

Since each literature program only lasts about twelve weeks, what can you hope to achieve in a few months? When setting up a program, then, you need to understand that the goals are both ambitious and modest. You can change lives, inspire new perspectives, energize thinking, and wrestle with important issues affecting the whole group. You can bring families together, heal wounds, and create community. And it is not just the offenders who change, but you, and the probation officer, and the judge.

CLTL has been the most rewarding experience in my life, more than one judge has said. But CLTL can only do so much. At its best, it can excite self-reflection, deep reading, and discussion; it can enhance verbal skills, personal revelation, and the power

> *You can change lives, inspire new perspectives, energize thinking, and wrestle with important issues affecting the whole group. You can bring families together, heal wounds, and create community.*

of imagination. It can give people a renewed sense of the past and hope for the future, the confidence and ability to create their own stories. Yet, it takes place over a very short time and, in this sense, can only offer a glimpse of what might be.

After a cycle of CLTL, the judges, the probation officers, and the facilitators move on to the next group. We can only hope that the offenders carry their new experience with them, seek out new community connections, meaningful work if they can find it, and educational opportunities. Their struggle remains more difficult than ours. When setting up a program, then, we need to think about our limitations and how success should be defined. (See Chapter 2 on issues of success and failure in CLTL.)

RULES AND GUIDELINES

Any question about rules, like so much else of value in the CLTL program, is open to discussion and debate. The idea of rules generates as many questions as answers.

Most team members agree that we want to avoid required tests or papers in the CLTL program; in other words, we want to discourage any reminder of the dark shadow of schooling. It is important to the meaning of CLTL, and consistent with the fundamental goals of the program, to create a positive and intellectually challenging experience that will move offenders beyond the stereotypes they hold of reading and education.

Many instructors argue that without tests and papers, reading and discussion become an end in themselves, an educational opportunity to liberate thinking and reflection. To read and discuss good literature in this way provides an enriched sense of the life of the mind and a chance to generate excitement about reading and thinking. These instructors enjoy participating in the program precisely because they feel they are free to engage in an intellectual environment, which is exciting, challenging, meaningful, and unhampered by bureaucratic measures of failure and success. Success, they argue, should be determined by means other than traditional standards of schooling.

Nevertheless, as part of the ongoing conception of the program, we have a few suggestions loosely formulated in response to inevitable questions:

❑ **Should we require students to have a minimum reading level before allowing them into the program?**

In general, we have set an eighth-grade reading level as a minimum. But our measurements to determine this level are always loose and informal. Can the student read a simple magazine article? Does the student demonstrate interest in reading? We realize that this requirement excludes a significant number of criminal offenders, but we believe that an eighth-grade reading level is a useful benchmark for anticipating a rewarding experience with the texts and discussions. We don't want to expose the offenders who can't read to another failure. Although we have held to this standard in general, some groups have successfully operated at much lower reading levels, using various strategies to include everyone in discussions. (See Chapter 10 on teaching strategies.)

❑ **Should we require a reading test for students?**

We have not adopted or designed any formal reading test to measure reading levels. Often, as part of the screening process, the probation officer will ask the offender to read a short article from a popular magazine simply to check on reading ability and to assess general comprehension skills. That informal test, coupled with an intuitive judgment about the readiness and desire of the offender to enter the CLTL group, is usually sufficient to determine the qualifications of the offender under the loosely constructed rule.

❏ **Should we restrict the CLTL program to certain categories of offenders?**

We established a rule at the beginning of the CLTL program that no sex offenders or murderers would be eligible for the program. Nor could any active drug user participate. We believed that people in these categories could not fully benefit from the reading and discussions. Distracted by their afflictions, they would not be able to focus on the texts or the exchanges around the table. In general, this seems to be the case. However, again there are exceptions. We have in fact allowed sex offenders into the program on occasion, and many offenders continue to struggle with their addictions while in the CLTL program.

Evidence suggests that almost everyone can benefit in some way from this program, and we are now convinced that anyone who can stay focused can find meaning in the process. Offenders with long criminal histories, with weighty crimes (armed robbery with a mask, for example), with violent backgrounds, have all done well. Offenders battling their addictions have also benefited. It is our belief that the reading and discussion of good literature can affect a violent offender as well as a nonviolent offender. As we have indicated throughout this text, evaluations of the program indicate that CLTL helps alleviate acts of violence at every level.

> *Evidence suggests that almost everyone can benefit in some way from this program, and we are now convinced that anyone who can stay focused can find meaning in the process.*

❑ **Should we provide books and transportation?**

Many groups have decided that students should be required to get their own books, either at a bookstore or a public library. It is their responsibility as part of the program. Others feel that the offenders have enough to contend with, so books should be provided. The advantage of having their own books to keep is that the offenders can write in them, mark them up, and engage with the text. The advantage of going to the public library is that students can get acquainted with a great institution and acquire a library card, not only for the CLTL seminar but also for the future. The books need to be returned unmarked, however.

Many groups also believe that students should be responsible for their own transportation to the college campus. However, in some cases, this is particularly difficult. The offenders often do not have a driver's license and sometimes live a considerable distance from the campus. As the first women's group developed in Lynn, Massachusetts, it was clear, given the distance between the court and the campus and other issues unique to the women's need for support, that transportation should be provided. When possible, we now use a van for transportation.

❑ **What about violations of the agreements made through the courts?**

Some programs ask offenders to sign a statement indicating their commitment and responsibility to the CLTL program. Whether there is an officially signed statement, most programs expect the offenders to attend every session, to read the stories carefully, to come prepared to participate in discussions, and, in general, to engage in the rhythm of the process. Violations of these expectations can lead to sanctions, sometimes a return to jail.

Probation officers ordinarily determine if a violation has occurred and what should be done as a result. If a student misses one class, for example, the probation officer might ask for a book report; two violations might disqualify the student from the current program, with the option of returning to the next program after sanctions. Sometimes, the offender has been sentenced back to jail.

We believe that it is important for everyone to understand that the CLTL program is as tough as the criminal offenders participating in it. It is a privilege to be chosen for these literature sessions, we argue, and that privilege should include a sense of worth, responsibility, and commitment. Yet we remain aware that flexibility, compassion, and the human heart itself are always at the core of important literature and deep discussions. Rules can undermine genuine success. Some CLTL groups have operated well without official rules for this reason. In the end, CLTL favors inclusion rather than exclusion and mindful compassion rather than harsh judgment.

❑ **Should all members of the group be the same sex?**

Although we encourage single-sex groups, mixed-sex or coed groups of offenders have also worked well. We tend to encourage single-sex groups because we believe that such groups often make the selection of books and the seminar discussions more focused and meaningful to the students wrestling with difficult issues.

However, even if you create a single-sex group, the three core team members might not all be the same gender. A group of women offenders, for example, might have a male judge actively involved in the discussions, or a male group of offenders might be led by a female instructor.

We also encourage visitors—such as other court officials, lawyers, professors, and friends of the offenders—to attend sessions. They too can be either male or female, despite the sex of the offender group.

Visitors should be required to read the stories in advance, though, and be prepared to join in the discussions. We do not want tourists.

GRADUATION

Once the literature sessions are completed, there is usually a graduation ceremony, which is a public ritual naming and validating every student and giving each a recognized place in the larger community. The ritual gives shape to the collective experience and to the students' personal experiences and, in a sense, helps reform each offender's story, making it part of the community story.

Like so much else in CLTL, the graduation takes various forms depending on the individual court, the team members, and the offenders themselves. Many groups now hold two graduations, one on the final day of class on the campus and one in the district court within the next day or so. At times, a member of the team will purchase pizza and soda for the class to celebrate the last night, after talking about the final novel or short story, and some of the offenders will bring family members or friends to observe the ceremony. The instructor will often prepare a signed university certificate, a diploma of sorts, with an official university seal and the name of each offender, along with the dates and the name of the program. Each participant will be called by name to the front of the room to receive the certificate, congratulations, and hearty applause. We realized the impact of these certificates when we saw them hanging on otherwise barren walls in offenders' apartments.

A more formal graduation takes place in the court, often in the same setting as the original sentencing. But now, the first row in the courtroom is occupied with proud family members, and the students are seated in a place of honor and distinction, such as the jury box. The judge is no longer perceived as the rigid authority figure in dark robes but as a complex human being who has contributed to a meaningful change in the offender's life. Often the judge will publicly praise the group for its achievement, followed by the instructor, who will talk about the challenge of the CLTL sessions, the power of literature to change lives, and the success and courage of the offenders who have gone through the program. The probation officer will review each person's achievement as he or she stands before the bench, recommending the agreed-upon reduced sentence to the judge. The judge concurs, and the certificates are awarded. At times, the students, individually or through a single representative, will offer their stories.

Evaluators of the CLTL program have indicated the importance of this formal graduation ceremony in the courtroom, and for those considering starting a program, plans for the ceremony should be included as a significant component of the CLTL story. As one evaluator explained it: "The recognition and certification offered by the Changing Lives Through Literature program may be what the participant needs to enable a transition to a conventional, non-offending style." In other words, the ritual provides the participant social verification for her or his reformation and redemption.

As a moment of public recognition, the graduation ceremony is also an opportunity to remind the community about the good work of the court and the ongoing struggle of the court to build an inclusive and just community of citizens. Often the court is crowded on the morning of graduation, filled with other offenders who will learn about the program through the ceremony, and with invited news reporters who are willing to write a story about how literature and justice can work together. It is a memorable moment worthy of community support, reflecting the democratic ideal.

8

Teaching Specific Texts: Novel, Autobiography, and Memoir

"Something extraordinary happened in our first group. Clients were not required to complete the class once their court order ended. But four students to whom this happened stayed on to complete the session. This tells me there's really something going on here. "

—*Brian Sullivan, Connecticut Program*

IN CHAPTERS 8 AND 9, we offer practical help for starting and running a program through list of texts and lesson plans. These resources were developed for facilitators of CLTL, but almost any instructor can benefit from the range of ideas here. Included is material that we each use in our programs but also material that has been successfully used by other CLTL facilitators to demonstrate the variety of programs and approaches. As previously mentioned, most CLTL classes are run for either men or women, but you should feel free to try these texts in coed classes. You also may want to consult our first book, *Changing Lives Through Literature* (University of Notre Dame Press), which includes selections from some of these texts and reader reactions, or explore the website *http://cltl.umassd.edu* from which these lesson plans are drawn.

LISTS OF TEXTS

We offer you a list of CLTL texts used across the country and in the United Kingdom and also draw from the many lesson plans developed by CLTL practitioners that are contained in full on *http://cltl.umassd. edu*. These plans have been adapted, but you will find that we still retain each person's voice, the particular plan they developed, and their approach to CLTL, all which we feel underscores the democratic process, the sense that CLTL is not an "it" but an "us."

The texts included are ones that we have found stimulated discussion, provoked insights, or in some other way approached the goals of CLTL that we discussed in earlier chapters. However, no book is foolproof. The group and its particular makeup should ultimately guide your choices.

In this chapter, you'll find information on teaching specific novels, memoir and autobiographies, all alphabetized by the author's last name. In Chapter 9, we cover teaching short stories and other material, also alphabetized and listed by genre. In Chapter 10 you'll find a discussion on teaching techniques.

In our list of texts, those marked with an asterisk have a lesson plan, and those for which additional material is provided are noted.

Novels

James Agee, *A Death in the Family*
Mitch Albom, *The Five People You Meet in Heaven*
Dorothy Allison, *Bastard Out of Carolina*
Margaret Atwood, *Alias Grace*
*Russell Banks, *Affliction*
Russell Banks, *Rule of the Bone*
Russell Banks, *The Sweet Hereafter*
Sandra Cisneros, *The House on Mango Street* (see Teaching Strategies: More Writing in CLTL on page 230)
Chris Crutcher, *Ironman*

Edwidge Danticat, *Breath, Eyes, Memory*

James Dickey, *Deliverance*

*Janet Fitch, *White Oleander*

Alexandra Flinn, *Breathing Underwater*

Jack Gantos, *Hole in My Life*

Jane Hamilton, *Map of the World*

*Kent Haruf, *Plainsong*

*Ernest Hemingway, *The Old Man and the Sea*

*Zora Neale Hurston, *Their Eyes Were Watching God* (see Teaching Strategies: Use of Questions on page 225)

*Ken Kesey, *One Flew Over the Cuckoo's Nest*

Barbara Kingsolver, *Animal Dreams*

*Barbara Kingsolver, *The Bean Trees* (see Teaching Strategies: Use of Questions on page 224)

Barbara Kingsolver, *Pigs in Heaven*

Harper Lee, *To Kill a Mockingbird*

Frances Lantz, *Fade Far Away*

Billie Letts, *Where the Heart Is*

Jack London, *The Call of the Wild* (see Teaching Specific Texts on page 171)

Jack London, *The Seawolf*

Lois Lowry, *The Giver*

Bernard Malamud, *The Assistant*

Bobbie Ann Mason, *In Country*

Joyce McDonald, *Swallowing Stones*

Ben Mikaelsen, *Touching Spirit Bear*

*Toni Morrison, *The Bluest Eye* (see Teaching Strategies: Use of Questions on page 222)

Toni Morrison, *Sula*

Gloria Naylor, *The Women of Brewster Place*

Tim O'Brien, *The Things They Carried*

Tillie Olsen, *Tell Me a Riddle*

George Orwell, *Animal Farm*

George Orwell, *Down and Out in Paris and London*

Gordon Parks, *The Learning Tree*
Sylvia Plath, *The Bell Jar*
Annie Proulx, *The Shipping News*
Anna Quindlen, *Black and Blue*
Daniel Quinn, *Ishmael*
J. D. Salinger, *Catcher in the Rye*
Esmerelda Santiago, *When I Was Puerto Rican*
Anita Shreve, *Strange Fits of Passion*
Scott Smith, *A Simple Plan* (see Teaching Strategies: Use of Film
    with Literature on page 233)
Aleksander Solzhenitsyn, *One Day in the Life of Ivan Denisovich*
John Steinbeck, *Of Mice and Men* (see Teaching Strategies: More
    Writing in CLTL on page 231)
John Steinbeck, *The Pearl*
*Anne Tyler, *Dinner at the Homesick Restaurant* (see Teaching
    Strategies: Use of Questions on page 223)
Larry Watson, *Montana, 1948*
Tobias Wolff, *The Barracks Thief*
Edith Wharton, *Ethan Frome*
*Richard Wright, *Black Boy*

Autobiography and Memoir

Maya Angelou, *I Know Why the Caged Bird Sings*
*Frederick Douglass, *Narrative of the Life of Frederick Douglass,
    An American Slave*
Viktor Frankl, *Man's Search for Meaning*
Zora Neale Hurston, *Dust Tracks on a Road*
Mary Karr, *The Liars' Club*
Frank McCourt, *Angela's Ashes*
Bill Russell, *Second Wind*
John Edgar Wideman, *Brothers and Keepers* (see Teaching Strategy:
    More Writing in CLTL on page 229)
Elie Wiesel, *Night*
*Malcolm X, *Autobiography of Malcolm X*

LESSON PLANS

We've included a number of specific plans to help you get started. Each plan gives you information about the genre, themes, and story summaries, as well as about how the work is used. They are alphabetized by the author's last name. We have adapted these lesson plans, but the full text written by each facilitator appears on our website at *http://cltlumassd.edu.*

Banks, Russell—*Affliction*

Genre: Novel

Theme: Affliction of family violence and drinking as they relate to male identity and growing up in small town

Class Type: Men

Lesson Plan by Robert Waxler

Waxler finds *Affliction* to be one of the more difficult yet rewarding novels in our CLTL program. It is used near the end of the literature series in New Bedford, often during the final week because it is such a challenging read. The story reminds the men—perhaps too often—of their own families and of the lives they have endured. They recall the revolving cycle of family violence, and they talk about the way such violence is perpetuated from generation to generation, as it is in the Whitehouse family in this novel.

The narrator of *Affliction*, Rolfe Whitehouse, tells a story about small town life and family violence in order to understand what happened to his younger brother Wade and to discover why it didn't happen to him. As the story opens, we meet Wade, who is middle-aged and divorced. He is a disappointed blue-collar worker whose best moments were back in high school (although even then he had to endure beatings from his father).

It is the beginning of the deer-hunting season in New Hampshire, and rituals of male violence permeate this small-town culture. Wade is frustrated, unable to gain respect or control in his personal relations and with his work. As readers, we eventually follow the narrative thread back to Wade's childhood, to his father's drinking and violence, to the father's inability to show compassion, and his relentless need for control. In the end, Wade spins out of control, killing the father, a desperate, almost tragic, attempt to release himself from the affliction of his life.

Ordinarily, Waxler limits the discussion of this novel to one session (two hours), but there is always more to be said, especially about such a richly textured and complex story.

The talk around the table often begins with the opening scenes that show Wade nervous and uncomfortable as he picks up his daughter, Jill, and takes her from Concord to his small town. Wade wants to love and care for Jill but also needs to feel he has control over her. He wants respect as a father but cannot discipline and respect himself. We want to know from everyone around the table what they have to say about Wade's opening struggle, whether they forgive him, whether we can understand his frustration.

Questions that Waxler might ask early on: *Why does Wade want control over others? Does he have control over himself? Does he actually control others? What does it really mean to have power?*

Such questions usually open the discussion to the relationship between power and manhood, and we are off and running as we move deeper into the story, exploring other characters, those who are in positions of power and those who are often manipulative and self-serving: Gordon LaRiviere (Wade's boss and powerbroker in the town), J. Battle Hand (Wade's lawyer for his custody case), Evan Twombley (labor leader shot and killed on his first day of hunting), Margie Fogg (Wade's lover and old friend), and Jack Hewitt (Wade's fellow worker who reminds him of his younger self).

As the discussion progresses, the group finally arrives at the core: Wade's relationship to his brother Rolfe and to his father Glenn. Rolfe—never connecting deeply to his emotions, never marrying or setting up a family of his own—has left the small town and gotten a job as a teacher. By contrast, Wade has struggled in his hometown, wanting to regain responsibility, at least as a father. Since childhood, though, both have been afflicted by the violence of their father.

Questions Waxler might ask at this point: *Who is more courageous, Rolfe or Wade? Who has set up more defense mechanisms against raw feeling and emotions? Is Wade a mirror image of his father despite his desire to escape the legacy of violence? Can he escape? Why does Wade kill his father?*

If time permits, participants also explore the shooting of Evan Twombley. It is never clear whether Twombley accidentally shot himself or was killed. The mystery is intriguing and evokes interesting discussion, often raising sophisticated issues about the telling of stories and the authority of narrative itself.

Final questions Waxler might ask: *Whose version of the story do we believe? Why? Do we trust those in power when they tell us something? Why don't we believe Wade's version of events? Why do we believe Rolfe? What is a good story?*

These are questions that are not only helpful in investigating this story, but also in investigating life itself. They underscore one of the central premises of Changing Lives Through Literature: good stories help us to change our lives because our lives are stories we can change.

Douglass, Frederick—*Narrative of the Life of Frederick Douglass, an American Slave*

Genre: Autobiography

Theme: In this famous book written in 1845, Douglass combines the story of his own life, up to age 20, with his indictment of slavery and slaveholders.

Class Type: Men

Lesson Plan by Taylor Stoehr

Although this classic text will shock and inspire any reader, just as it did when it first appeared in 1845, it has been chosen by the Dorchester program because it still speaks to the problem of racism in contemporary America, a concern that confronts Dorchester students every day in their ordinary lives. To read about Douglass's bondage to the slave system of his day can be especially stirring for men bound over to probationary status in a criminal justice system that weighs so heavily on people of color in our own times. Douglass's discovery of the meaning of freedom can help probationers find new hope for their own lives.

Taylor Stoehr says that Frederick Douglass is an excellent model for historical awareness of how one's personal plight has roots in larger public issues, opening up the possibility of new roles to play in society and a new sense of responsible citizenship. For example, when Douglass taught himself to read and write as a boy of nine, it was because he realized even then that literacy was the key to personhood and to his vision of freedom. Young Douglass overheard his master warning his wife that if a black man was taught to read, "It would forever unfit him to be a slave." Douglass did learn to read, and it did inoculate him against the slave mentality. This was his first step in understanding his condition and thereby taking a hand in his own fate.

Later, when a white farmer named Edward Coveys was determined to break his spirit to fit him for field labor, Douglass fought back because at age sixteen he had begun to understand what was at stake: not simply another beating, but a defining moment aimed at making him "a slave for life," as he had now learned to phrase it. "This battle with Mr. Covey was the turning-point in my career as a slave. . . . My long-crushed spirit rose, cowardice departed, bold defiance took its place; and I now resolved that, however long I might remain a slave in form, the day had passed forever when I could be a slave in fact."

Finally, after his escape four years later, Douglass devoted himself to the abolitionist movement, telling these stories over and over because he understood that his own destiny had depended on seeing beyond personal suffering to its significance as part of the slave system.

Douglass's gradual discovery of the power of historical consciousness is one of the fundamental themes in the CLTL program and can lead to insights for probationers. Consider, for instance, what one of them wrote about Douglass and Malcolm X a few years ago: "I feel that these black men show the meaning of courage because of the way they lived their everyday lives. Knowing that what they say and do can change their lives in a split second. Not only their lives. But the people in their own time."

Stoehr says that the probationer who came to these conclusions was a stolid man of thirty, built like a tank, a family man whose arrests on drug charges had thrown his life into confusion but who was beginning to pull himself together by the time he came to the program. He was Hispanic. He worked as an auto mechanic, went to the movies, read the sports page, and smoked pot. From outward signs, he was not someone you would expect to possess much knowledge of history. In fact, he was not much given to reflection of any kind. He was just an average guy, responding to Douglass's story with surprise and admiration.

Douglass's *Narrative* is the central text in the Dorchester program. Although written a century and a half ago by a runaway slave who had never been to school and who taught himself to read and write, the book is as clear and readable as today's newspaper and serves Dorchester well with a student body that often ranges from the barely literate to the college-educated. It is not too difficult for the former or too simple for the latter. They read just a few chapters a week, combined with short excerpts from other works that help highlight the key issues. For example, they might read selections by Malcolm X from *The Autobiography of Malcolm X*, Maxim Gorky from *Notch*, Richard Wright from *Black Boy*, or Fyodor Dostoyevsky from *House of the Dead*. In this way, they get to know Douglass very well, talking about him over the entire semester and comparing his virtues and strengths, as well as his hardships, with those of other heroic figures like Malcolm X or Martin Luther King, Jr., and with struggling protagonists in fiction by Tolstoy and other classic Russian authors.

It is useful with readers who are nervous about their ability to read literature to tell them at the outset to glance at the prefaces by white abolitionists William Lloyd Garrison and Wendell Phillips before starting to read Douglass. The contrast is reassuring, and students are much more willing to read so colloquial a stylist after a taste of the preachers who introduced and authenticated him.

Taylor Stoehr asks questions like the following: *How do people learn to face the things that life will demand? Where do people get their courage, self-esteem, and righteousness?*

Fitch, Janet—*White Oleander*

Genre: Novel

Themes: Overcoming adversity; finding one's voice or one's strength; inheriting patterns of behavior

Class Type: Women

Lesson Plan by Gail Mooney

White Oleander is a long, compelling story about Astrid, a young girl whose mother, Ingrid, is a self-involved and vaguely crazy poet and artist. When Astrid is 12, her mother murders a boyfriend who has left her and is sent to prison, thus beginning the girl's entry into the foster care system: She lives in five foster homes in six years. She is sexually seduced at thirteen, mistreated, starved, and, in one home, loved and nurtured before the foster mother commits suicide. It is a story about loss and strength. What gets Astrid through her teenage years is her art and ultimately her sense of being "above it all," a skill she inherited from her mother.

It is a tale of development: sexually, emotionally, intellectually, and culturally. Astrid goes from the formless years of adolescence to the rage and alienation of the mid-teen years and, finally, to the acceptance of self, that maturity of late teens and early twenties, all amidst a backdrop of chaos and insecurity, living with nothing in "the land of plenty."

She is beautiful and doesn't know it, she is extremely intelligent and is never given a chance to use her intelligence, and she is a gifted artist but no one cares except for the one foster mother who makes all the difference. This woman, however, cannot save herself from her own monsters, which is the pivotal point of the girl's life and of the book.

Mooney reads this story midway through the course, and it usually turns out to be one of the favorites because it is a great read and because of the issues it raises for the women as a result of these questions Mooney might ask: *Where do teenaged girls get their strength? How much can an adult influence a young girl? When girls picture themselves, from what sources do they get positive images? How is it possible both to hate and to love someone? In what ways do women allow men to define them? Where do girls find the strength to resist peer pressure and media influences? How do violence and poverty inform the choices we make in life?*

Hemingway, Ernest—*The Old Man and the Sea*

<u>Genre:</u> Novella

<u>Class Type</u>: Men

<u>Theme</u>: A fisherman looks deep within to summon the courage necessary to get through the triumphs and tragedies that life—represented by the sea.

<u>Lesson Plan</u> by Orian Greene

In preparing for her CLTL program, Greene debated whether *The Old Man and the Sea* was fast-moving and timely enough to appeal to a dozen men in their twenties whom she would not have characterized as easy readers. The discussion was lively, however, and some of the observations from the men surpassed anything she had gotten teaching her college classes. At the end of the program, she asked the men to name their favorite selection from the program and was astonished when two-thirds of them put *The Old Man and the Sea* first.

At the beginning of this last session, she asked the students to write for about ten minutes on the following question: *What is the hardest thing you have ever done?*

Before they began discussing the story, she read them an excerpt from an April 1936 article by Hemingway in *Esquire Magazine* in which Hemingway tells of an old man fishing alone who hooked a 1,600-pound marlin and had struggled with that fish for over two days, unwilling to give up the fight. In spite of being attacked by sharks that ate much of the marlin, the old fisherman stayed with his boat, clubbing sharks and fighting them with an oar until he was picked up by another fisherman. Hemingway said while sharks still circled the boat, the old man felt grief and was "half crazy from his loss."

Greene points out how Hemingway used this story to create his novel. She says that one of her focusing questions is: *In the beginning, the old man is hoping for a big fish that will bring him a lot of money. What is he hoping for at the end?*

She breaks the class into groups of three or four, with each group taking four questions. She asks students to mark the pages on which they find the answers so they can refer to them quickly if needed. Some of the questions she asks include: *What are the old man's recurring dreams, and what do they mean? How does the old man first view the fish, and what changes come over his view as the story progresses? What physical and mental resources does the old man summon to deal with the repeated attacks of the sharks? What is the difference between humiliation and humility? Which characterizes the old man at the end and why?*

The classroom discussions generally focus on whether Santiago was wise to row out so far and/or to let the fish drag him so far out. It usually happens that a few of the men in the group fish, and they share their knowledge and observations very freely, often pointing out places where Hemingway has it exactly right. The class also generally spends quite a lot of time comparing the literal story with the novel and discussing the differences between truth and fiction. The discussions are lively and interesting.

Before dismissing the class, Greene asks the students to answer the following question: *Is Santiago a winner or a loser—and why do you think so?* Most see him as a winner; many say that if they had been asked that question at the beginning they would have characterized him as a loser, but after the discussion they began to see his behavior as much more courageous and admirable.

A very interesting exchange took place during the discussion of *The Old Man and the Sea* in Greene's second group of probationers, a group characterized by their young age and general immaturity. One young man, who we will call Andy, identified himself as someone who hated reading, had never finished a book until this program, and wouldn't have been finishing them now except that he wanted to get his probation cut in half.

Andy was with Greene when they broke into small groups. Naturally, he hated *The Old Man and the Sea*; it was too long, too boring, had no action and no point. However, he had finished the book, and he spoke especially scathingly about Santiago's stupidity in dragging that fish carcass all the way back to shore when it wouldn't do him any good.

Trying to find a hook, Greene asked Andy what he had written when asked to tell about the hardest thing he had ever done. He said it was something that had occurred that fall. Hunting with a bow and arrow about a mile from the road where he had parked his car, he had killed an eight-point stag, the biggest deer he had ever caught. Since it was illegal to leave the carcass in the woods, he had had to drag it all the way back to the car. It was huge and heavy, he said, and the antlers kept getting caught on the bushes, so it took him forever and left him exhausted.

She asked Andy why he hadn't cut off the head to make it easier. He looked dumbfounded. He wouldn't do that, he said, because then no one would believe he had killed such a huge stag.

After a long silence, Andy said, "I guess that's kind of like Santiago."

We're not going to claim that this insight or CLTL changed Andy's life, but we do think it made him think in a new way, look at himself more thoughtfully.

When Greene asks her groups at the final session what they have gained from the program, she gets a surprising unanimity in their answers that convince us that the program has affected their thinking. They say they learned that people have choices. For these men, seeing others' lives as a series of choices may help them see the choices in their own. We hope so anyway.

Hurston, Zora Neale—*Their Eyes Were Watching God*

Genre: Novel

Themes: A woman's quest for autonomy; self-discovery; an African-American woman's struggle in a white man's world; what love is

Class Type: Women

Lesson Plan by Jean Trounstine

This poetic book is one of the mainstays of Trounstine's women's CLTL group. It is used every year after the group has bonded and has experience with reading other novels. This text involves dialect and the language of imagery, and getting through that means having some positive experiences with reading ahead of time.

The story is told from the first-person perspective of Janie, a young woman who starts her life dreaming about love and how it can save her. The book begins and ends with a conversation, after the death of Janie's third "husband," Teacake. Sitting on her porch, Janie has come home and tells the tale while her best friend, Phoebe, listens. Most of the rest of the book is Janie's flashback of a life in the 1930s, during the course of which she loses her grandmother, moves several times, has three husbands, and ends up an independent woman in her middle years with a home and business of her own.

The story evokes a variety of responses:

One student said, "It was tough to start, and at first, I didn't have a clue but tried to get ahead. It was about empowerment. In the end, I loved the book and the jokes, innuendos and phrases, and I respected Janie."

Another student said: "Like Janie, I don't want to be anyone's slave or servant, nor do I want to be someone who's just around for convenience. I want to be treated as an equal. I've had too many experiences already where guys want you for your money, car, or sex and only treat you nicely when you're providing them with those things. As Janie said, there are two things everyone has to do for themselves and that's go to God and find out about living on their own."

A third said: "Janie wasn't to be pitied. . . . She soon learned that Logan was a typical black man at that time and thought all he had to do was put food on the table and provide shelter for her, and she would be the perfect loving wife. I feel that a lot of guys I meet today have the same attitude. They think just because we're going out they can run the show, appear when they feel like it, go out whenever they want, but always expect me to be there whenever they call."

The discussion always delves into questions allowing the class to explore the notion of empowerment that underscores Janie's growth throughout the book. Conversation explores the language of the book, how Janie's voice is different from the men's voices, what it must have been like for Nanny—Janie's grandmother who raised her—growing up during slavery, and the fact that Janie's mother was raped. Maureen, a young white woman, called her experience with this book approaching "a whole different culture."

The discussion always ultimately involves grappling with the question of love. Trounstine asks: *What does Hurston show us of love and where we find it? How do we know it? Why are we afraid of it or willing to live in its illusion, share it, refuse it, build on it, or hurt in its name?*

Questions Trounstine might ask also include: *What is Janie searching for? Does she find it? Can a woman ever be equal to a man in Janie's world?*

When Janie meets the man she thinks is the love of her life, the class asks: *Does Teacake really love Janie? What about the fact that he steals from her, cheats on her, and hits her? What should we make of all that?*

Trounstine wonders *what does Zora Neale Hurston mean when she has Janie say, "She was too busy feeling grief to dress like grief?" What does the title mean?*

Participants also spend time talking about what this book tells us about community and history. The women always ask Judge Dever, who is at the discussion table: *"Would you have given Janie any time for killing Teacake?"* His answer is as provocative as their question: Would you?

Haruf, Kent—*Plainsong*

Genre: Novel

Themes: Community; finding love; giving love

Class Type: Women

Lesson Plan by Gail Mooney

This is a spare, easy-to-read book that explores relationships in a small town, centered upon the predicament of a teenage pregnant girl and two elderly bachelors who take her in when her mother throws her out. It also quietly weaves together the lives of a single father bringing up two young sons and an unmarried English teacher caring for her father who has Alzheimer's disease.

This novel changes point of view so that the reader is able to see the world through the eyes of many characters, and, ultimately, the town itself becomes a primary force, since it is all about community and family and how they both define and nurture us.

The question Mooney always starts the class with is a written response piece: *In the novel* Plainsong *by Kent Haruf, the pregnant teenager, Victoria Robideaux, goes to her teacher Maggie when she finds herself homeless and from there to the McPheron brothers' farm. None of these people judges her: They simply help her. Can you describe a time in your life when you needed the help of others and not their judgment? What was the help you needed, from where did you get it, and how did you avoid feeling judged?*

The discussion of the book centers primarily on the importance of community, of feeling part of a larger whole. They talk about how alienation casts us all adrift, how this sense of not belonging leads us all to make poor decisions, and about where and how we can find or create a community for ourselves. Mooney ordinarily saves this novel for the end of the course when, in fact, the women agree that the class itself has become a community wherein they feel accepted and heard and never judged. Everyone loves this book for its beautiful prose and calm revelations about character and setting. It is a very healing way to say goodbye.

Kesey, Ken—*One Flew Over the Cuckoo's Nest*

<u>Genre</u>: Novel

<u>Themes</u>: Identity, freedom versus established authority; leadership; independence versus dependence

<u>Class Type:</u> Men

<u>Lesson Plan</u> by Robert Waxler

Waxler usually uses this novel near the end of the seminar sessions, often in the next-to-last week, after students have become a community much in the way Mooney describes.

The story is interesting and well paced, and because of the ongoing battle between the highly energetic McMurphy and the authoritarian Big Nurse, the book seems to hold everyone's attention. However, the story is told through the consciousness of Chief Bromden, and so, at times, the distinction between what is imagined and what is actually happening becomes puzzling to the reader.

The story opens with Randle Patrick McMurphy (RPM), an optimistic counter-culture figure, entering the mental ward controlled by the cynical Nurse Ratched, whose job seems to be to maintain the status quo, the "established order." The Nurse has the power and the control, and her strategies are all designed to get the patients to conform to the bureaucratic apparatus—the dehumanizing schedules that bring comfort to the weary but rob human beings of their independence and courage. By contrast, McMurphy's strategies are designed to bring everyone together, to make them believe in themselves and their potential.

The Chief observes the struggle between McMurphy and Ratched, and it is as if that struggle is the equivalent of the internal struggle going on inside Bromden himself—a battle between dependence and independence, freedom and authority, security and risk, joy and despair. In the end, McMurphy will die, a crucifixion of sorts, but the Chief will grow to his full height and potential, breaking free from Big Nurse, thanks to McMurphy, as he heads out on the open road.

Several issues are explored in the discussion of the story. The main focus is usually on the meaning and implications of the battle between the rebel figure (McMurphy) and the established order (Big Nurse). Most everyone agrees that McMurphy is heroic, willing to take a chance, a gambler who shows the importance of taking risks and the joy of life itself. The group identifies with him and admires his individuality and sense of freedom, his openness and tolerance. But, on occasion, someone in the group will try to defend Big Nurse, not in the details of her tyranny, but with an argument that suggests McMurphy needs to be given limitations, that we all need some boundaries. Readers don't like Big Nurse, but perhaps she too is a reminder of something we all have to grapple with, both outside and inside of ourselves.

In a similar context, the class often explores the contrast between the way McMurphy and Big Nurse lead. They both would claim they are helping the patients. But are they? McMurphy seems to work on boosting self-esteem, playing to the strengths of others. Big Nurse seems to work on emphasizing weaknesses, making people feel small.

But, at times, some will argue that McMurphy is really selfish, putting others in danger, interested primarily in his own gain. This is Big Nurse's argument, of course, and most disagree with it. But Big Nurse would say that she is protecting the patients, keeping them out of harm's way.

Chief Bromden is always part of the conversation. When he thinks about McMurphy, he also thinks about his own father, a Native American who was victimized by the White Established Order. In a sense he is seeking his father, his roots, just as he is in pursuit of his own deep self. That his mother was white, and that he is known by her name, complicates his journey and raises important questions about his mixed heritage and about identity in general. In terms of the story, it is as if Chief Bromden must return home to the "name of the father" before he can truly know himself. But he must also symbolically kill the father figure (McMurphy) before he can be set free.

The fact that the novel was written in the 1960s is also important. Kesey was a central figure in the counter-culture; in many ways, the book itself reflects the hope and vision of that era. *Is it a vision worth holding on to today?* Waxler might ask.

Toward the end of the session, the group considers some final questions raised by the novel: *Who is sane and who is insane? How do we determine such things?* Waxler might ask: *Who makes those definitions real? Is it right to say that those who have the power control the language?* This last question is particularly important in a program engaged in changing lives through literature.

Kingsolver, Barbara—*The Bean Trees*

<u>Genre</u>: Novel

<u>Themes</u>: A relationship with a child literally can lead a woman to a new life. What does it mean to be "human," fight past fears of hurt and attachment, learn to take emotional risks, and be open to love, despite the pain such openness invites?

<u>Class Type</u>: Women

<u>Lesson Plan</u> by Jean Trounstine

This is a very accessible novel, an easy 232 pages, and one used early in the semester because it grabs the women immediately with its coming-of-age theme and its direct clear prose. The women love this book, and there are many characters and situations in it for them to relate to. Taylor comes from rural Kentucky and a poor family and wants to get out, not just out of poverty but out of a dead-end existence. This in itself provides conversation. *What is a dead-end existence? How do you know? How do you get out or should you? How do we determine what is worth the risk of changing our lives?*

Taylor leaves in an old car with bad tires and finds herself in a Cherokee bar in Oklahoma and, once outside, is confronted by an Indian woman who desperately thrusts a child into Taylor's arms. Taylor discovers that the child has been severely abused and so she feels she has to keep her. Another issue: *How does this child change Taylor, and, more universally, how do children change us? What does it take to raise a child, and what sacrifices do we see in Taylor's new world?*

As Taylor finds a place to settle down, she meets an eventual room-mate, Lou Ann, and has more to learn from her about friendship. *What,* Trounstine asks the women, *does it mean to be a friend? Is Lou Ann a better friend to Taylor than Taylor is to her?*

Taylor eventually gets involved with a widowed owner of a tire store, whose other business is helping political refugees enter the United States illegally, and this brings politics into the book. The group gets a chance to talk about values and what is right. *Is the law always more important than morality? How do we make that decision?*

Other questions from a Barbara Kingsolver website that also may be used with the book include discussing the theme of being an outsider: *In what ways are various characters outsiders? What does this suggest about what it takes to be an insider? How and why do the characters change, especially Lou Ann, Taylor, and Turtle?* In many ways, the novel is about "the education of Taylor Greer." *What does she learn about human suffering? About love?*

London, Jack—*The Call of the Wild*

Genre: Novel

Theme: Survival

Class Type: Men's group, inexperienced readers

Lesson Plan by Cherie Muehlberger

Class is opened with background about the author, Jack London: his search for adventure in Alaska; his short stint in jail; his determination to have a better life, which sent him back to school; his highly successful and disciplined career as a writer; his alcoholism; and his financial difficulties and eventual death, possibly a suicide.

After discussing the descent of Buck who was a highly refined judge's dog and became a sled dog prospecting for gold in the Klondike, conversation concentrates on his survival in an unfamiliar environment. Muehlberger says that students look at Buck as the center of the story and discuss all the ways he learns to survive. They talk about change brought on by outside forces and his adaptation to them. The discussion considers the concept of "survival of the fittest." Some talk about the trust and love of his final master for him, and Buck's choice to return to the wild.

Finally, the group concentrates on the skills and characteristics we humans need to survive in the twenty-first century. This activity is done first by the individual on paper and then as discussion, looking at the attributes each of us utilizes for our own success.

Malcolm X (as told to Alex Haley)—*The Autobiography of Malcolm X*

Genre: Autobiography

Theme: The famous hoodlum who converted to the Nation of Islam in prison, and whose subsequent career made him a national icon as celebrated as Martin Luther King, Jr., although for opposite reasons

Class Type: Best with male students, especially groups that are racially mixed

Lesson Plan by Taylor Stoehr

Taylor Stoehr says that although this book has been taught in its entirety in the Dorchester Program, ordinarily only excerpts are read, matched to passages in other works (and especially to chapters in the core text, Frederick Douglass's *Narrative of the Life of Frederick Douglass, an American Slave*). The course begins with an emphasis on childhood experience and typically combines readings about Douglass's essentially parentless childhood with passages from Malcolm's autobiography that tells, among other things, of his father's death and his mother's sufferings and ultimate breakdown. Sometimes assigned for its ironic parallels is an excerpt from Booker T. Washington's *Up from Slavery*, which also tells of his own fatherless childhood. Usually included are passages from Bill Russell's autobiography, *Second Wind*, in which his luck having two strong parents contrasts with these other fates.

Questions Stoehr asks students to think and write about may include the following: *What are the most important things a child needs in order to grow up "normal"—as a healthy, happy, worthy person?* Douglass grew up without his parents, Washington without a father, and Malcolm X lost his father at a young age. Yet all three became great men. *Is having a father necessary? How do people learn to face the things that life will demand? Where do people get their courage, self-esteem, and righteousness?*

These questions are spread out over the several weeks that the class is devoted to thinking about childhood, gradually moving into issues of self-determination and schooling. When the discussion includes the latter, the students focus on the same authors, choosing passages in which they describe learning to read and write—including Malcolm's extraordinary account of training himself as a public speaker by mastering the dictionary while serving time in prison. Often added is a passage of contrast describing Muhammad Ali's very different literacy, which is a combination of minimal reading skills and quick-witted verbal eloquence.

Some other questions Stoehr considers for thinking and/or writing: *What should a parent's role be in teaching? What is society's responsibility in setting and enforcing educational standards? Can a genuine desire to learn be encouraged through coercion—enforced attendance, assignments, etc.? How did you learn what you needed to know in your childhood?*

Malcolm's example works as an implied challenge in the background of such questions, but Dorchester does not exhort students to model themselves after him, nor does it ever draw attention to problems of literacy in student writing. If they are to make any progress in such areas, Stoehr says it will be because the urge comes strongly from within, not from any agenda imposed from the outside.

Many probationers have seen the Spike Lee film about Malcolm X and are already familiar with his career, so that a few excerpts from the *Autobiography* can bring up a wide range of concerns. Sometimes the group talks about his prison experience and his religious conversion. More often, conversation heads toward Malcolm's challenge to Dr. King's nonviolent activism, a debate that dominated civil rights discourse in the 1960s. All of this is useful for getting some distance on issues of self-respect and social responsibility, says Stoehr, and helping probationers form new attitudes toward their own problems. Dorchester's experience suggests that the most fruitful conversations come from comparisons between Malcolm's story and similar accounts from other authors such as Douglass and King.

Morrison, Toni—*The Bluest Eye*

Genre: Novel

Themes: Love and longing in a racist world; overcoming the cycle of despair; sexual abuse; alcoholism

Class Type: Women

Lesson Plan by Jean Trounstine

The story details the life of two young girls as they seek to understand their growing up and the community around them. It contrasts the worlds of rich white Ohioans with the poor blacks of rural Lorain; the tough but normal childhoods of sisters Claudia and Frieda McTeer and the traumatic growth of their friend, Pecola; the trust and playfulness of youth in the face of adult alcoholism, racism, and sexual abuse. Pecola yearns for blue eyes; that is, she yearns for what she, as a black girl, cannot have. Raped by her father and unprotected by her mother, Pecola eventually "gets" those blue eyes. It is Claudia and Frieda, and thus the readers, who learn from her sad tale. Implied is that we are the ones who can change the cycle of despair.

When the book is assigned, before the discussion begins, Trounstine tells students a bit about Toni Morrison and some of the difficult subjects of the book. It seems important to let students know that they will be reading about the roots of racism and abuse so that they might recognize the book's potential power on their psyches. Trounstine also thinks it is important to establish a class community before introducing this book since the text asks us to tackle issues about which the students have strong feelings. Trounstine suggests waiting to use it until the middle of the course since taking on the tough issues first requires trust and a certain degree of bonding.

Morrison's language, poetic and filled with a sense of place, draws students in but also demands a focused reader. Because they are so drawn to Pecola's yearnings, women probationers often lose pieces of Claudia's story. Trounstine has found that giving students questions about Claudia as the narrator helps to broaden the book for students, and allows them to reflect on their lives in connection to its themes. They get engaged in the idea that because of Pecola's sacrifice, there is hope for the community.

When the group has gathered, participants begin by each taking a turn responding to the text. No one interrupts while each reader has a chance to say whatever she feels and thinks about whatever aspects of the text she chooses. The initial comments give students a chance to hate Cholly, the rapist father; pity Pecola; ignore the sisters; wonder why they are reading such a "depressing book"; or, occasionally, ask for what more they can read of Morrison's. This is where the conversation really begins, with the intention to let them discover that all of us have a right to opinions; we all have responses that should be valued; we each need to listen as well as be heard.

Since Morrison plays with the idea of the American Dream gone very wrong for the folks in Claudia's world, Trounstine uses a "Dick and Jane" reader from the 1950s to show how the American Dream was imaged in that text: a stay-at home mom, a dad who went to work in a suit, three smiling children, a dog, a cat, even a house with a white picket fence. The "Dick and Jane" reader is also used because Morrison employs pieces that are similar to the old fashioned "Dick and Jane" readers to set up her chapters, but adds a twist. Her words begin "normally," and then are run together so that a passage of jumbled letters seems a "dream gone wrong." This opening, a sort of "Dick and Jane" run wild, repeats itself throughout *The Bluest Eye*. Morrison takes the idea of the American family and shows how most of us do not have "white picket fence" perfection.

As Trounstine reads aloud, using show-and-tell pictures, asking students to consider what Morrison is doing with the opening of her text, students discover that most have overlooked this because they didn't understand it. After the passages are clarified, they begin to see that looking closely is valuable. Someone always says, "There is no perfect house, no white picket fence, and certainly no perfect family." They start to enjoy finding all the broken passages in the text that they overlooked the first time around.

Trounstine also asks them to think about the difference between Claudia's background and Pecola's. They surprise themselves by remembering details: Claudia's mother took care of her when she was sick; her family took in Pecola; her father protected them when the boarder, Mr. Henry, "touched" Frieda. They begin to think about Claudia as more than teller of the tale. Each character comes under scrutiny as the group attempts to uncover the multitude of Morrison's truths.

Questions may include: *How do we learn to feel ugly? What does Pecola's life show us?* As rapidly as the questions come, students begin to fill in the blanks with "mean neighbors like Maureen," or "parents that tell us we're worthless like Pauline." Often, Trounstine asks them to underline language that they like, phrases that stick out. Maureen Peal, the little girl who taunts Pecola, has "lynch rope braids," someone will always say, and then comment that Pecola is taunted by both the black and white community.

It would be easy if we could let our students rest with partial understandings of reality, but great literature does not afford that. Morrison allows us to understand Cholly, the father, the husband, and the rapist in a way that makes us see him as a human being. Asking the women what happened to Cholly forces them to look past their anger and hate at their own abuses. They don't have to forgive, but they have to see.

As they begin to see Cholly, too, as a troubled soul, a black man beaten down by a white society, they open themselves to more than one way of looking at the world. Other characters, too, present them with dilemmas.

Questions present themselves about Pauline, Cholly's wife: *Why does she physically abuse her child? How do you explain that beautiful passage of tenderness between Cholly and Pauline? What does Morrison want us to think about their relationship?*

One woman was so furious at Pauline for staying with Cholly that she said she would have preferred indentured servitude as a maid to the white missus rather than live in a house with "that man." The class challenged her insistence on that way of seeing, but in the end, Morrison makes us recognize that there are no easy answers.

As the women sort through their new understandings from the discussion, they begin to offer new responses. They comment on how hard it is for all these characters to survive. They talk about a society that promotes the illusion that a black child can ever have "blue eyes." They talk about how even the bluest eyes don't bring happiness or ensure fitting in. They stop considering some characters "bad" and others "good." Even Soaphead Church, the minister-gone-wrong who provides Pecola with her prized eyes, has a story worth telling. And hating a character says something about the hater as well as about the character.

Where is the beauty in this book? Trounstine asks them over and over, not with that exact question but with all the questions, insisting that a book so well written can help us explore the darkest moments, unsilencing the silenced for all of us. "Claudia is a tree, and all the rest of them are bamboo," one woman said at the end of a class. Another replied, "It may be too late for Pecola, but it is not too late for us."

Steinbeck, John—*Cannery Row*

<u>Genre</u>: Novel

<u>Themes</u>: Relationships; institutions; dependency; wealth; death; living life to its fullest

<u>Class Type</u>: Male, different age groups, most with chemical dependency or violence issues

<u>Lesson Plan</u> by Trudy Schrandt

Trudy Schrandt describes this as a story of a group of social misfits surviving by their wits (legal and otherwise). Their lives are lived in and about the affluent community of Monterey, California. They are mere flies in the social lives that spin around them. However, they are full and dimensional characters with much to say and teach.

The novel is set at the edge of the fish canneries. It introduces the neighborhood grocery owner, Lee Chong, and shows us his business sense as well as his heart. It is from him that Mac and the boys procure a place to call home. Dora and her girls practice the oldest profession in the world but have connections to the community that no social worker could ever imagine. Doc's biological laboratory rounds out the group. Other characters are tangential to this group and add to or underscore the themes.

The underlying action in the novel centers around planning a party for Doc. The false starts and missteps they make attempting to achieve this are at once funny, sad, and revealing of the human heart. Rationalizations for actions, guilt regarding motives, rehabilitation, and success are played out to their fullest. Great wealth becomes not what one has but with whom it is shared. Schrandt says that ultimately the story gives insights into understanding what motivates each of us and what functions to complete us.

Throughout the story each character opens a chapter of actions and reactions about decisions we make in life and situations we are presented with. Along with their consequences, we see many of our own foibles and mistakes played out.

At the end Schrandt says that we can understand how the inhabitants of Cannery Row are "whores, pimps, gamblers, and sons of bitches [meaning] saints, and angels and martyrs and holy men."

There is an immediate connection between the participants and the characters in the book. Often, however, Schrandt has found that it takes ten to fifteen minutes for some of the participants to admit how much they like one character or another. Although it is obvious that the characters are not the standard-bearers of society, the class members aren't sure whether that is good or bad. Once they realize that the characters' flaws are being investigated, not to cast judgment, but to elevate their standing, they relax and enjoy the discussion and bring quite a bit to it from their own perspectives and experiences.

The book begins by defining itself as a "poem," so Schrandt takes each chapter and treats it like a stanza, or at least that is always the intent. Schrandt takes special time with the Introduction as this opens the door to looking at people differently from their stereotypes.

Throughout the discussion, many questions beg to be asked: *What is the symbolic importance of collecting? How is success defined? What is the function of violence (suicides, deaths, and even in the party mode)? What does it mean to be a part of a neighborhood or a community? Why might family be a troublesome concept?*

A word of caution: It is very easy to make this a discussion of the evils of alcohol and, by extension, addiction. While this certainly is a part of the story, it is only a small part. Schrandt says that the varying themes are far too important to lose sight of substance abuse as the controlling issue. These characters are not the pillars of society or even its middle-class. Many of them are on the bottom run of the stereotypical ladder of American success. It behooves us to look at them through the glasses that Steinbeck offers and consider what makes then honorable men. They have a lot to teach, or maybe we have a lot to learn.

Tyler, Anne—*Dinner at the Homesick Restaurant*

Genre: Novel

Theme: Through Pearl Tull, her two sons, and her daughter, Tyler takes us into the notion of how families both wound and heal each other. A great book to use to teach point of view—not in a literary sense, necessarily—but to discuss how events and relationships differ, depending on who is telling the story.

Class Type: Women

Lesson Plan by Jean Trounstine

Pearl Tull is on her deathbed when the book begins, and through her eyes, as well as through the eyes of her children, readers come to understand why her husband left her, what kind of a mother she was, who her children are, and what ties they each had with Pearl.

Judge Dever loves to tell a story about how one woman in the Lynn-Lowell class said that Pearl Tull was a really witchy mother, and then with a straight face, as the light bulb went off inside her head, she said, "just like me." Inevitably, women will identify with Pearl or say that their mother is like Pearl. Some find her to be a mother they admire, while others actually hate her and feel she is responsible for all the problems that the children have. When Judge Dever points out that the kids are all "successful" by the world's standards, with decent jobs, the students still will open up about their perspectives.

One student said, "She's a strong woman facing hard times by herself."

Another student said, "Married to Beck Tull, a perfectionist with a large ego and a man who felt his family was an albatross around his neck, she had to be strong-willed, but as strong as I found Pearl, she was not a fighter."

And a third said, "Pearl had to bring the kids up alone and she knew she made a lot of mistakes and she was even cruel and distant."

Such comments take us into the nature of mothering as well as into the understanding that each of us has different points of view; for this reason, Trounstine uses the text early in the semester. Although the chapter progression does need clarifying (because each chapter changes point of view, and that can be confusing to the students if it's not explained before they start reading the book), this is a great book to see who identifies with what character and to learn from each other about how to connect. It allows for multiple perspectives: Students also learn to see what they value most.

One of the women wrote the following insightful comment when asked to tell what happened in this book:

> I think the turning point was when before Pearl died, she told Ezra to invite everyone in the book, including Beck Tull, the father who left, to the funeral. It was quite a shock when Beck showed up. When Beck poured out his side of the story to Cody, they learned he felt that Pearl drove him away but that he secretly watched them from across the street and knew the kids would be all right.

That particular woman had been left by her father; it was interesting when she realized that Beck actually thought about his children after leaving Pearl.

There are a variety of comments about each character during class discussion, and conflicting opinions make for a great and sometimes heated conversation. Some of the women hate Cody. Some love him. He's handsome. He's money hungry. He's insecure. He's a mean son-of-a-bitch. He's the most wounded of all the children. He's a survivor. They have the same variety of opinions about Ezra and Jenny. The richness in Tyler's writing and her ability to show us full human beings help this book remain a classic in Trounstine's class.

Other suggested questions: *What does the book teach us about home? About families? What's the importance of family dinners to the book? Of food and nourishment? How are different characters nourished or hungry? Sick for home? Sick of home? What is nostalgia and how do we all ache for the idealized home?*

The class also looks at all the houses in the book and discusses them, their differences, and what they say about the people who live in each—the Baltimore house, Cody's farm, Jenny's house, Ezra's restaurant. And as students consider the archery accident for each of the characters, they ask: *Will Beck stay for dinner at the end of the book?*

> **Wright, Richard—***Black Boy*
> <u>Genre</u>: Autobiographical novel
> <u>Theme</u>: Wright's slightly fictionalized account of growing up in the
>   Deep South; cruelty and punishment; manliness and violence
> <u>Class Type</u>: Probably best with African-American men's groups
> <u>Lesson Plan</u> by Taylor Stoehr

This text works both as an entire book and in excerpts. In the Dorchester Men's Program it has been used both ways. In the suggested questions and writing prompts listed, some of the possible uses of Wright's work can be seen. There are many other sections of *Black Boy* that lend themselves to the themes that come up in a CLTL curriculum, especially one with minority students. One passage may indicate some of these possibilities. Early in the book, the boy Richard is ordered to the blackboard on his first day in school but is so frightened that he is unable even to write his name, though he is in fact already quite literate and, of course, destined to be a famous writer. The passage might be read in combination with the chapter in *Narrative of the Life of Frederick Douglass, an American Slave,* recounting his own discovery of reading and writing, or the section of *The Autobiography of Malcolm X* in which Malcolm sets himself to master the dictionary during his incarceration. Given the fact that students are often anxious about their own degree of literacy, passages like these have special impact.

On the theme "Cruelty and Punishment," Taylor Stoehr uses an excerpt from *Black Boy* in combination with selections from Maxim Gorky (*Notch*) and Fyodor Dostoyevsky (*The House of the Dead*). For that assignment, Stoehr asks these questions: *What causes cruelty? Why do people inflict pain on others? Is it out of anger and hatred, or for other reasons? What's the effect of cruelty on the person who is cruel? On the victim?*

In this assignment, Stoehr uses this prompt for an in-class writing exercise, discussing what punishment does to its victims and what it does to the person who does the punishing. *Can a person inflict pain and suffering on someone else without being cruel? Does it make any difference whether or not the punishment is deserved?*

On the theme "Manliness and Violence," Stoehr uses an excerpt from *Black Boy* in combination with selections from Langston Hughes ("Last Whipping," from *The Best of Simple*) and Bill Russell (*Second Wind*). When he reads Chapter 10 of the central text, Frederick Douglass's *Narrative*, included in the assignment is the following question: *To what degree is it necessary to use force to defend one's rights against oppression or injustice: In public life? In private life? Can you think of examples in your own experience?*

9

Teaching Specific Texts: Short Story, Essay, Article, and Poem

"The program gives you a chance to get a positive attitude about life. It gets you going in the right direction."

—Student
Barnstable Men's Program

CHAPTER 9 CONTINUES OUR VARIED APPROACHES to texts, and here we include many of the short stories, essays, articles, and poetry we have used in CLTL. Most of these texts have been found by individual instructors in anthologies or in story collections by the author. Some can be found in our text, *Changing Lives Through Literature* (University of Notre Dame Press). Teaching ideas are also provided for some of these materials. The texts here are alphabetized by the author's last name; those marked with an asterisk have a lesson plan.

SHORT STORIES

Dee Axelrod, "River"

James Baldwin, "Sonny's Blues" (see Teaching Strategies: More Writing in CLTL on page 230)

Marta Brunet, "Solitude of Blood"

Toni Cade Bambara, "Gorilla, My Love"

Toni Cade Bambara, "Raymond's Run"

*T. Coraghessan Boyle, "Greasy Lake"

*Karel Capek, "The Last Judgement"

Ray Carver, "Cathedral"

Ray Carver, "So Much Water Close to Home"

Ray Carver, "Tell the Women We're Going" (see Teaching Strategies: Identifying with the Stories on page 212)

*Ray Carver, "What We Talk about When We Talk about Love"

Ray Carver, "Where I'm Calling From"

Willa Cather, "Paul's Case"

John Cheever, "The Five Forty-Eight"

*John Cheever, "The Swimmer" (see Teaching Strategies: More Writing in CLTL on page 230)

Kate Chopin, "The Storm"

Kate Chopin, "The Story of an Hour"

*E. L. Doctorow, "Jolene: A Life"

*Roddy Doyle, "Ask Me, Ask Me, Ask Me" (see Teaching Strategies: Inspiring Student Writing on page 226)

Andre Dubus, "Giving Up the Gun"

Louise Erdrich, "The Shawl"

William Faulkner, "Barn Burning"

Tim Gautreux, "Little Frogs in a Ditch"

Charlotte Perkins Gilman, "The Yellow Wallpaper"

Susan Glaspell, "A Jury of Her Peers" (see Teaching Strategies: More Writing in CLTL on page 229)

*Maxim Gorky, "Notch"

Ernest Hemingway, "Hills like White Elephants"

Langston Hughes, "Last Whipping"

Zora Neale Hurston, "Sweat"

Shirley Jackson, "The Lottery"

Gish Jen, "In the American Society"

Neil Labute, "Layover"

D. H. Lawrence, "The Rocking-Horse Winner"

*Ursula Leguin, "The Wife's Story"

Doris Lessing, "Woman on a Roof" (see Teaching Strategies: More Writing in CLTL on page 230)

William Henry Lewis, "Shades"

Luke, the Bible, "The Parable of the Prodigal Son," Chapter 15: verses 11–32

Katherine Mansfield, "The Garden Party"

Katherine Mansfield, "Miss Brill"

Alice Munro, "Boys and Girls"

*Rita Marie Nibasa, "A Line of Cutting Women"

Thisbe Nissen, "Grover, King of Nebraska"

Joyce Carol Oates, "Christmas Night, 1962"

Joyce Carol Oates, "The Lost Child"

Joyce Carol Oates, "Politics"

Joyce Carol Oates, "Where Are You Going? Where Have You Been?" (see Teaching Strategies: More Writing in CLTL on page 230)

Tim O'Brien, "On the Rainy River"

Tillie Olsen, "I Stand Here Ironing" (see Teaching Strategies: More Writing in CLTL on page 230)

Dorothy Parker, "Big Blonde"

Dorothy Parker, "A Telephone Call" (see Teaching Strategies: More Writing in CLTL on page 230)

Edgar Allan Poe, "The Cask of Amontillado"

John Steinbeck, "The Chrysanthemums"

Michael Thompson, "The Last Time I Seen My Father" (see Teaching Strategies: More Writing in CLTL on page 230)

Leo Tolstoy, "The Death of Ivan Ilych"

Leo Tolstoy, "God Knows the Truth but Waits"

Leo Tolstoy, "Korney Vasiliev"

Alice Walker, "Everyday Use"

Eudora Welty, "A Worn Path"

Tobias Wolff, "The Chain"

Tobias Wolff, "Hunter in the Snow"

*Tobias Wolff, "The Rich Brother"

ESSAYS AND ARTICLES

Maya Angelou, "My Name Is Margaret"

Claudette Colvin, "Refusing to Move Back"

Epictetus, "Enchiridion"

Arthur Huff Fauset, "Sojourner Truth"

Robert Lipsyte, "'I Don't Have to Be What You Want Me to Be' Says
    Muhammad Ali"

John Stuart Mill, "On Liberty"

Grace Paley, "Traveling"

Rosa Parks, "A Bus to Freedom"

Plato, "Apology"

Plato, "Crito"

Plato, "Euthypho"

Plato, "Phaedo"

Howell Raines, "My Soul Is Rested"

Brent Staples, "Just Walk On By: A Black Man Ponders His Power
    to Alter Public Perception"

POETRY

Gwendolyn Brooks, "We Real Cool"

Lucille Clifton, "Miss Rosie" (see Teaching Strategy: Use of Poetry
    on page 231)

Sandy Coleman, "Rhyme and Reason"

Langston Hughes, "A Dream Deferred"

Langston Hughes, "Mother to Son" (see Teaching Strategy: Use of Poetry on page 231)

Barbara Helfgott Hyett, "In the Theater at Harvard Square" (see Teaching Strategy 11 on page 236)

Galway Kinnell, "St. Francis and the Sow" (see Teaching Strategy: Use of Poetry on page 231)

Philip Levine, "What Work Is"

Sharon Olds, "The Abandoned Newborn" (see Teaching Strategy: Use of Poetry on page 231)

Sharon Olds, "My Son the Man"

Mary Oliver, "Wild Geese"

Marge Piercy, "To Be of Use" (see Teaching Strategy: Use of Poetry on page 231)

Theodore Roethke, "My Papa's Waltz" (see Teaching Strategy: Use of Poetry on page 231)

Sonia Sanchez, "Blues"

William Shakespeare," Let Me Not to the Marriage of True Minds"

William Carlos Williams, "This Is Just to Say" (see Teaching Strategy: Rap to Poetry on page 232)

LESSON PLANS

Capek, Karel—"The Last Judgement"

<u>Genre</u>: Short story (an ironic Czech parable)

<u>Theme</u>: Judgment and punishment

<u>Class Type</u>: Men's group

<u>Lesson Plan</u> by Taylor Stoehr

Taylor Stoehr uses this story in Dorchester's final class, usually in combination with another story (recently, Tolstoy's "God Sees the Truth but Waits"). The basic text for Dorchester is Frederick Douglass's

Narrative of the Life of Frederick Douglass, An American Slave, which is read in small segments coupled with supplementary texts, nonfiction and fiction, matched thematically with Douglass. At the end of the semester, however, students will have finished Douglass before coming to this final assignment. The thematic material of the previous week's meeting has to do with "hitting bottom," despair, and forgiveness—themes that are now picked up in Capek's story from a different angle. The story raises questions about the right of any human being to judge another, while at the same time acknowledging that such judgment is necessary in the modern social order.

In the story, a murderer dies and faces judgment. God appears, not as judge, but as witness, knowing everything. When the murderer asks why God is not his judge, the reply is that knowing everything about a man precludes being able to judge him. The story is very short and straightforward though it has this rather sophisticated message. Stoehr says it can give rise in the classroom to considerable excitement in students who, after all, have recently been judged, because it brings into a new focus the problems of guilt and innocence and the nature of judgment and punishment. Sometimes students express anger at society, sometimes they experience a new sense of compassion, or a new conception of the nature of justice. He says it's hard to predict.

At one graduation ceremony, a student made a speech while accepting his diploma, and in the midst of it, he turned to the judges to tell them the plot of this story, and charged them to remember that they were only human beings too, judging other human beings. This is a good story for getting some closure on problems of "re-entry" into civil society after having been judged and punished by its representatives. If you have a judge sitting in on your classes, it's an especially provocative selection, says Stoehr.

Suggested questions and writing prompt: *Who has the right to sit in judgment on others? Is the way our society deals with judgment and punishment just? How else could it be done?*

Carver, Ray, "What We Talk about When We Talk about Love"
<u>Genre</u>: Short story
<u>Theme</u>: Love; friendship; conversation
<u>Class Type</u>: Men or women
<u>Lesson Plan</u> by Robert Waxler

Two married couples—the narrator Nick, his wife Laura, the cardiologist Mel, and Mel's wife Terri—are sitting around the kitchen table, drinking gin, and talking about love. The heart doctor, Mel, does most of the talking (he thinks he's entitled to), although it becomes increasingly clear through the gin-soaked discussion that he doesn't quite know what he's talking about.

A seminarian before attending medical school, Mel claims that "real love" is "nothing less than spiritual love," an absolute love that seems to reflect his own desire to find permanence and stability in a world saturated with flux and change.

At the beginning of the conversation, Mel insists that Terri is wrong when she asserts that Ed, the man she used to live with who was a violent abuser, actually loved her. Both Laura and Terri believe that people love in their own individual way and that we cannot judge another's situation. "Sure sometimes he may have acted crazy," Terri says about Ed. "But he loved me. There was love there, Mel. Don't say there wasn't."

Is it possible for someone to love another person and still physically abuse that person? Waxler ask the students.

Responses include:

"Yes, I think Ed did love Terri. Maybe he didn't know how to express it though."

"Terri just wants Mel to acknowledge that someone else could love her."

"Mel says he loved his first wife, but now he wants to kill her."

"There are all kinds of love—spiritual, chivalric, sentimental, carnal, physical—the story shows that."

As the four characters in the story continue to drink their gin, Mel emerges as a man struggling with fear, wrestling with contradictions. Waxler might ask Mel: *How can you say you loved your first wife, Mel, and now you don't, then at the same time insist that love is always absolute? How can you say you love your son, but not call him and talk with him? Why do you really like those medieval knights, Mel? Because they believed in love or because they wore that protective armor?*

As he keeps drinking his gin, Mel tells a story about an elderly couple deeply in love who are rushed to the hospital after a near-fatal car accident. They are put in a hospital room together, but in hard casts, so they cannot turn to see each other. The couple's relationship seems to meet Mel's expectations of "spiritual love," but he dismisses their behavior as foolish and absurd.

"I mean, it was killing the old fart just because he couldn't look at the fucking woman," Mel says as he concludes his example with an undertone of his own growing frustration and violence.

What does Mel seem to be wrestling with? Waxler asks the CLTL group around the table. *What does he fear?*

Responses include:

"He's all ego. Thinks he's better than everyone else."
"He's protecting himself. That's why he says he likes the medievel knights with their armor. He believes they can't get hurt."
"Yes, he's afraid that he'll lose Terri like he lost his first wife."
"He doesn't want to make himself vulnerable. But even the knights in their armor got trampled sometimes, as Nick reminds him."

As the light of the late afternoon fades into evening, and the gin is gone, Nick finishes the narrative: "I could hear my heart beating. I could hear everyone's heart. I could hear the human noise we sat there making, not one of us moving, not even when the room went dark."

What do you make of the ending?" Waxler asks. *Is there any hope in this darkness?*

"They must be very drunk."

"It must be night, and they can't even get up to switch on the lights. They're stoned."

"But Nick hears the heart beat. They are together."

"It's the conversation they've had that binds them together."

Cheever, John—"The Swimmer"

Genre: Short story

Themes: Impact of alcohol on the life of the alcoholic and those around him/her; inability to see the truth/reality

Class Type: Men—a range of ages—most with chemical dependency or domestic violence issues

Lesson Plan by Sandi Albertson-Shea and Ray Shea

The Sheas say that this story needs preparation at the previous class because the surrealism is initially frustrating for immature readers. However, by the end of the discussion, the story is almost always viewed positively by students. This class might begin with a look at some of Sharon Olds' poetry dealing with her alcoholic father: "I Go Back to May 1937," "The Guild," and "Saturn." When students then turn to "The Swimmer," there is initial whole-group discussion of major elements, such as *Setting: Time and place?* and *Timeframe: How long does this story take?* Then they break into small groups for discussion of specific assigned questions.

Some of the questions the Sheas might include: *What are some adjectives to describe Neddy Merrill? What is Neddy's goal/project when he leaves the Westerhazys' pool? What is Neddy's attitude/philosophy about swimming? What are changes in Neddy's physical condition and behavior as the story ends? What is the role of alcohol in the story? What signs show that Neddy has lost social status? What is your explanation for Neddy's discovery at the conclusion of the story?*

After a break, the groups share their answers to one or two questions that they have selected to report on. They also discuss: *What's really going on with this guy? What do we learn about Neddy at each swimming stop? What facts/truths has he not acknowledged?*

A small video clip from a Raymond Carver PBS documentary is shown in which Carver reads the poem: "Photograph of My Father." Then the group discusses three other Carver poems: "To My Daughter," "Gravy," and "Late Fragment."

The last 20 minutes of the class are spent doing reflective writing from a list of suggested topics, with reading aloud (optional) after everyone has finished writing. The Sheas offer four possible writing prompts: *(1) The effects of alcohol on the lives of those around the person who is drinking. (2) A time when someone you know was so caught up in a world of alcohol or drugs that this person could not see what was happening around him/her. (3) A time when you so repressed unpleasant facts that you damaged your sense of the truth. (4) Like Carver or Olds, speak the truth to a photo of one of your parents.*

Doctorow, E. L.—"Jolene: A Life"

<u>Genre</u>: Short story

<u>Theme</u>: Growing up female; broken family; American dream

<u>Class Type</u>: Coed, ages 18–25

<u>Lesson Plan</u> by Jane Hale

Doctorow recounts the difficult life of a girl named Jolene who marries at fifteen to get out of her latest foster home. For the next ten years she lives through adulterous affairs, the suicide of a spouse, commitment to a psychiatric hospital, multiple bad marriages to losers and abusers, occasional prostitution, a series of menial jobs along with a few good ones, a brush with the mob, and being accused of kidnapping her own baby and subsequently losing him. She is a talented artist who develops her drawing skill throughout the story almost in spite of herself, yet at the end, she dreams only of becoming a famous movie star so she can be reunited with her child.

Jane Hale has used this story on the first night of class, along with T. Coraghessan Boyle's "Greasy Lake." Students received the stories in the mail two weeks before class started and were asked to read them before the first night. Since Hale has a coed class, the heavily male orientation of "Greasy Lake" is balanced with an equally complex tale of female experience of violence and bad choices.

Students understand the story and respond positively to it. They decide that Jolene made all kinds of bad choices in her life, and that the problems she has are mainly her own fault. However, they don't always make the connection between her unrealistic dream at the end and her past failures until it is pointed out to them.

Hale's suggested discussion questions include: *Does Jolene change, learn, grow over the course of the story? What does art mean to her? How does it weave as a theme throughout the story? Why does Jolene go from one man to another? Does she have other choices? Are any of the men she lives with good to her? Is Jolene a victim or a victor, or both?*

The class also looks closely at the text. Doctorow writes that Jolene looks "hard." *What does that mean? How does a person get that way?*

When Sal is killed, Jolene's "life changes, as lightning strikes, and in an instant what was is not what is." Hale asks, *Have you ever had such a moment, when your life changed suddenly, as if lightning struck it?*

Doctorow writes that Jolene "liked the way she felt" on her own. She had "come of age." *So why doesn't she stay in this good spot in her life? Why does she get involved with Brad? Did you know from the beginning that he was bad news? How?*

At the shelter for battered women, Jolene had been told "it happens once, that's it, you leave." Hale asks: *Do you agree with this advice? Why didn't Jolene take it? Why is her baby so important to her? What do you think lies in store next for her?*

At the end of the discussion, Hale asks students to write about the two stories and talk about which they enjoyed most. She also asks:

What kind of stories would you like to read in the course? Do you have any titles to suggest? From the half of the group that votes for "Jolene," come the following comments:

> "This story reminded me of some of the ups and downs I went through growing up—how I realize I shouldn't rely on others to be happy or to wait for that one moment that you thought was good and in the end you regret it."
> "It was fast-moving. She made mistakes and poor choices, but she had lots of spirit and never gave up. . . . I liked how she moved all over the country and met so many different people."
> "I could relate to some of the choices she made. Also it didn't really leave off with a sense of needing more."

Finally, Hale may ask for additional writing prompts such as: *Pretend you are Jolene; write a letter to "Dear Abby" asking for advice; write Abby's response, too. Write the next chapter of Jolene's life.*

Doyle, Roddy —"Ask Me, Ask Me, Ask Me"
Genre: Short story
Themes: Domestic violence; alcoholism; romantic love; community and family
Class Type: Women
Lesson Plan by Ann Brian Murphy

Roddy Doyle's short story is taken from his novel, *The Woman Who Walked into Doors*. It's a first-person narrative of Paula, an alcoholic, battered woman. The story opens when the police come to the door to tell her that Charlo, her estranged husband, has been killed by the police in an attempted robbery. The story then alternates between present and past, as she reacts to his death and remembers falling in love at their first meeting, and repeatedly circles around the first time he hit her, finally acknowledging their long, terrible life of violence and drink.

Ann Brian Murphy says that the story is complex and challenging, but these very complexities offer great opportunities for discussion. Doyle spends considerable time, for example, establishing the deeply misogynist culture of Ireland in the 1960s, and the students are often shocked by that culture, as they are by society's silence about domestic violence, the failure of family and church and healthcare providers to ask Paula about her wounds. So it's possible to have great discussions about the U.S. society and the ways that many still marginalize women and enable violence. Similarly, the confusing structure invites discussion about why her reactions are so confused and how the story's structure conveys Paula's shock and post-traumatic stress disorder.

Some of the questions Murphy asks early on: *Discuss the scene when Paula and Charlo first meet. What is the vision of romantic love in this scene? How does that vision of romantic love connect with Paula's tolerance of Charlo's beatings?*

As students continue to look at Paula and Charlo's relationship, they consider: *How many times does Paula describe the first time Charlo hit her? What is different in each version? Why do you think she keeps coming back to that event? And how does her awareness change each time she describes it?*

When the class discusses the way Paula describes her family and life in adolescence, Murphy asks: *What is the attitude toward women in this society? How did this attitude contribute to Paula's sense of herself and her reaction to Charlo's violence? What connections do you see between the way Paula's father treats her and the way Charlo treats her?*

Murphy uses a writing prompt to further help students process the story, noting that the story is set in Ireland in the 1960s and '70s, and requires some discussion of both language and setting. Since the structure can be confusing, and the narrative shifts back and forth between past and present, a writing prompt may include: *Write for five minutes on your reaction to the way this story is written. What makes it confusing? Why do you think Doyle chose to write it this way? What does it tell us about Paula?*

Murphy also may ask students to: *Pick one scene you find powerful or puzzling and write about your reactions to it. What does it reveal about Paula or Charlo? About their society? How would it be different—or similar—in our own society?*

Finally, students may write on: *What question would you like to ask either Paula or Charlo? What do you think they would say in reply?*

Faulkner, William—"Barn Burning"

Genre: Short story

Theme: Justice

Class Type: Male, different age groups, most with chemical dependency or violence issues

Lesson Plan by Trudy Schrandt

Set in the post–Civil War South, Faulkner creates a family that is at once self-centered and cunning. This is a story of one man's conviction regarding the righteousness of his own actions and the life-altering decisions this creates for his youngest son's sense of decency as it conflicts with his sense of loyalty to the family. The father burns barns as revenge for what he feels is injustice. Sarty, the boy, is coming of age and must either accept the father's view of justice and society or choose a path that is defined differently.

The story is told from the point of view of the young boy co-existing with a narrator somewhat removed from the action; the boy's emotional stress intensifies and he reaches the point where he must choose "justice and society" over "father and family." This is a complex story and needs to be carefully taught. The intrusions from the narrator are meant to show the reader that the boy can't quite comprehend his situation.

It is imperative that the reader understand both the father and the son. So Schrandt begins by asking participants to discuss Abner Snoops and their opinions of the man, stressing his role as a tragic hero: *What values does he live by? In what ways can you admire him? What is his downfall? What exactly is his code? How does he break his own code?*

After that Schrandt moves on to Sarty, asking students: *What is your opinion of Sarty? What is his dilemma? Does he understand his situation? Does he understand his father? Are his actions justified? What does his future hold?*

Schrandt says there are some powerful descriptions in this story, and the class spends time dissecting the description of the father and the description of the son (along with his italicized thoughts), the DeSpain mansion, and the final eulogy given by Sarty. The remainder of the class is spent discussing that this is a history of justice, inquiring into the concepts of justice that emerge from the story. Finally, the group can explore similar situations in today's society and how they deal with them.

Gorky, Maxim—"Notch"

<u>Genre</u>: Short story (nine pages, easy reading)

<u>Theme</u>: Cruelty and its sources, in relation to punishment

<u>Class Type</u>: Men

<u>Lesson Plan</u> by Taylor Stoehr

Written in the first person by an assumed ex-convict (as Gorky himself was for political offenses sometimes labeled "vagrancy"), this story concerns the dynamics of a Russian prison yard, where a prisoner nicknamed Notch has established a reputation as jailhouse clown, always thinking up new jokes and buffoonery to entertain his fellow prisoners. One day a stray kitten, taken on as a mascot of the yard, steals his thunder until Notch thinks of a crude entertainment that will destroy his rival. He proposes dipping the kitten in a bucket of green paint—a comic experiment that everyone agrees to heartily. Then, once accomplished, it becomes apparent that the poor kitten will die, and the men turn on Notch savagely, beating him without mercy. At the end, he is battered and bleeding, still performing his pathetic pantomimes, and recovering his fickle audience. The kitten will be seen no more.

Taylor Stoehr says that this story is best used in combination with other short works or excerpts. Stoehr pairs it with two, both of which also deal with cruelty and punishment in different amalgams. One, a passage from Fyodor Dostoyevsky's "House of the Dead," not only has the obvious similarity of being set in a Russian prison camp, where the author was himself an inmate, but also deals with the way people who are punished themselves tend to be cruel to others who happen to fall into their power, passing along the suffering and humiliation by whatever means they can.

The second is a passage from Richard Wright's *Black Boy*, recounting how Richard, no older than five, executed a stray kitten with a noose hung on a nail. Richard's cruelty was his perverse way of defying his father, who routinely treated the boy with offhand contempt, as if he were a stray kitten.

These three works offer many approaches to the central questions of cruelty and punishment, and Stoehr leaves it relatively open as to which connections students start with. The reading assignment is matched to Dorchester's ongoing core text, Frederick Douglass's *Narrative of the Life of Frederick Douglass, an American Slave*, exploring chapters dealing with the cruelties of slavery.

In assigning these texts, questions to students include: *What causes cruelty? Why do people inflict pain on others? Is it out of anger and hatred, or for other reasons? What's the effect of cruelty on the person who is cruel? On the victim?* Students write brief answers to these questions, says Stoehr, but an opening exercise covers much the same ground to ensure that everyone has meditated on the issues before the discussion begins.

Further questions include: *What does punishment do to its victims? What does it do to the person who does the punishing? Can a person inflict pain and suffering on someone else without being cruel? What difference does it make if the punishment is deserved?*

Dorchester does not attempt to probe the texts themselves to any depth, preferring to deal with the issues as they arise in class discussion and not wanting to leave out any students who have neglected the reading, for good or bad reasons. Stoehr says that an area that seems most problematic in discussing the texts themselves is the difficulty students have putting their finger on the motives of the various punishers in these stories. The authors have typically left it to the reader to draw his or her own conclusions, and indeed the etiology of cruelty and the ideology of punishment are not easy to identify or justify. Dorchester often frames its conversations around the problem of exacting obedience from children, when attempting to teach the difference between right and wrong.

LeGuin, Ursula—"The Wife's Story"

<u>Genre</u>: Short story

<u>Theme</u>: A very surprising science fiction story that reverses the werewolf idea: Man is just as frightening as beast. LeGuin teases us with issues of child abuse, male-female relationships, life in a small town, and sisterly devotion.

<u>Class Type</u>: Women

<u>Lesson Plan</u> by Jean Trounstine

Trounstine often starts a Lynn-Lowell CLTL program with this text. In the first session, participants should feel successful; using a story that gets them excited and intrigues them is important. Trounstine reads "The Wife's Story" aloud; this works particularly well, for as students follow along, they begin to think, wonder, doubt themselves, get confused, and ultimately burst out with comments. "The Wife's Story" also forces them to read closely, and they see how that pays off as they come to understand the story and ponder the meaning behind the wolf's transformation. Certain questions appear immediately: *Who is telling the story? How do you know? What do we know about the narrator? Her husband? Her sister?*

Before the class breaks into discussion, Trounstine asks each person to say something about the story. This technique—"The Go-Round" is discussed in greater detail in Chapter 10. As participants comment, one by one—students, probation officers, the judge, all on equal footing—Trounstine takes notes in order to return to their comments. This particular story gives participants a chance to talk to each other and argue about what they believe early on, and it sets the scene for the kind of discussions and work they will be doing throughout the program.

As the class discusses this story, Trounstine asks: *Where does the story seem to change? What's your reaction to the male violence in the story? What is LeGuin telling us about women in relationship to that violence? Is there female violence as well in this story? What is your reaction to that? What do the children feel about their father?*

Once the group sees that LeGuin has intentionally tricked them into believing that a woman was telling the story instead of a female wolf, they begin to think why the author has used such a technique and to what end.

Trounstine asks: *If you could rewrite this story, would you change it in any way? If so, what would you change? If not, why not?*

Finally, this story offers a chance to discuss more global questions that set up discussion for other texts that will be read later in the program: *What makes a story satisfying to us? Is this a satisfying story? Why or why not? How does your understanding of a story change when others give their impressions?*

Nibasa, Rita Marie—"A Line of Cutting Women"

Genre: Short story

Theme: This is a crossroads story about choice versus pre-determination and cycles of violence. Can these cycles be broken?

Class Types: Women and Men. Also used with the Vulnerable Male Prisoners Unit (sexual predators, police, etc.) in the United Kingdom.

Lesson Plan by Jean Trounstine

This is a contemporary story about a young woman whose mother was a "cutter." Darlene is the "bad" girl and her sister, Mary, the perpetual helper. Trounstine says that in the story, we meet several characters who each represent a possible life choice. The mother has made her choice before the story begins and passes down the legacy to her daughters, causing Darlene to wonder if her mother has it right and if all men are the same. Mary takes in her wild sister and tries to teach her how to be what she wants her to be, and this, of course, is great fodder for discussion. Darlene, the unruly sister, gets hit by Ricky, a boy she calls "the son of a wife-beater" and defends herself by knifing him. The story then moves through Ricky and Darlene's meeting at which they each are faced with how they want to live and what they will do with blood on their hands.

The first time Trounstine used this story, during a Lynn-Lowell initial class session in which stories are always read aloud, its shock value alone carried the group into a great discussion. The women identified with Darlene, and if they didn't, they knew friends like Darlene. Everyone felt this story was "reality." Comments ranged from "The brutality of it struck me when Darlene says 'After all, I had a legacy to uphold,'" to "You see as a child what you learn." The students talked about how lifestyles get perpetuated, and the women had as much compassion for Ricky, the hitter, as for Darlene, the cutter. Both, they said, have a chance to change—if they want to.

Starting the class with the idea that all characters deserve compassion helps set the stage for what is to come. It allows the discussion to begin exactly where the students are. It doesn't scold. It lets the story open the door to discussion about the idea of change. It is a great example of allowing the text to be the teacher. Trounstine prods thought to help the group consider: *What does it mean to change? What would it take for these characters to change?*

This story also has power with male students. They focus on Darlene in much the same way as the women do, considering her lifestyle and her choices, but they identify with Ricky. Good conversation ensues when the group talks about Ricky's background, which they piece to-gether from clues in the story and from their own imaginations. *What was it like for Ricky at home? Why does Ricky feel the need to show off and hit Darlene?* Trounstine was taken by the depth with which this story hit male students as they considered what it must feel like to be challenged by a woman and to strike her. Some wondered what cutting was all about, for the woman and for the man. *Why does Ricky come to see her after Darlene has cut him?* Others wondered *what will happen to Ricky?* The question *"Does he have choices?"* propelled the class into a discussion on what makes change possible.

Mary, the sister, brings up the most conflict with both men and women. Some people hate her. Others say, "She is the only one who shouldn't be locked up." Mary also allows us to consider why people who come from the same household turn out so differently. And fi-nally, Mary makes us ask if being protective serves her or if she too is running from something.

Walker, Alice—"Everyday Use"

Genre: Short story

Themes: Reality vs. illusion; society's artificial boundaries; prostituted
   ideals (movements); love defining beauty and giving it meaning

Class Type: Men or Women

Lesson Plan by Trudy Schrandt

This is a story of a poor black family preparing for and living through a visit from the "successful" daughter (Dee). The mother has lived off the land and by her faith. She raised two daughters. One daughter (Maggie) was badly scarred in their house fire. The other is a beautiful, well-educated, "successful" woman living in the big city.

When Dee returns home, Momma and Maggie are afraid of her and a bit in awe of her. Throughout the story, Dee's values and commitment to her new life are revealed. By the end of the story, Momma has a new perspective on which daughter understands the world, its trials, and how to succeed in it as a true person.

Trudy Schrandt spends considerable time on comparison and contrast, as this holds the key to understanding the story. The conflicts are seen between Momma and what Dee wants of Momma; between Dee and her new persona, Wangero; between Dee and her sister, Maggie; and between Wangero and her companion. Many words are unfamiliar: *Polaroids, bench, butter churn, quilts, dashiki.*

Once these have been discussed, the story is pretty much laid out on the table. Schrandt can then begin discussion of Dee's flawed statement, "You ought to do something with yourself; it's really a new day for us." The question, "When is progress a step backward?" opens up a wonderful conversation.

The concept of what is real is an important part of the discussion. Following the crowd versus defining one's own self and standards often leads to good introspection by the class participants. More often than not, the concept of true love not being skin deep enters the conversation. Many of the participants have been rejected, and they feel scarred like Maggie. To discover the moral victory Maggie achieves because of who she is, not what front she presents, is often very rewarding, says Schrandt.

Although this is a story about a black family at the time of the Civil Rights Movement, it is much deeper than that. Its lessons easily resonate in the present day, and it presents many issues the participants deal with as they confront drugs, alcohol, decaying family values, and violence.

Wolff, Tobias—"The Rich Brother"
Genre: Short story
Theme: Sibling rivalry; family relationships; the meaning of "success"
Class Type: Men
Lesson Plan by Robert Waxler

"The Rich Brother" is a story about two brothers, Pete and Donald. Pete, the older brother, is an American middle-class success story, with money from real estate, a wife, two daughters, a house, and a sailboat. Donald, the younger brother, lives alone, paints houses, sometimes stays in an ashram in Berkeley, and always owes his brother money.

When the story opens, Donald has been tossed out of a communal farm, and Pete, as usual, goes to pick him up. In the car, Pete gives Donald $100 to hold, and they talk briefly about childhood memories, focusing on the times Pete babysat for Donald after Donald's operation. Pete, apparently, would purposely hit Donald on the parts of his body most vulnerable because of the recent operation.

"Do you remember when you used to try to kill me?" Donald asks.

"Kids do those things," Pete replies.

Donald wants to know about Pete's interior life. Does Pete ever dream about them? Pete would never tell Donald such intimate details of his life. But, in fact, he does have a repetitive dream in which Pete is blind and needs Donald's help.

As the group talks about the richness of this relationship, they begin to wonder about the richness of the story itself. Waxler may ask: *Where do we situate ourselves in the midst of this story? Should we celebrate Donald's sensitivity and vulnerability more than Pete's sense of distance and exterior success? If Pete really needed to ask Donald for help, would Donald be able to actually give it to him?*

As the story moves on, the two brothers pick up Webster, a man who tells them a mythic tale about his own experiences with dreams and relatives, gold mines and greed, family and friends. Eventually Donald gives the $100 Pete gave him to Webster in exchange for a share in a mythic gold mine; when Pete finds out what Donald has done, he throws his brother out of the car. More questions: *Would we do that? Where do we draw the line?*

The story is not quite over. As Pete drives away alone, listening to the music on the radio, he is already "slowing down" his thought process as well as the car, turning back, and thinking about his wife standing "before him in the doorway of his home," asking, "Where is he? Where is your brother?" Waxler says that Wolff's story resonates with Biblical overtones—Cain and Abel, Jacob and Esau, the Prodigal Son—reminding readers that sibling rivalry is an ancient story as well as a modern one, part of the family romance, deeply embedded in the human condition.

"Why does Pete pick on Donald when they are growing up?" Waxler asks. The responses vary:

> "Because he's jealous of Donald."
> "That's what older brothers do."
> "Their parents must have given Donald more attention because he was sick."

"And what about Webster?" Waxler wonders aloud.

> "Pete is right: Webster is a con artist."
> "Donald trusts everyone—that's his problem."
> "Pete trusts no one—that's his problem."
> "Webster takes advantage of people."
> "Webster is like Donald—he needs people to help him."

Near the end of the discussion, Waxler raises the crucial question of the story: *"Who is the rich brother?"* Most of the students say they assumed when first reading the story that Pete was clearly the only choice, but now they are not so sure. They are ready again to renew the conversation:

> "Pete has the resources; he's the rich one."
> "Pete is the responsible one; he wants to help his family, even his brother."
> "Pete has worked hard; he deserves his material success."
> "But Pete desires something more than he has—that's why he goes skydiving, for example."

"Yes, Donald needs Pete, but does Pete need Donald?" Waxler asks again, reminding the group around the table about the recurring dream Pete tells Donald about. Yes, perhaps Donald is the rich brother, some say. Carefree, trusting, spiritual. He has depth, an interior self. In any case, the two brothers need each other. They are part of the same family—as we all are.

10 CLTL Teaching Strategies

> *"This program opened up a whole new area of my life I never thought possible. I greatly appreciated the chance to be a part of it.*"
>
> —*Student,*
> *Kansas Program*

THE PROCESS OF FINDING ONE'S VOICE can take a lifetime, but through CLTL's skillful facilitation and support we help our students as they delve deeply into their lives and reconsider their choices. As teachers, our methods of approaching our students vary according to the instructor and the class and its dynamics. But we do have some tested strategies that might work for you; the ones listed here are adapted from facilitators' writings on the website at *http://cltl.umassd.edu.*

These strategies are not drawn from a particular educational or philosophic theory, but simply from experimenting with what might work in the classroom. They come out of a matrix that emphasizes fundamental CLTL beliefs. And in some ways they show different approaches that seem contradictory. In fact, each facilitator adds his or her own stamp to the strategies, and each group is filled with different voices.

Whether we are thinking about how to encourage reading itself or discussion of the reading, we in CLTL are always thinking about how verbal skills can be enhanced. For us language helps shape human identity, create stories, and build good communities. We have often observed significant leaps in literacy skills within a short period of time because people have made just this kind of connection among language, themselves, and the world that surrounds them. The stories we read and the stories we talk about help shape new life stories, just as the stories we bring to the table help us understand the stories read. The entire CLTL process is infused with this sense of language and story, and we are convinced that much of what we do reflects this kind of interaction. We offer in this chapter a few of the strategies that facilitators have found to be helpful in this regard.

STRATEGY 1: THE GO-ROUND

Trounstine has developed a pre-discussion strategy called the "Go-Round." Although it can be used with any group, it works best when most or all of the participants have read the material, and it should probably be reserved for those kinds of classes. It also works beautifully if you read a story aloud in class (a method Trounstine always uses on the first night of class—see Teaching Specific Texts: "A Line of Cutting Women" on page 202). Reading aloud ensures that everyone has read the material, but since the levels and understandings vary throughout a group and from group to group, Trounstine uses the Go-Round to aid participants' close reading skills.

Before discussion begins on any piece—story, novel or work of non-fiction—start by going around the table and eliciting each person's opinion on the text, one by one, with no other comments coming from other members. The idea is to give each person space to say exactly what she or he thinks, to let the diversity of opinions stand in the room before discussion begins. In other words, this technique allows listening as well as speaking, and it promotes an eventual civil dialogue.

Begin the Go-Round by posing a question such as: *What did you find most interesting (touching/angering/disturbing/important to you or whatever you choose) in the book and why? Or, Let's hear any reactions and thoughts you had about the book.*

Trounstine always asks a global question on the Go-Round for several reasons: It gives everyone a chance to figure out what they have to say; it also enables the facilitator to get a sense of how students understand the material and what is most important to them, and thus, offers stepping off places for the later discussion.

Trounstine always takes notes as they go around the table and comes back to the ideas, subjects, themes, characters, confusions (it is important to talk about the latter), and stories that participants bring up on this first pass. The facilitator may draw students out a bit, but there is no dialogue. When students want to argue, Trounstine asks them to hold their thoughts until each person has a chance to respond to the text. This also teaches them not just to react with their own ideas, but to consider each other's positions. Trounstine says this enhances, and never stifles, the upcoming discussion because it offers possibilities.

Beginning the class this way helps students know that they are responsible for the material, for having ideas, and for their participation in the class. They may feel afraid at first, but Trounstine also uses this time to be extremely positive about anything they say, and to nod and encourage the thoughts they voice. For the students who want to go on and on, the facilitator might gently let them know that they will have other opportunities later to talk. This also helps anchor the class and provide a focus.

As an example of the Go-Round technique, when Trounstine used *To Kill a Mockingbird* one semester, she asked: *What is it in this book that is most compelling to you? What themes or ideas draw you in the most?* That question seemed as useful to someone who had read the book several times (the probation officer and the judge, as well as a visitor and one student) as it was to the student who had slept through the book discussion in high school. In that initial conversation, one person said how much she loved the father, Atticus Finch, and his relationship with his children. The next class participant said how the father was anything but real, an absolute "fantasy father." Another brought up race relations and the impact that the book had on her in that area and completely ignored the father; another said that because she lived with an African-American man, she knew racism from another angle and saw the book through those eyes.

Part of what makes the Go-Round important is the fact that a question without a set answer really has the most power in provoking a discussion of literature. Trounstine says that as all of us come from our own unique perspectives, we begin to see how different we are, how much we take in as individuals, and yet, at the same time, how others' insights resonate with us and often reveal our common humanity.

STRATEGY 2: IDENTIFYING WITH THE STORIES

For Waxler, too, there is no meaning without context; one strategy developed in the New Bedford program emerges from that notion. Waxler believes that we find ourselves in the stories we read and discuss, gain perspective on our own relationship to something beyond ourselves, and so begin to understand where we are and where we might be headed. This presents a significant challenge for the CLTL facilitator: how best to get everyone talking and how best to get each person to articulate perspectives and still preserve the story itself.

Waxler assumes that everyone on any night has read the same story and is eager to talk about it with the group. But each participant has also read the story in his own way, mapping his own story onto the one just read. Waxler wants to listen to and honor each voice, each version of the story, and at the same time deepen the context of the written text to make the story a genuinely communal one.

One strategy Waxler uses to achieve this goal is to continually repeat the important points that come up in the discussion. It is a way of re-contextualizing the story over and over again, giving it increased depth and dimension. Waxler doesn't want to interfere with the other voices around the table, doesn't want to bend the conversation too much to one perspective. But the facilitator's voice is filtering the other voices, so Waxler suggests remaining as sensitive as possible to the goal of creating a mutilayered context that is inclusive.

A short, disturbing story provides an example of this strategy: Raymond Carver's "Tell the Women We're Going." Waxler might ask to begin the conversation about this troubling tale of male violence, *What do we know about Bill Jamison and Jerry Roberts, the two male characters in the story?* The facilitator wants to hear the participants' voices first before he speaks and the multidimensional responses to the questions:

> "They shared everything growing up—same girls, same teachers, same clothes, same jobs, same cars."
> "Yes, they were like blood brothers."
> "Jerry dropped out of school senior year, though, and got married to Carol."
> "Right, and Bill got married a few years later, when they were twenty-two, to Linda."
> "Yes, and Jerry and Carol have two kids, with another one 'in the oven.'"

Waxler listens and then begins to move the story and the discussion forward. "Okay. Now early in the story Bill and Linda are going over to see Jerry and Carol on the weekend—like they usually do. *How come? Why don't Jerry and Carol come to see them?*" And more voices around the table:

> "Jerry and Carol have too much stuff to drag around."
> "And Bill seems always to be following Jerry anyway, since they were kids."
> "Jerry seems depressed too. He isn't talking much."
> "They're drinking beer, just the two of them."
> "The women are together in the kitchen."

This is the beginning, the conversation taking shape. Waxler helps provide context and direction, but the voices are all interesting and diverse. Waxler doesn't want to lose the energy or the arc of the discussion at this point but now wants to pause, create an opportunity to begin to reflect on the implications so far, deepen the texture of the talk, and enhance the self-reflective nature of the talk itself. This strategy is to summarize what has been said, weave a few of the facilitator's own thoughts into the conversation, and then focus on a couple of the threads dangling out there.

"So we have two guys who have known each other much longer than they have known their wives: a male friendship, a male bond that seems to precede their relations with women. This is not unusual." Waxler might suggest moving the conversation ahead after repeating several other main points of the discussion.

And then, the facilitator looks for something more concrete, closer to the details of the text itself: "And Jerry isn't talking very much. He's getting 'deep,' Bill thinks. They tell the women they're going, and they are out on the road, headed to the local bar."

Hoping to further turn up the plot ground and the intensity of the discussion, Waxler might ask, *And then what happens?*

"They go to shoot some pool in the local bar."
"They drink a lot of beer in the bar—almost two six packs."
"They talk to Riley, the bartender, about girls."
"Jerry mashes his beer can."
"There are no girls in the bar."

How to further deepen the context at this point? For Waxler, the story is revealing a pattern embedded deep in American culture: male bonding, male brooding, male drinking, males driving on the road, and males together in the bars—all of which the students have talked about. Now they see that such patterns can be contrasted with marriage, wives and children, family, home, and domestic space—other parts of the story already raised in the discussion thus far.

Waxler might think, *What is the analogy? Is there a way of connecting this story now with larger social and cultural patterns?*

Although perhaps not obvious at first, Waxler might suggest that the story as discussed so far seems similar to the classic American Western: freewheeling cowboys together in the bar, thinking about bar girls, troubled by the Sunday school teacher from Boston who just arrived on the stagecoach to "civilize" them. Waxler feels this is a story about American male perception, the American male frontier shaping our violence, the American mythic story of the West. All of this enhances the context, demonstrating that stories map onto other stories, that the context of one story can be another story, that the story of our lives is multidimensional and rich in possibilities.

"So we have two scenes here so far. One at home (domestic space) where Jerry is troubled. One in the bar (frontier space) where Jerry and Bill drink and shoot pool together," Waxler might suggest now. And then, another question moves the conversation forward: *"But what about Jerry—why is he so troubled?"* And then, the other voices:

"His wife is pregnant."

"He is weighted down at home."

"He never had a chance to finish sowing his wild oats in high school."

"He doesn't want all that responsibility—wife and kids and job."

"He is tired of working so hard."

"He wishes he was back in high school with Bill."

Those voices now resonate with the depth of all the contexts mentioned, of all the stories hinted at.

Waxler then moves to the third scene of Carver's story, focusing on a few details: Out on the road again, Jerry spots two girls on bicycles.

The two guys stop, try to pick the girls up, eventually follow them to Picture Rock.

And then Waxler will comment on how the language of the story from now until the end grows increasingly violent. Waxler will read a passage directly from the text to secure the point: "But it started and ended with a rock. Jerry used the same rock on both girls, first on the girl called Sharon and then on the one that was supposed to be Bill's." But then another moment of self-reflection, another question: *Why does it happen?* And the voices wrestle with all that has gone out, the depth of the reading and the discussion:

"The girls don't want to have anything to do with these guys."
"Jerry feels rejected."
"Jerry blames the girls."
"He thinks women are the problem."
"He won't take responsibility for his problems."
"He wants to show Bill he is in control."
"Jerry is out of control because he feels he has no power."
"Jerry hates himself and needs somebody to blame."
"Jerry hates all women and blames them all."

If this strategy has succeeded, no one has been left out. Waxler has helped to weave new connections between this story and other stories, has allowed everyone to live through language, and has helped shape that language to lead away from violence toward community.

STRATEGY 3: SPEAKING UP IN SMALL GROUPS

For Taylor Stoehr, it is the discussions that make CLTL so important, so he likes to use small groups as a central teaching strategy. Following is an adaptation of what Stoehr wrote for *http://cltl.umassd.edu.*

Stoehr feels that under traditional classroom conditions, a few bolder students often lock horns over some issue, while everyone else sits back to watch the show. This can be fun, but it doesn't usually lead anywhere. These debates tend to arise and pass like miniature tornados, all wind and noise one moment, empty silence the next. In a group like Stoehr's CLTL, "there will always be a few gifted orators who enjoy a rousing argument in front of an audience, often over very minor differences of opinion. Sometimes there is a compulsive talker who handles his own public anxiety by going into a street-corner mantra, or someone who has had a conversion experience of one kind or another, often in prison, and needs to reassure himself by telling others: 'I was a sinner but now I'm saved!' "

The challenge to listeners is to hear the depth of that voice, but the call can ring hollow, and the line between authentic self-renewal and ritual self-dramatization is sometimes very thin. In Stoehr's classes he hears both the true voice and the false one, sometimes in the same person at different times during the semester. Usually the other students wait respectfully until the orators run out of steam or begin to hear themselves rambling. But when there are three or four such platform speakers in Stoehr's class, they invariably fall into debating style, and testifying becomes wrangling, each man trying to hold the floor against all comers. A teacher usually has to out-shout them all to get back on track.

Stoehr remembers one loud four-way argument in which no one was listening or trying to find common ground, when, in the midst of his rant, one of the participants abruptly held up his hand like a traffic cop and called himself to a halt: "Why are we yelling at each other like this? It's part of our problem, it's why we have so much trouble in our lives. We don't know how to listen!" Stoehr doesn't remember his exact words, but his sudden insight brought everyone in the room to a thoughtful silence. Sheepish grins broke out on the faces of the worst offenders.

Stoehr says that at the other extreme, there are always a number of painfully shy probationers who sit in the corners or near the door, hoping to survive ten weeks without being called on. They too have their moments of self-discovery, just like the preachers and performers. Of course most of these tight-lipped students want to join in the conversation, and they envy the talkers with whom they chat easily enough before and after class. They arrive every night resolved to raise their hands and say something, but the opportunity never seems to arise. Even when a man gets up his nerve, chances are that the topic will shift before he can put in his two cents.

Stoehr says he will never forget the last meeting of a semester, when a 40-year-old recovering alcoholic in the back corner raised his hand. Never before had he had the guts to volunteer a single word in a schoolroom, but class had finally freed his tongue. Now at last he was breaking his long silence; he had found his voice! No one realized how desperately he had been trying to speak up.

After everyone else had gone home that night, the probation officers and Stoehr lingered, marveling at this testimony. But even then it never occurred to Stoehr to think about what this event implied for a whole row of other students in the back of the room. The hindrance to speaking up wasn't really in the students, but in the traditional school-oriented approach to public discourse. But it took Stoehr a long time to realize that it would be better to do away with the general class discussion altogether and find an alternative format in which it would take less courage to offer an opinion.

Even for those students who are not shy, the typical class discussion presents serious logistical problems. As the opportunity to speak moves back and forth, moderated by the instructor, each remark may get people thinking, but the perspective keeps shifting slightly with every new contribution. That can be engrossing for those who are content to sit and listen, but it can be frustrating for the student with a bright idea or counter-argument, who finds that the topic has changed by the time he or she gets a chance to speak. Stoehr says most people give up; only a few keep waving their hands to yank the discussion back to where it was five minutes ago. Even the best moderator will have trouble keeping a topic alive long enough to canvass all opinions, usually by virtue of controlling the movement of thought with a constant stream of interpretation and recapitulation.

In recent years, Stoehr says, there has been a shift in colleges toward small-group discussions, mostly in Freshman English and English as a Second Language classes, stemming from the radical pedagogy of Paulo Freire and his disciples, who regard literacy training as a means to self-empowerment. Paradoxically, in Dorchester, Stoehr and the others came to their own small-group strategy not to get the voiceless people to speak so much as to shut up a few loudmouths.

Stoehr still remembers the moment of decision, in the middle of a Tuesday night class years ago. He was moderating a class of fifteen, with three probation officers. There happened to be four or five monologists in the class who were competing with each other, not letting anyone else say a word. It had been interesting the first few weeks—a talkative class!—but now it was boring and frustrating. The only good effect was that their harangues made others want to talk. But try as he might, Stoehr couldn't clear any space for genuine discussion.

It occurred to him that he could divide the class into four small groups, with all the vociferous ones off in a corner together. Stoehr put a probation officer in each of the other three groups to spark conversation if necessary, and he sat up on the front desk to watch the results. It worked like a charm: From then on, a portion of every class was set aside for small-group conversation, varying the mix of students and probation officers each time and letting the segregated orators work out their own rules for sharing the floor.

Of course, Dorchester facilitators recognize that small-group conversations can be just as digressive or polarized as general discussions, but it makes a huge difference to have the speakers right there next to you, where you can take in other faces at a glance and make eye contact when you disagree with someone. Issues may shift and the focus may wander, but you feel like you're getting somewhere when you can keep track of what each one has been saying. Stoehr points out that two or three people can be talking at once, and you can still make sense of it, whereas in a large group that's just a shouting match. Similarly, if a man sits silent, it means something entirely different in a small group than it does in a larger one. His eyes tell you whether he's listening, and he's part of your group no matter what, whereas in a larger body the non-speakers disappear in the background.

In making such comparisons Stoehr does not mean to say that a larger forum has no advantages, but prior spadework in small groups helps general discussion bear fruit. Once a reflective mood and conversational rhythms have been established, it's much easier for participants to move to public assembly without being stifled by the more formal situation. Arriving at consensus in a small group means that people have to listen to each other and make compromises.

Once issues are framed and positions identified, something is at stake for everyone, and the simple fact that the chairs are still arranged in small circles helps people feel part of a constituency when the larger discussion is reconvened. Somebody from a group is always ready to back up others, and that in turn gives each a place in the larger forum. It's this net of pro-tem allegiances woven in face-to-face conversation that the Dorchester group relies on to make "safe" the scary public performance.

Stoehr says that once they lose their fear of the spotlight, even the most bashful and inarticulate CLTL students sometimes blossom into astonishing eloquence. But the success of the program is not to be measured by its drama, though it makes a good story. Stoehr is satisfied with a modest increase in earnestness and self-respect. If a student is moving in the right direction, inching forward is better than a risky leap he or she is not really ready for, even if there is a safety net. Perhaps most important, students complete Dorchester's class having experienced what it is like to participate in a genuine public forum where ideas are treated seriously and everyone has a voice. Stoehr feels that's a key step toward being a responsible citizen in a society based on shared experience and mutual support.

STRATEGY 4: USE OF QUESTIONS

One of Trounstine's favorite quotes is from *Night* by Elie Wiesel, author of the Nobel Prize-winning book about his experience as a child in the Holocaust. In *Night,* he says that the power of a question lies less in its answer than in the sheer fact that it exists. Finding questions that provoke real conversation and real thought are what makes the CLTL classroom ring with truth. Some questions aren't answerable, but trying to answer them make us dig into our psyches and leads us toward a deeper self-examination and awareness of community.

Using questions in the classroom is as old as teaching itself. Who can imagine the great philosophers teaching their students without asking thought-provoking questions? And who among us cannot think of a time when someone asked us a question that took us into our inner selves? Questions help organize the discussion of texts, and they certainly help us link texts and themes. But Trounstine particularly likes questions that help students link the texts to their own lives—questions they may come back to a few weeks later or think about at home.

Some of the more provocative questions Trounstine has used from a few select books follow. Some of these books are also referenced in Chapters 8 and 9. When we ask questions about the text, everyone has the opportunity to talk in-depth about the text itself; inevitably the conversation goes beyond the text, and the direction it takes often depends upon the probes.

Included here is the basic version of each of Trounstine's questions. But inevitably a question needs fine-tuning, depending on the group, and some follow-up to help the responders engage more deeply with the text. That is all part of using questions to get to deeper ground. So in some places, Trounstine also indicates a way to get the question rumbling around inside by enclosing the additional questions you could ask in parentheses.

The Bluest Eye, **Toni Morrison**

1. Toni Morrison says this is a woman's story. Do you agree with her? Why or why not? (What does it mean to be a woman's story? Is there a difference between a man's and a woman's story? Have you felt your story to be gender-based? The story of your friends and family members?)

2. How do we learn to feel ugly? (What is ugly? Is it defined universally? Is it different in different cultures? How do we get ideas about what is ugly or what is beautiful? From what sources?)

3. If you had "the bluest eyes" or something that meant as much to you as the blue eyes do to Pecola, would they make you happy?

4. Do we give up things in this society in order to fit in? Do we have to give up things in order to fit in?

5. What does it mean to be a victim? Who are the victims in this book?

6. What does it mean to be abused? To be an abuser? Who is abused, and who abuses? Does Cholly think he is actually loving Pecola? Do you think he is loving Pecola?

Dinner at the Homesick Restaurant, **Anne Tyler**

1. What does it mean to be nostalgic for home? (Define nostalgia. When have you felt it? Think of these words put together: *home* and *sick*.)

2. Why do we go to restaurants? What are we looking for when we do?

3. What do we learn in this book about dying and death? (What does the word *dying* seem to mean to each of the characters? How do you know?)

4. Which character do you have most sympathy for in this family saga? Who will have happiness, and who won't? Who will have success? Who will live a life of regret? Who is most like you, and who would you want to be?

5. What does it mean to be wounded? What does it mean to be healed? (Think about wounding. Think about the archery incident and what gets wounded. Think about healing. Where do you see healing in the book?)

The Bean Trees, **Barbara Kingsolver**

1. What do we learn from this book about friendship? About family? About community?
2. What does it mean to be a good mother? A bad mother? (Define the qualities of mothering. Do you need to be a biological mother to be motherly? To be unmotherly? Think of men who are nurturing. Is there a difference?)
3. (This question would be asked after discussing the Cherokee Nation and the Guatemalan Civil War of the 1960s.) What is your reaction to the hiding of refugees and the way in which Taylor ultimately keeps Turtle?
4. What would draw us to go on a search across the country? What would be the dangers of doing so? What would compel us to leave and to stay?

Their Eyes Were Watching God, Zora Neale Hurston

1. How do we learn through our failed dreams? (What makes a dream, a dream? What's the difference between a dream and a fantasy? Do women dream about different things than men dream about? What makes a failure or a success?)

2. What is love? What does the book tell us about love? Does this story leave out the suffering in love? (Does love require suffering?)

3. What does this mean: "They seemed to be staring at the dark but their eyes were watching God?"

4. What does this book show us about being a woman? (What have each of the books we've read shown us about being a woman?)

5. What does it mean "to grow?" How does Janie change? Is her growth in any way familiar to you? How do we know when we've changed?

STRATEGY 5: INSPIRING STUDENT WRITING

Tam Neville facilitates discussions in our Dorchester, Massachusetts, women's program. She writes on *http://cltl:umassd.edu* that writing and reading are closely tied together. She has developed a teaching strategy using a passage from a text to inspire students in their own writing. Neville wants reading and writing to become infectious.

She starts with one or two students reading an especially good passage aloud from the text they are focused on. After a brief discussion of the passage, she asks the students to freewrite on the subject of the passage as inspiration. The students can also write in imitation of the style of the passage.

The technique can be used with almost any form of literature: fiction, poetry, or memoirs. The passage should be one the facilitator really likes so she can communicate her enthusiasm to the class.

Neville has used the following passage from "Ask Me, Ask Me, Ask Me" by Roddy Doyle to inspire the students to write:

> Where I grew up—and probably elsewhere—you were a slut or a tight bitch, one or the other, if you were a girl, and usually before you were thirteen. You didn't have to do anything to be a slut. If you were good-looking; if you grew up fast. If you had a sexy walk; if you had clean hair, if you had dirty hair. If you wore platform shoes, and if you didn't. Anything could get you called a "slut."

She likes the strong and direct spoken voice behind it.

STRATEGY 6: MORE WRITING IN CLTL

Jane Hale also uses writing in her CLTL sessions. She makes it a practice to include a short writing assignment in each session, for the same reasons that she emphasizes writing in her teaching outside of the program. For Hale, spoken and written language are both evidence of and tools for the organization of thoughts; they make order out of the disorder inside our heads. She says that to the extent we can formulate into spoken and written words whatever is troubling or confusing us, we can look at it more objectively and calmly. The ability and desire to control—or at least give some form to—the chaos of our minds through language can save us from becoming absorbed into the random internal monologues and raw emotions that draw us away from compassion for and understanding of others.

Hale says it is no secret that the ability to write well is key to success in our society today. In fact, those who do not write well often keep this fact their own shameful and painful secret. Giving students the opportunity to formulate their thoughts leads them to discoveries in their writing and helps them practice and perfect this aspect of their linguistic power. Likewise, the discussions that form the core of the class experience help students achieve the eloquence and clarity associated with effective perspectives.

It is essential to the cooperative, non-hierarchical spirit of the CLTL group that all participants, including facilitator, judge, and probation officers, participate fully in Hale's writing assignments. Nobody in her class is exempt from doing everything they can to formulate their thoughts as eloquently and clearly as possible, even if they do not wish to share them.

Writing assignments also vary the activity and pace of the CLTL class, says Hale, affording everyone five or ten minutes of quiet introspection in an individualistic endeavor that is subsequently put to work in group conversations. While nobody is required to share his or her writing with the group, most students do so willingly. Hale makes sure to let group members know that they will read and exchange their papers with other group members, as well as to turn them in to her, so they might wish to refrain from writing down painfully confidential information that they would rather keep private.

Hale encourages everyone to use personal journals. She gives them the option of giving her their writing with the notation "confidential" written on the top of the page, so she will not share their words with the rest of the class or publish them in the end-of-term souvenir booklet that Hale puts together.

Hale places writing at different points in the class period, depending on where each assignment best fits the discussion and on her desire to vary class structure to keep things from going stale. Sometimes students write at the beginning of the evening to have some formulated thoughts to refer to as the discussion begins. This is especially useful for shy students who hesitate to contribute to discussions because they "can't think of anything to say." Sometimes students write just before break, and leave the room individually or in pairs as they finish.

When they all come back to finish the session, incorporating what they have written into the discussion is a good way to increase class participation and personal revelations as the evening proceeds. Hale may ask students to read what they or their neighbor have written to the class, to share their writing in pairs or small groups, or to use their written thoughts to inform their oral interventions. Sometimes she ends the evening with a written assignment to give a reflective closure to what has often been a lively and spirited exchange. This final placement of the individual writing assignment highlights the importance of the students' personal perspectives on the discussion, allowing them to have the last word, at least for that evening. Hale then collects the papers and reads them. She opens the next session by reading aloud excerpts from the previous week's writing, so students can benefit from the thoughts of their peers, and so they can all get the themes of the course—and of each group member's life—back on the table for continued consideration.

At the end of the course, Hale publishes excerpts from student writing assignments, along with the syllabus, book list, and suggestions for further reading (from both her and the students) for each class member to take home as a souvenir, as well as a concrete affirmation of the value of their written words to their teacher and fellow classmates.

Sample writing questions used for various texts and purposes are listed.

> ❑ At the end of the first night, after several stories have been read, Hale asks:
>
>   1. Which of tonight's stories did you enjoy most? Why?
>   2. What kind of stories would you like to read in the course? Do you have any titles to suggest?
>
> ❑ *Brothers and Keepers* (Hale asks students to choose one to answer.)
>
>   1. "It's like I wanted things to be easy, and misguidedly tried to make everything that way, blinded then to the fact that nothing good or worthwhile comes without serious effort. . . . Always wanted things to be easy; so instead of dealing with things as they were, I didn't deal with them at all. I ducked hard things that took effort or work and tried to have fun, make a party, cause that was always easy."
>
>   Comment on how Robby's tendency to "take the easy way" wound up not being so easy after all for him.
>
>   2. Tell about a time in your life when you tried to take the easy way.
>   3. Tell about something good or worthwhile that has come about in your life from serious effort.
>
> ❑ "A Jury of Her Peers" *(*Again, Hale asks students to choose one to answer.)
>
>   1. If you were on the jury for Mrs. Wright's trial for killing her husband, how would you find—guilty or not guilty? If guilty, what sentence would you recommend? Explain. (Assume you have been presented all the evidence given in this story, that you know everything that both the women and the men do.)
>   2. Finish this statement: "If a jury of my peers judged me. . . ."
>
> ❑ In "The Lottery," The author is trying to show that. . . .

- "A Woman on a Roof" shows the following about men and women:
- "Where Are You Going, Where Have You Been?" shows the following about men and women:
- Neddy Merrill (in "The Swimmer") is the kind of man who. . . .
- In "The Last Time I Seen My Father":
  1. If I were the narrator, I would have. . . .
  2. The worst family holiday of my life was when. . . .
- For "I Stand Here Ironing":
  Pretend you are your mother (or father, or grandmother, etc.—some person who raised you). Describe what you were like as you were growing up, from their perspective.
- For "Sonny's Blues":
  1. My possibilities in life are. . . .
  2. The neighborhood I grew up in. . . .
  3. How do you account for the very different outcomes of the two brothers' lives?
  4. What's missing inside of Sonny?
  5. Why doesn't the narrator give his own name?
  6. What does Sonny want?
- For *The House on Mango Street*, write about:
  1. A house you lived in during your childhood.
  2. Your name.
- For "A Telephone Call":
  1. Describe the type of male-female relationship shown in this story. Is it a healthy one? Is it a common one?
  2. Pretend you are an advice columnist. The woman in this story writes you for advice about what to do: whether to call the guy, whether she's in a healthy relationship. Write her letter and your response, or, if you want, just write your response.
- For "Sexy":
  In one class, Hale says that the last page of this story was omitted by mistake when copies were handed out to students. So the

first thing they did in the class when the group discussed it was to make up endings. Then they checked out what the author had written and compared participants' imaginations to hers.

- ❏ For *Of Mice and Men:*
    1. Close your eyes. Which scene in the book springs to mind? Describe it.
    2. Tell of a dream you have had (or still have) that's as important to you as George and Lennie's is to them.

STRATEGY 7: USE OF POETRY

Ann Brian Murphy knows that poetry works especially well in CLTL classes. She asks students to read a short poem on a contemporary issue and then to respond to it with questions, comments, and reactions. She says that by doing so they'll discover that the process of reading—even something as intimidating as poetry—can be exciting, interesting, and challenging. And we find that they ask fresh and original questions, leading them often into the heart of the text, illuminating the poem for all.

Murphy started using poetry in the CLTL class to introduce students to ways of reading literature on the first night. She found, however, that the students do great poetry readings. They have very few preconceptions about what they are "supposed" to say, for one thing, so they often ask insightful questions and cut straight to the heart of the poem. Further, poems are compact and complete, difficult but ultimately accessible, and reading them gives students a sense of pride and accomplishment. So now Murphy does poems in almost every class, often selecting ones that enhance or comment on the essay, story, or novel they are reading.

First, Murphy reads the poem aloud, pausing at the end of each line or thought, and asking students to write their comments, questions, ideas, and reactions. If they don't know what to say, she tells them to write what they think the poem is saying.

Once they finish reading the poem, Murphy invites them to discuss their reactions and to read aloud phrases or sentences they find powerful or puzzling. This allows her to stress that being puzzled is not a sign of failure but an opportunity to ask questions and find connections.

After they discuss their reactions to the poem, they turn to the reading questions they have developed: *Who is the speaker? What is the setting? Where do we see imagery?* They discuss how those questions illuminate or complicate the poem. And finally, Murphy asks them to write what they see as the main themes and ideas of the poem, and they discuss all the reactions to those ideas.

Some suggested poems include: "The Abandoned Newborn" by Sharon Olds; "Miss Rosie" by Lucille Clifton; "Mother to Son" by Langston Hughes; "My Papa's Waltz" by Theodore Roethke; "To Be of Use" by Marge Piercy; and "St. Francis and the Sow" by Galway Kinnell.

STRATEGY 8: RAP TO POETRY

Jean Flanagan also loves poetry and has developed an interesting teaching strategy using rap music to teach poetry. Students are asked to bring their favorite compact disc (CD) to class and to discuss why they like the particular music and lyrics.

Flanagan begins class by playing the CDs and asking the students what they like about each CD—the music, lyrics, or both. At the same time, they are given a packet of poems written by contemporary local area poets. They go over these poems and discuss the meanings, examining where the power comes from. They analyze poems using these ideas and discuss whether the lyrics are a poem.

They also go over class poems. Students are asked to write a rap song and to then imitate "This Is Just to Say" by William Carlos Williams and "We Real Cool" by Gwendolyn Brooks by using lines from these poems to create their own.

STRATEGY 9: USE OF FILM WITH LITERATURE

Cherie Muehlberger from our Kansas CLTL Program believes that because we are a visually oriented society, using film with literature is a good teaching strategy. We can give a visual dimension to a piece of literature we have read and perhaps lend another interpretation. The video will provide further discussion.

Muehlberger has used this strategy with the novel *Of Mice and Men* (the film title is the same), *Man's Search for Meaning* (the film title is *Life Is Beautiful*), and *A Simple Plan* (the film title is the same). After thoroughly discussing *Of Mice and Men*, she shows the last 20 minutes of the film starring Gary Sinese and John Malkovich. It is a touching recreation of the theme of the novel—friendship—and provides a poignant and memorable ending to their session.

Muehlberger discusses the concentration camp experience through *Man's Search for Meaning*. Then she shows *Life Is Beautiful* (the subtitled edition), and the CLTL group views the concentration camp experience from a different perspective: the father/son relationship. They then discuss the sacrifice and love that are evident in the film.

For *A Simple Plan*, Muehlberger discusses the implications of trust and collaboration when crime is involved. Then, as a group, they go to the theater to watch the movie. The ending of the film was changed, so that is discussed as well as some of the film's interpretations of events.

STRATEGY 10: THE ROLE OF THE JUDGE IN THE CLTL CLASSROOM

Taylor Stoehr says that probationers come into our program brooding on their personal experiences in court or jailhouse. Whatever their awareness of their own innocence or guilt, there are always some students who view the entire social order as rigged against them, though they rarely have more than newspaper headlines for arguments or their own lives as evidence. For these angry men—and perhaps even more for those who passively accept their fate—it can be a salutary shock to realize that the criminal justice system is not a cruel and unrelenting instrument of retribution, but an evolving institution open to criticism and change.

Stoehr says if we want to encourage a more balanced and reflective view of their situation as criminal offenders, one tactic is to try to demystify the system itself by presenting ourselves as its personal embodiment—a little group of real people who serve as teachers, probation officers, and judges in society's impersonal institutions. For many of our students, this may be the first time in their lives that a teacher or other authority figure has entered into open-ended dialogue with them, outside the rules of role and format. This does not mean that authority relationships vanish in the classroom—a teacher is still a teacher, a judge still a judge—but these are not the faces we wear as we sit with the students.

In the Changing Lives classroom, teachers and probation officers inevitably remind students of all the admonishers out of their past, but it's much more emphatic when we add a judge to the row of authorities. By virtue of his or her title and office, the judge certainly does represent the court, and some of the probationers in our group may have been tried and sentenced before this very judge! But in the CLTL classroom, a judge's authority usually sits so lightly that students are not intimidated.

The important thing, Stoehr says, is that the judge who participates in a CLTL program comes to class without black robes and is not towering over us from the bench, but is sitting in the midst of everyone on equal footing in discussions and doing the homework like the rest of us. Reminders of the judge's authority may hover round the person like an aura—the judge is often the only one in the room who isn't called by a first name, for instance, but is addressed simply as "Judge." Yet by and large it's the actual man or woman and not "Your Honor" who is participating in the group.

Stoehr points out that in graduation ceremonies at the end of the semester, judges invariably take the opportunity to say why they value the program so much. They explain to the probationers and the entire courtroom that contact on a personal level with those who come before them to be judged reminds them they are dealing with human beings, not "cases." Guilty or innocent, their lives are full of pain and suffering, mistakes they regret, anger and self-pity they yearn to be done with—just like the rest of us. As a judge pronounces these words from the bench, he or she brings the semester to a close with a sobering message about the nature of public justice, those who administer it, and those who come before it as offenders.

Judges can be a calming influence without robbing a young man or woman of pride. Stoehr says "a young dude could ask Tom May in Dorchester about his own experience in the streets, in the Marines, as a father, as a citizen angry at the politicians, as a judge worried about injustice. He could argue with him about Malcolm X or the jury system. Often the liveliest conversations would occur in these small groups, where the younger probationers are finding their tongues for the first time in a classroom. One could hear Tom's even voice alternating with their excited speeches."

The core problem of the CLTL classroom is how to preserve a probationer's individual autonomy in a high-stakes encounter with authority and its representatives. It is possible to carry authority without brandishing it like a scepter or a club, and sitting across from one another week after week, in earnest conversation, strips away initial illusions and uncovers authentic grounds of respect in all of us. Stoehr says that each man or woman acquires his or her own moral authority as we hammer out an ethical consensus regarding issues we all know something about, probationers as much as staff.

Although carefully chosen readings can focus group discussion on crucial personal behavior issues for our students, Stoehr believes that the essential factor in the CLTL approach to moral growth and self-respect lies in this public exercise of the ethical imagination, deliberating on problems of social, economic, and criminal justice with the actual authorities responsible for them—judges and probation officers who are revealed as striving and fallible human beings just like the rest of us.

STRATEGY 11: A SYLLABUS AS A TEACHING STRATEGY

While our syllabi not only demonstrate the kinds of texts we use and include suggested time periods for CLTL classes as well as our expectations, they can also provide clues as to how we might get students engaged in thinking from the beginning.

Trounstine always begins with the same poem at the top of the syllabus, using this poem, which seems simple at first but becomes more complex on the second and third read. This takes the Lynn-Lowell women through a close reading that initial night and helps them understand what is expected. After a brief introduction of the program and introductions, Trounstine asks, *What do you need to know in order to understand this poem?* They then read aloud this poem by Barbara Helfgott Hyett from *In Evidence:*

> At the University Theatre in Harvard Square,
> I went to see The True Glory and I was still in uniform.
> When they showed the films of Dachau,
> the woman who sat beside me said, "That's a lie."
> I was rugged in those days. I just couldn't take it.
> I said, 'Lady I've been there. I still smell the stench.'
> And I said it loud and all the people heard."

The poem prompts students to read and re-read, to mention things they want to understand, such as "Dauchau," "Harvard Square," or "*The True Glory*," pictures they have in their heads of black-and-white documentary footage of bodies, words that need interpretation such as *rugged.* They have to think about the meaning of words as they wrestle with who the poem's speaker is and why he (or she as they question at first) is still in uniform. They come up with images of the theatre where this scene takes place and the woman who says, "That's a lie." Through questions and coaxing, Trounstine helps them put meaning around their images.

As the CLTL group works on this poem together, they also begin to deepen their reactions to the speaker. Trounstine does not tell them until the end of the discussion that the speaker is the voice of a soldier who liberated concentration camps during the Holocaust. As each participant adds something to the discussion, they also learn that they are smarter together than alone, that our individual sense of the world is enriched by others' perspectives. The poem is read a second time after the discussion, and everyone always remarks how much more they now understand.

After that discussion, students say that they feel more confident. This hands-on demonstration also shows them they can be successful with text.

The group proceeds through the syllabus, as Trounstine reads aloud. The rest of the syllabus provides some comments, turning the experience into an interactive one.

> This is a poem, indeed a powerful poem, that asks us to respond. It is a piece of literature, and one that raises questions. It expects us to know about the Holocaust and to be aware of Dachau. Perhaps it leaves us glad that the poem exists, that someone speaks the truth.

> In Changing Lives Through Literature, we will be discussing many pieces of literature that ask you to respond, to think, to question, and to feel. You are expected to engage yourselves in the texts and to be prepared to offer what you see in the readings. Reading closely is the first step. As you progress, you will become involved with the characters and have strong opinions about the books. They may disturb you or make you laugh. But all in all, literature is a way for us to examine our own lives and to feel less alone in our journey.

After going through these more philosophical understandings about the text, students have an easier time understanding what is expected of them by "reading closely." In addition, the actual requirements are clearly stated so students see their responsibilities spelled out. It is important to take students step by step to this point so that there is more willingness and less fear when they arrive at what they are required to do. When the classroom tone is warm and accepting, it is easier to move into the more demanding aspects of participation:

> You are required to attend all seven sessions and the graduation session, to read all the materials, and to contribute to the class conversations. You must call your probation officer if there is a problem and make up work missed. Missing a class may cause you to be dropped from the program.

Trounstine always allows the demands to settle in gently. Everyone knows that there is something required, more responsibility to this program than some may have bargained for; others realize that they will have to push themselves to attend, show up, and be present. But now, after the small syllabus exercise, they see why: They recognize that something might actually happen to them in this class.

Trounstine sees heads nodding when asking students if they have trouble when they first begin a book. They all share tips, suggestions, and reveal their own ways of getting into texts. Trounstine tells them the next part of the syllabus can help them along:

> Read a little each night so you finish the book in your two weeks. Books are handed out in class, and they are yours to keep. I recommend that you make notes on the book before coming to class each time. These notes should include in particular your observations about the characters. What kind of people are they? Why do they do what they do? Do they change during the story?

After they go through this together, Trounstine goes over the particular texts with each class—very generally, reminding them that they are in a college and that this is a college reading list. Students like this; it makes them feel special and proud, right away. For example, the fourteen weeks may look like this:

SYLLABUS (Readings due on the date listed)

Tuesday, September 26:
Joyce Carol Oates, "Where Are You Going, Where Have You Been?"

Tuesday, October 10:
Sandra Cisneros, *The House on Mango Street*

Tuesday, October 24:
Anne Tyler, *Dinner at the Homesick Restaurant*

Tuesday, November 7:
Harper Lee, *To Kill a Mockingbird*

Tuesday, November 21:
Toni Morrison, *The Bluest Eye*

Tuesday, December 5:
Barbara Kingsolver, *The Bean Trees*

Tuesday, December 19:
Zora Neale Hurston, *Their Eyes Were Watching God*

Graduation at the Lynn court to be announced—transportation from Lowell provided.

Once they go through the syllabus, there is a notable relaxation in the class. It's as if they have been shaken loose. The next move is to read a story aloud to them, and inevitably because the path has been paved for their comfort, conversation erupts in the best sense of the word.

For a final note on the power of CLTL teaching techniques to enhance all participants—judges and probation officers as well as students—we give you the voice of Judge Joseph Reardon of the Barnstable Massachusetts District Court who says that "Hank Burke and I have become reinvigorated and vested with new zeal for our work in the trial court as we realize that we are part of a rebirth of critical thinking and decision-making by our probationers."

Changing Lives Through Literature changes all of us.

Works Cited

BIBLIOGRAPHY OF TEXTS IN LESSON PLANS

Banks, Russell. *Affliction.* New York: Harper Perennial, 1990.

Capek, Karel. "The Last Judgment." In *Great Modern European Short Stories.* New York: Ballantine, 1996.

Carver, Ramond. "What We Talk about When We Talk about Love." In *What We Talk about When We Talk about Love: Stories.* New York: Vintage, 1989.

Cheever, John. "The Swimmer." In *The Stories of John Cheever.* New York: Vintage, 2000.

Doctorow, E. L. "Jolene: A Life." In *Sweet Land Stories.* New York: Random House, 2004.

Douglass, Frederick. *Narrative of the Life of Frederick Douglass, an American Slave.* New Haven, CT: Yale University Press, 2001.

Doyle, Roddy. "Ask Me, Ask Me, Ask Me." In *The Woman Who Walked into Doors.* New York: Vintage, 1998.

Faulkner, William. "Barn Burning." In *Collected Stories.* New York: Vintage, 1995.

Fitch, Janet. *White Oleander.* New York: Back Bay Books, 2000.

Gorky, Maxim. "Notch." In *The Collected Stories of Maxim Gorky.* New York: Citadel Press, 1988.

Hemingway, Ernest. *The Old Man and the Sea.* New York: Scribner, 1995.

Hurston, Zora Neale. *Their Eyes Were Watching God.* New York: Perennial, 1998.

Haruf, Kent. *Plainsong.* New York: Vintage, 2000.

Kesey, Ken. *One Flew over the Cuckoo's Nest.* New York: Signet Books, 1989.

Kingsolver, Barbara. *The Bean Trees.* New York: HarperTorch, 1998.

LeGuin, Ursula."The Wife's Story." In *Changing Lives Through Literature.* South Bend, IN: University of Notre Dame Press, 1999.

London, Jack. *The Call of the Wild.* New York: Aerie, 1990.

Morrison, Toni. *The Bluest Eye.* New York: Plume Books, 2000.

Nibasa, Rita Marie. "A Line of Cutting Women." In *A Line of Cutting Women.* Corvallis, OR: Calyx Books, 1998.

Steinbeck, John. *Cannery Row.* New York: Penguin Books, 1993.

Tyler, Anne. *Dinner at the Homesick Restaurant.* New York: Ballantine Books, 1996.

Walker, Alice. *"Everyday Use."* In *Changing Lives Through Literature.* Notre Dame, IN: University of Notre Dame Press, 1999.

Wolff, Tobias. "The Rich Brother." In *The Collected Stories of Tobias Wolff.* Bloomsburg Publishing PLC, 1997.

Wright, Richard. *Black Boy.* New York: Perennial, 1998.

X, Malcolm. *The Autobiography of Malcolm X.* New York: Ballantine Books, 1987.

SECONDARY SOURCES

Jablecki, Lawrence T. "Changing Lives Through Literature." *Federal Probation* 62, no. 1 (June 1998): 32–39

Jarjoura, Roger G., and Susan T. Krumholz. *An Evaluation of the Changing Lives Through Literature Program,* October 1993, *http://cltl@umassd.edu* (prepared for CLTL).

Jarjoura, Roger G., and Susan T. Krumholz. "Combining Bibliotherapy and Positive Role Modeling as an Alternative to Incarceration." *Journal of Offender Rehabilitation* 28 (1998): 127–39.

Kane, Robert, and Robert Waxler. "Changing Lives Through Literature Program." *Community Corrections Report: On Law and Corrections Practice* (January, February 1993).

William R. Kelly. *An Evaluation of the Changing Lives Through Literature Program: Brazoria County CSCD,* February 2001, *http://cltl.umassd.edu* (prepared for CLTL).

Manguel, Alberto. *A History of Reading.* New York: Penguin, 1997.

McLaughlin, Meghan, Jean Trounstine, and Robert Waxler. *Success Stories: Life Skills through Literature.* Washington: Office of Correctional Education, U.S. Department of Education, 1997.

Trounstine, Jean "Throw the Book at Them." In *The Book Group: A Thoughtful Guide to Forming and Enjoying a Stimulating Book Discussion Group,* ed. Ellen Slezak. Chicago: Chicago Review Press, 1995.

Turner, Mark. *The Literary Mind: The Origins of Thought and Language.* Oxford: Oxford University Press, 1998.

Vaughan, Susan. *The Talking Cure: The Science behind Psychotherapy.* New York: Owl Books, 1998.

Waxler, Robert P. "Journey down the River." In *The Book Group: A Thoughtful Guide to Forming and Enjoying a Stimulating Book Discussion Group,* ed. Ellen Slezak. Chicago: Chicago Review Press, 1995.

Waxler, Robert P., and Jean R. Trounstine, eds. *Changing Lives Through Literature.* South Bend, IN: University of Notre Dame Press, 1999.

Index

Massachusetts, University of, at Dartmouth, xiv, 2, 71–72

Massachusetts Foundation for the Humanities: support for CLTL program, 4

Massachusetts Institute of Technology Laboratory for Nuclear Science, 30

Mastrosimone, William: "Bang, Bang, You're Dead," 117

May, Robert E. (judge), 39, 108

May, Thomas (judge), 101

McBride, James, 125

McCourt, Frank: *Angela's Ashes,* 130, 154

McDonald, Joyce: *Swallowing Stones,* 116, 153

McDonnell, Kathleen: *Loon Boy,* 130

McLean, Lenny (probation officer), 118

McLellan, Kathy (facilitator), 116

Memoirs: use of, in CLTL program, 94, 154–55. *See also specific*

Middlesex Community College, 3, 84, 86, 99–100, 112, 113

Mikaelsen, Ben: *Touching Spirit Bear,* 116, 153

Mill, John Stuart: "On Liberty," 188

Miller, Arthur: *The Crucible,* 117; *Death of a Salesman,* 117

The Miracle Worker (Gibson), 117

"Miss Brill" (Mansfield), 187

"Miss Rosie" (Chifton), 188, 232

Monro, Alice: "Boys and Girls," 98

Montana 1948 (Watson), 112, 154

Mooney, Gail (facilitator), 38–40, 114; lesson plan for *Plainsong* (Haruf), 166–67; lesson plan for *White Oleander* (Fitch), 160–61

Morrison, Toni: *The Bluest Eye,* v, 90–91, 93, 97, 110, 153, 174–77, 222, 239

"Mother to Son" (Hughes), 189, 232

Muehlenberg, Cherie (facilitator), 14; lesson plan for *The Call of the Wild* (London), 171–72; use of film with literature as teaching strategy, 233

Munro, Alice: "Boys and Girls," 97, 187

Murphy, Ann Brian (facilitator), 102; lesson plan for "Ask Me, Ask Me, Ask Me" (Doyle), 196–98; use of poetry as teaching strategy, 231–32

"My Name Is Margaret" (Angelou), 188

"My Papa's Waltz" (Roethke), 189, 232

"My Son the Man" (Olds), 189

"My Soul Is Rested" (Raines), 188

Nagle, Robert (probation officer), 126

Narcotics Anonymous, 88

Narrative of the Life of Frederick Douglass, an American Slave (Douglass), 103, 154, 157–60, 172, 182, 189–90, 200

National Endowment for the Humanities Grants, 4, 61

Naylor, Gloria: *The Women of Brewster Place,* 97, 153

Negative capability, 33

Neville, Tam (facilitator, Dorchester Program), 48; use of student writing as teaching strategy, 226

New Bedford Juvenile Court juvenile program, 125–26

New Bedford Men's Program, 3–4, 61–81, 101; choosing participants for, 63–65; *Deliverance* in, 75–76; evaluation of, 79–80; first group in, 71–73, 77–78; first literature seminar in, 68–78; forming

Acknowledgments

FOR THE IMPORTANT WORK THEY HAVE DONE to develop our Changing Lives Through Literature program over the years and especially for granting us permission to use their material drawn from our CLTL website *(http:/cltl.umassd.edu)*, we wish to give thanks to: George Albert, Sandi Albertson-Shea, Ean Alleyne, Filomena Aresco, Charles Ashe, Anita Barnes, Megan Barrett, James Blackstone, Bettina Borders, Henry Burke, Idella Carter, Michelle Carter-Donahue, Jill Carroll, John Christopher, William Cleaver, Joan Dagle, Laurie DeBower, Kelly DeSouza, Joseph Dever, Dorothy Donnelley, Patty Fairweather, Anthony Farley, Melanie Fenske, Jean Flanagan, Donald Friar, Ed Gaffey, Neil Galbraith, Marjory German, Matt Gibson, Moses Glidden, Robert Greco, Orian Greene, Jane Hale, Sydney Hanlon, Clive Hapwood, Robert Hassett, Charles Henry, K. Randall Hufstetler, Marie Jackson, Robert Kane, Valerie Karno, Deirdre Kennedy, Anne-Marie Kent, Greg Kincaid, Larry Jablecki, Linda Jacino, Carolyn Labun, Bernard Lafayette, Michael Leahy, Eliabeth Lehr, Babara Ann Loftus, Robert May, Tom May, Lenny McLean, Kathy McLellan, Cherie Muehlberger, Gail Mooney, Ann Brian Murphy, Robert Nagle, Tam Neville, John Owens, Theresa Owens, Joseph Reardon, Stella Rebeiro, Caroline Rickaway, Heather Rocheford, Ann Schneider, Trudy Schrandt, Ray Shea, Edith Shilue, Marlys Shulda, Edward R. Sirois, James "Bobby" Spencer,

Wayne St. Pierre, Mary Stephenson, Herbert Stern, Taylor Stoehr, Brian Sullivan, Linda Trigg, Julia Walking, Gail Weinberg-Krause, Joseph Wickliffe, Charles Zalewski, and Elliott Zide.

We hope we have done justice to them and to the CLTL program as a whole.

We would also like to thank the National Endowment for the Humanities for their generous grant enabling us to create the CLTL website. Thanks also to the Gardiner Howland Shaw Foundation and the Massachusetts Foundation for the Humanities for believing in us—and for the ongoing support from the wonderful Library of America who consistently provide us with books for our graduations. Thanks also to the University of Massachusetts, Dartmouth, and Middlesex Community College—and, of course, to the Massachusetts State Legislature for providing funding for the CLTL program.

We also want to recognize the hard-working staff at the University of Michigan Press and our families and good friends who are always there for us, sharing the vision, the conversation, and their love of literature.

6 - time some criteria

7 :

133 get started as soon as possible
136 don't worry about details
     planning